The Aesthetics of Survival

The Aesthetics of Survival

A Composer's View of
Twentieth-Century Music

Edited and with an Introduction by William Bolcom

GEORGE ROCHBERG

THE UNIVERSITY OF MICHIGAN PRESS

Ann Arbor

To Mims, Chessie, Geno, and Jacob

Library of Congress Cataloging in Publication Data

Rochberg, George.
    The aesthetics of survival.

    Essays.
    Bibliography: p.
    1. Music—20th century—Addresses, essays,
lectures.   I. Bolcom, William.   II. Title.
ML60.R62   1984   780'.904   83-16878
ISBN 0-472-10037-8

Acknowledgments

Grateful acknowledgment is made to the following journals and publishers for permission to reprint copyrighted material.

Belmont Music Publishers for Arnold Schoenberg, *Pierrot Lunaire*, "Mondestrunken," No. 1; Variations for Orchestra, Op. 31; and Five Pieces for Orchestra, Op. 16, "Premonitions," No. 1. Used by permission of Belmont Music Publishers.

College Music Society for "The Composer in Academia," from *College Music Symposium*, 1970. Reprinted with permission of The College Music Society.

Current Musicology for "Reflections on the Renewal of Music," *Current Musicology* 13. © 1972 *Current Musicology*, Columbia University. Reprinted by permission of the publisher.

European American Music Distributors Corporation for Luigi Nono, *Il Canto Sospeso*; Alban Berg, Lyric Suite for String Quartet; Anton Webern, Concerto for Nine Instruments, Op. 24 and Piano Variations, Op. 27; Pierre Boulez, *Le Marteau sans Maître*, "Bourreaux de Solitude," No. VI.

Kraus Reprint for "Indeterminacy in the New Music," *The Score* 26 (January, 1960).

New Literary History for "The Avant-Garde and the Aesthetics of Survival," *New Literary History* 3 (Autumn, 1971).

Perspectives of New Music for "The New Image of Music," *Perspectives of New Music* 2, no. 1 (Fall-Winter, 1963); "Reflections on Schoenberg," *Perspectives of New Music* 11, no. 2 (Spring-Summer, 1973).

G. Schirmer, Inc., for Arnold Schoenberg, Fourth String Quartet. Copyright © 1939 G. Schirmer, Inc., renewed 1967.

Springer-Verlag New York, Inc., for "The Structure of Time," in *The Study of Time*, vol. 2, edited by J. T. Fraser and N. Laurence for the International Society for the Study of Time.

University of Toronto Press for "Duration in Music," in *The Modern Composer and His World* (Toronto: University of Toronto Press, 1961).

Music calligraphy by Mark Fasman.

Introduction

We are in the 1980s, and it is generally accepted among most artists that modernism is on the wane. What is happening now is less a new movement— although critics have been quick to name it postmodernism—than it is a movement away from movements, those schools and isms that have bedeviled art and led toward its current sclerotic self-consciousness. It is not easy for an artist to cut adrift from a style like modernism that has had such social approval and pressure behind it. No previous style was nearly so politically adept, nor so total in its power to sway and hold the majority of artists, as modernism; the style still has the power to rail against its defectors (through modernist critics), and it will continue to require courage on the part of individual artists to take alternate courses, no matter what they may be. Apparently no critic alive, and not even every artist, seems to understand that *all true artists are, and must be, laws unto themselves.* Anything less, and art will not survive.

George Rochberg is a composer of moving and powerful music. We have been good friends for many years. I am grateful to him for showing "alternate courses" to me when I was still recovering from my experience with the post-Webern movement—which is the form modernism took in the world of music in the decades after World War II—and I feel that his example gave me courage to strike out on my own.

In quite another way from Rochberg the composer, Rochberg the essayist shows the dangers of pursuing a course alongside, divergent from, and sometimes in direct conflict with, modernism. Where a piece of music must be a fait accompli, a point of arrival, a self-sufficient organism, a book of essays such as this can be a journey, a transition between points, a traveling correspondent's diary. Where Rochberg the composer shows you where he is, Rochberg the essayist shows you (in part) how he got there. Hence the value of these essays, and why they may well be necessary reading for artists struggling for freedom in their own ways. It is perhaps more common in Europe than here to find thinly disguised puff pieces written about artists and passed off as objective monographs (André Hodeir's *Since Debussy*, discussed at length in the body of Rochberg's text, strikes me as but one of many such books—in that case one written in support of the late composer Barraqué). I want it clear that my purpose in urging the publication of the present volume is emphatically not in that spirit, and that my editing these essays does not indicate nor constitute total agreement with George on all points. Happily, there is nothing in these lectures and articles that argues for one's becoming a composer just like the writer (no disciples need apply); what they are as a body of writing is an account of the explorations of an inquiring mind, bringing an extremely wide scope of reading and thought into focus on the question: whither music?

While I edited these essays, a question stuck in my mind: Will it be necessary for the general reader to know very much about the various submovements of modernism in music—aleatoricism, total organization, and so forth—that George discusses from so many different angles? Two things are true after all about these submovements: (1) hardly anyone outside the realm of serious modern music knew or cared much about them when they were new; (2) already, even the younger composers of today know extremely little about the submovements of thirty, twenty, or even ten years ago. So why the fuss, you may ask, if each of these submovements proved as ephemeral as they in fact have been? Because all these faces belonged to the same body of thought, which held that the past is dead and must be buried—the chief tenet of modernism.

In swiping heads off this hydra with his literary sword, George is working toward the heart of the beast. It is simply true, for example, that the produced musics of two diametrically opposed methods of composition —aleatoricism (or "chance" music) and total organization (wherein every quality of music was submitted to external numerical control)—sound almost indistinguishable one from the other; why? What, for another question, has turned composition into an activity for specialists for the delectation of other specialists? Behind the battles in each essay one glimpses the shape of the war, and I am taking the chance that the general reader will divine this without long preamble or overexplanation—it is the war that counts. Anyone interested in the battles can follow up the many sources quoted and discussed throughout the book by referring to the essay notes and to the bibliography.

Each section of the essays is arranged chronologically. It is interesting to follow the progress of a thought through several essays on the same subject over a period of years; very striking in this regard are the two essays on Schoenberg, separated by nearly twenty years. Some of the essays are of course addressed mostly to musicians; many others (such as "Humanism versus Science," which actually is the text of a lecture given to scientists) deal globally with the question of music in our world in a way not intended only for the music specialist. Perhaps the potentially most useful documents for composers are the essays on musical time and space that, like some of Busoni's writings, could point to profound developments in new music. But any reader, musician or not, will find most of the essay, "The Fantastic and the Logical" so relevant to the terrifying world situation of today as to belie its 1973 date. One of the pleasures of the book is the variety of approaches and tone in each essay, particularly in view of the fact that they all confront the same basic questions.

I am thankful to George for his cooperation and help in the editing process. Our wives, Gene Rochberg and Joan Morris, have been extremely supportive throughout the strenuous business of putting together such a book, and they deserve our inestimable thanks.

William Bolcom

Contents

On the New Image of Music

Indeterminacy in the New Music

Human consciousness and thought in the twentieth century have discovered the essential irrationality of the premises on which they are based. That the old world of illusory certainties has disintegrated in the face of new conditions which govern contemporary existence is acknowledged by all who are seriously concerned with man's destiny, including the physicist, the theologian, and the philosopher. The falling away of values founded on the illusion of rationalistic certainty has left man exposed both to the waywardness of his own nature and to that of the universe around him. Man can predict nothing today except on the basis of statistical probability and this brings him little comfort in his new and painful awareness of his condition. This is the time when, according to Zen Buddhism, "mountains no longer look like mountains, and rivers no longer look like rivers."

Afflicted by irrationalism, uncertainty, and indeterminacy, we are suffering collectively what Pascal suffered individually centuries ago.

> We sail within a vast sphere, ever drifting from end to end. When we think to attach ourselves to any point and to fasten to it, it wavers and leaves us; and if we follow it, it eludes our grasp, slips past us, and vanishes forever. Nothing stays for us. This is our natural condition, and yet most contrary to our inclination; we burn with desire to find solid ground and an ultimate sure foundation whereon to build a tower reaching to the Infinite. But our whole groundwork cracks, and the earth opens to abysses.[1]

What for Pascal was a painful individual intuition is for us a terrifying collective apprehension based upon the physical discoveries of our time and the Freudian discovery of the unconscious. If man's reason is the true measure of reason, ours is a nonrational world. Still there are those who must have certainty in order to act, any certainty that seems to ensure the possibility of a rational order. In their haste to seize upon rational certainty, the first thing they sacrifice is subjective freedom, because it is this possibility of inner freedom, now deprived of its supporting buttresses, which is so painful to bear. Not only are we surfeited with political examples of this, in both Communist and Fascist states where freedom of the individual is sacrificed to power, bread, and security; we see evidence of an analogous kind in the divorce of subjective freedom from objective rational standards in twentieth-century art.

Erich Heller, discussing this same problem in his essay on the "Hazards of Modern Poetry," says:

> The human affections are the only instruments of recognizing and responding to values. By treating the affections as the rascals in the school of reason, and as the peace-breakers in the truth-bound community, reason—the rationalist's reason—has set up a kind of truth which leaves the human affections as idle as do, by general consent, the "objective" methods that lead to its discovery. The workshops in which our truths are manufactured are surrounded by swarms of unemployed affections.[2]

Heller refers to the "theory of the 'impersonal' character of poetry, of the poet as a neutral agent bringing about the fusion and crystallization of nameless experience." As he says, "These theories merely express, and express significantly, the spiritual depreciation of the real lives that real selves lead in the real world."[3] The divorce of the poet from his poetry is a spiritual and moral defection in favor of order, objectivity, technical certainty. And as Heller comments, "Truth is likely to be untidy, the *enfant terrible* in the systematic household."[4]

In music, this divorce between the human affections—subjectivity—and the operations of reason is fully revealed in the works which have been recently issued under the slogan of "total organization"—a completely rationalized system of serial composition which, so its practitioners mistakenly believe, leaves nothing to chance. On the other hand, in an attempt to make unpredictability itself a principle of composition, there are those who, like John Cage, compose "chance" music. In the one case, indeterminacy enters by the back door, disturbing the careful microcosmic calculations of the composers and upsetting their "systematic household." In the other, indeterminacy is the root principle; but because it, too, proclaims a personal detachment from what will happen, the doctrine of "chance" music is as incapable of entering into the subjective human world as is the doctrine of "total organization." Here is Cage on experimental music: "Where attention moves toward the observation and audition of many things at once, including those that are environmental, becomes, that is, inclusive rather than exclusive, *no question of making, in the sense of forming understandable structures can arise* (one is tourist)——"[5] Even more to the point:

> A sound does not view itself as thought, as ought, as needing another sound for its elucidation, as, etc.; it has not time for any consideration—it

is occupied with the performance of its characteristics: before it has died away it must have made perfectly exact its frequency, its loudness, its length, its overtone-structure, its precise morphology of these and of itself.[6]

Cage thus denies any living connection between "sounds" made and their maker, their human agent. Nothing could illustrate more perfectly the "impersonality" of the composer and his subjective withdrawal from what he makes than Cage's idea that "sounds" live in, of, and for themselves. And, as with the composers of totally organized music, the *materiality* of the materials of music, that is, their reification, is clearly seen to be the self-sufficient and sole end of music making. Without relationship either to the composer as human being–artist, or to the world of man as a culture-process, such music making is hermetically sealed by its own laws of order, shut off, and shutting itself off from anything beyond itself. Such notions are the ultimate consequence of a failure to recognize that, on the one hand, the reification of the material of music, and, on the other, absolute control of that reification do not satisfy the conditions of art as an existential act. Art as an existential act is understood here as the state in which a subjective consciousness—aware of its own existence in itself (Jacques Maritain) and of its relation to other existences, human and natural, outside itself—seeks to express the truth of its awareness through materials viewed, not as material per se, but as an expressive medium.

The abdication of subjectivity in favor of technical certainty sums up the position of the avant-garde rationalists.[7] But because truth is the *"enfant terrible* that upsets the systematic household," and *our* truth (or my truth) lies in an awareness of the uncertainty and indeterminacy of existence itself, the rational order of advanced serialism has paradoxically fallen prey to indeterminacy. Though it seems paradoxical to speak of indeterminacy in connection with this music, yet it is precisely through this paradox that the rationale and techniques of this new music can best be understood.

The term *indeterminacy* suggests words like *indefinite, vague,* and *nonspecific.* Its implied tendency to formlessness would seem to contradict the extraordinary degree of self-avowed objectivity and rational control characteristic of the work of Boulez, Stockhausen, Nono, and others, that is based upon the principles of *total organization*—serialism pushed to its furthermost limits and investing every aspect of composition with a predetermined mathematical certainty. The question arises: How can a total serial approach to composition, so rigorously systematized, result in "indeterminacy"? Isn't there something wrong with the equation? And if such an approach to composition *does* produce an effect of "indeterminacy," how does this contradiction between the technical means employed and the musical results achieved come about? Are there hidden factors which must be elicited in order to resolve the paradox? If so, what are they?

It will be very useful, in seeking to resolve this paradox, to invoke, for descriptive purposes only, the physical concept of *entropy*. Entropy, which plays a large part in the world of probability depicted by twentieth-century physics, is the measure of the tendency of nature toward disorder, non-differentiation, and a final state of static equilibrium. According to Norbert Wiener,

> as entropy increases, the universe, and all closed systems in the universe, tend naturally to deteriorate and lose their distinctiveness, to move from the least to the most probable state, from a state of organization and differentiation in which distinctions and forms exist, to a state of chaos and sameness.[8]

Entropy then is the statistical tendency toward disorder in isolated systems in which energy remains constant. Unless a new source of energy is freshly supplied, the tendency to entropy will steadily increase and a drab uniformity result. Order, that is, the tendency to differentiation, is nonentropic.

There is no question but that in total organization a certain kind of order exists; and, if order is a decrease in the tendency to entropy, then we should not expect to find entropy here. But it is precisely this kind of order which does produce entropy. Total organization is based essentially on an *equivalence principle:* all elements are granted equal status in their ordering by the proportions of measurement determined in advance. T. W. Adorno describes this method of composition as an effort

> to extend the rigor of the serial system to the metric and other aspects of composition so that, in the end, the art of composing is replaced by a system of serial arrangements which guarantee objectively and control arithmetically, from one end of a score to the other, the exact position of every sound according to pitch and every interval and metric or dynamic value. The result is nothing more nor less than an integral rationalization (apparently without precedent) of the art of composition.[9]

He goes on to make the comment that such a system is "based on a static conception of music: all the exact ratios of equivalence and symmetry decreed by extreme rationalization assume that the identical (or exactly analogous) things that appear in different places in the score *are*, in fact, identical (or exactly analogous)."[10] In this sense pitch, intensity, duration, and timbre, subject to identical procedures, become analogous aspects of a unified field of composition. This is so essential to the doctrine of total serial organization that without it there can be no such thing. Karlheinz Stockhausen is reported to have said of his *Kontrapunkte:* "The contrasts may be so arranged that a state is created in which only one unity and one infinity are audible." Pitch is now a proportion of time, and vice versa. Pitch no longer, according to this view, moves through time, expressed in values of dynamic level and timbre; rather, it now joins with segments of proportioned time, linked to a related degree of intensity and color to form objective sound structures in a unified acoustical space. To quote Herbert Eimert: "The identity of time and pitch was first stated exactly by Schoenberg, who saw the unity of 'musical space' as a play of vertical and horizontal forces that were in substance identical."[11] Eimert's misinterpretation of Schoenberg's idea will not detain us now.[12] His remark, however, confirms the essential equivalence of pitch and duration viewed in the light of total organization.[13] If, then, equivalence prevails, no real distinctions in value can be made between pitch, time, intensity, and timbre. They are now objective quantities, aspects of a unity. As such, no one aspect can be accorded more value than any other since each shares equal status in this unity—the filling of acoustical space. Since no hierarchy of value or function is operative, we can only speak of an order of equivalents. This ordering of equivalents is analogous to the equal distribution of energy in closed physical systems, and therefore, by the same analogy, tends to entropy. Were the order governing total organization an ordering of functions of different values—the contradiction in terms is self-evident—the tendency to entropy, to a loss of distinctiveness, would be reversed; but it is precisely because this order is based on equivalence and identity that it produces its opposite tendency—entropy. It is an order which seeks to establish an equilibrium within a musical space which is identical with the material that fills it. In music produced in this fashion it is virtually inconceivable to have melodies and accompaniments (even in the manner of Schoenberg) because they would immediately set up a hierarchy of values in which, for example, the identity of pitch and time claimed by Eimert would no longer exist. In totally organized music, then, the equivalence principle tends to reduce differentiation to a minimum; and by creating a kind of musical entropy brings on itself the condition of indeterminacy. In Adorno's words:

> In the end the rationalization of form results in an absence of form. . . . It results, too, in the regression of music to the pre-musical, pre-artistic stage of raw sound; it is only logical that the next step should be concrete or electronic music. And so, as a result of wishing to control everything, they lose control in the end because the dynamism inherent in music, intolerant of a too precisely regulated static order, overthrows the order—or at any rate renders it inoperative in the particular sphere in which it is primarily intended to function—namely the unfolding of music in time.[14]

The rigorous exclusion of subjectivity in any form, insofar as it represents the nonrational and therefore the unpredictable (both conditions dangerous to a carefully calculated rational system) has led to the view that pitch, duration, intensity, and timbre are material elements capable of precise quantitative measurement. The avowed purpose of serial composition is to treat these objectively as quantitative elements whose notation is not potential but actual, whose functional equivalence is predetermined by fixed patterns of permutations and ratios of proportion. Accordingly, pitch, only one of several equivalents, is a structural element of which the interval constitutes the irreducible musical cell. No longer expressive of purely melodic values, intervals have become quantitative relationships of sound structure which are ends in themselves, and therefore remain fixed objects, incapable of radiating value or meaning. The same is true of dynamic values since they no longer relate to expression (and therefore should not be called "dynamic" any longer!) but merely indicate a particular degree of volume or amplitude of sound. Under such conditions *pp*, or its numerical analogue, has no meaning as a mark of expression because it now stands for a quantity of measurement.[15] This process of objectifying and materializing the so-called elements of music has its inevitable consequences: music, based solely on predictable patterns of order, becomes "structure." Eimert, waxing almost lyrically subjective, says that "only in the newest developments and the development of the newest composers have the invisible doors burst open, revealing a world of measured quantities, of intervallic mensural-fields, of complex forms of organization replacing by 'structures' the material which, taken out of its usual context, has been, as it were, 'de-materialized.'"[16] Again he says:

> In music, measurement is an operation on prearranged material: at the same time it is more than that; with the advent of "proportioning" it is transformed directly into structure. Thus, finally, the "ideal" of structure becomes the composer's inspiration—this is one of the points closely preceding the practice of *pointilliste* and electronic music, and at the same time the very heart of the musical process.[17]

Even though opposed in views, Adorno and Eimert both confirm that electronic music is a product of the new aesthetic; the difference is that what for Adorno is a regression to a preartistic condition is for Eimert an advance to the "very heart of the musical process," as he calls it.

It was in his Symphony Op. 21, that Webern (unknowingly?) established the equivalence principle. Contrasting Webern's method with Schoenberg's, Eimert says, "[Webern] is the only one who in his music organized *more* than the stratum of pitch-levels; the only one who was conscious of the structured spatial dimension where the antithesis of vertical and horizontal no longer exists."[18] It is precisely in this work that Webern prepared the way for the new aesthetic:[19] the creation of the idea of a homogeneous musical space defined by interval-motives which penetrate through the whole time-space without essential differentiation of function. The remarkable degree of interval-order attained (canon being the technique par excellence of distributing interval-motives and durational proportions) tends to produce acoustical entropy (Stockhausen's "state . . . in which only one unity and one infinity are audible"). Through this work entropy, and therefore indeterminacy, first entered the contemporary musical scene, the *negative consequence* of "integral rationalization," as Adorno calls it. In the works composed "after Webern," as the degree of integral rationalization increases so does entropy and indeterminacy. The generation of young composers that came after Webern chose to model themselves on his instrumental works, and on the rational principles they deduced from these works. This, so they thought, would give them complete control of the precompositional situation and therefore of the compositional situation as well. But in their preoccupation with the extreme rationalization of the internal order they lost sight of external order, i.e., of the external architecture of their music (as well as Webern's own).

It is important in this connection to examine in some detail the techniques by which durational proportions are subdivided in order to achieve the suspension of any feeling of pulsation or beat. The sense of an overall architectural articulation of time has disappeared almost entirely from the new music, further establishing the condition of indeterminacy. The suspension of beat in a physical sense is achieved either by a careful avoidance of regular metric groupings or, if regular metric groupings are employed, by avoiding the natural accentual weight inherent in them. In the music of Mozart and Beethoven, external formal considerations were so important that they organized individual metric pulsations and rhythmic phrase pulsations so as to achieve the large shapes required. But since shape in this sense is foreign to the new music, temporal divisions need not be related to external shape. To suspend pulsation and beat—thus circumventing the natural tendency of regular pulsation to organize itself into ever larger units and shapes—certain techniques have been devised, chief among them the Webernian contribution to the art of the suspended beat based primarily on the interaction of sound and silence. (The complexity Webern achieves within basically simple bars of 2, 3, and 4 is well known.) A favorite device of the Boulez-Stockhausen-Nono group is that of arithmetically increasing or decreasing the number of subdivisions within a regular bar-length. For example in 3/8, it is common to observe groups of 2, 4, or 5; in 2/4, 3 and 5; in 4/4, 7 and 9 and so on. In the *Kontrapunkte* of Stockhausen, for instance, there is only one time signature throughout—three eighth-notes per bar. But the simplicity of this time value is lost in the maze of subdivisional complexities; the beat is entirely suspended. Much the same may be said to be true of Luigi Nono's *Il Canto Sospeso* where, though there are different and frequently changing time signatures, the differences and changes mean next to nothing perceptually, because the internal subdivisions destroy the possibility of establishing a beat. In the *Structures for Two Pianos* of Boulez, one finds bracketed groups of 5 in 6/32, with the indication "pour 6" over the bracket; or a group of 7 and the indication "pour 6." In some of his earlier piano pieces Stockhausen uses ratio proportions: for example [4 : 5], meaning 4 divisions played in a bar given as 5/16; or [7 : 6], meaning 7 divisions in a bar of 6/32; etc. Thus a regular bar-length is rarely heard as such. It exists rather for the composer as a basis upon which to project irregular subdivisions, so that the simplicity or regularity of the bar-length has no possibility of emerging. The constant and purposeful obscuring of the simple metric values which the eye can distinguish in the score, but the kinesthetic sense can know nothing of perceptually, is a tendency toward indeterminacy. For when metric pulsation is clearly articulated, it can also be clearly perceived, and there is a natural correspondence between the order in which it is articulated and the order in which it is perceived.

The technique of the suspended beat thus has a direct bearing upon the most important issue to which a discussion of indeterminacy in music must inevitably lead—namely the relation between the external order and the internal order of music; in other words, the relation between the macrocosmic and microcosmic aspects. Microcosmic durational proportions are the means out of which form develops and becomes perceptible. Whether these are accentual or nonaccentual determines perceptibility to a great extent. In the music of the eighteenth and early nineteenth centuries, for example, in which the design of the external architecture was of primary importance, the microcosmic details of the inner order were in direct relation to the ultimate macrocosmic shape sought by the composer. As the nineteenth century advanced and forms grew larger in relation to time span, the charge of formlessness was brought more and more frequently, primarily because of the composers' inability to cope with increases in time span as well as with an ever-increasing number of harmonic innovations. Until the new music of the mid-twentieth century, this macrocosmic view dominated the composer's consciousness; and microcosmic order, i.e., the conscious rational determination of detail, was looked upon not as an end in itself but in relation to the macrocosmic aspect of the music.

With the emergence of serialism and total organization in our time a shift has taken place toward a primary concern for discrete, quantitatively determined sound structures without regard to their relation to the articulation of an external order. This microcosmic view, antithetic to the dynamism of duration in time, attempts to arrest time flow by equating it with so-called acoustical space; hence Eimert's remark about the identity of time and space. There are indications, however, that the problem of extended duration in time is seriously engaging the attention of some of the composers of the new music.

Boulez, discussing electronic music, poses three problems which he says must be solved: "The perceptibility of the duration, the definition of *tempo* and the continuity of non-formulated time."[20] In an article on structure and experiential time, Stockhausen remarks that the composer "who, for all his determining of individual details, holds fast to his aural conception of a complete, pre-experienced time-organism" is one whose art "has received that indispensable essence that alone gives sense to 'structure.' "[21] He describes Webern's String Quartet as a "multiplicity . . . welded together" becoming "time experienced through sound"; therefore "it becomes music."[22]

With all attention and energy focused on a self-enclosed microcosmic order it becomes impossible to shape the external architecture of music; under such conditions the end product can only be true formlessness, macrocosmic indeterminacy. If, then, the microcosmic structure of the new music leads to indeterminacy through its tendency to entropy and, because of its nonrelation to the articulation of external architecture, results in macrocosmic indeterminacy, the paradox with which I began is no longer a problem for us: indeterminacy in the new music is a fact—the *"enfant terrible* in the systematic household."

But we are involved once again in a paradox; this time as a result of comparing the traditional macrocosmically oriented past with the new microcosmically oriented present. Intuition is a nonrational faculty of man. Through intuition, we suddenly know something or see relationships existing between phenomena where previously it seemed none existed. Man proceeds as much by his intuition as by his reason, and when intuition is guided by reason we have the wedding of man's two great potential resources for acting from within himself and on the world around him. The new paradox then is this: In those eras dominated by the macrocosmic view of music, composers operated intuitively, using their reason only as a controlling guide, a final check on what their intuition projected into their musical consciousness. Because the expanding vocabulary of the eighteenth and nineteenth centuries was the result of a continuous cultural process, composers did not have to rationalize every stage of this process. The constant interplay of intuition and reason, subjective projection and objective purpose, produced the clearest, most sharply defined determinate shapes we know in music, including, as I pointed out before, those of Webern. In the new music, intuition—representing subjectivity, the nonrational in man—having been rejected as an unwelcome intruder, has had its revenge by returning as indeterminacy. Though largely intuitive, the melodies of the old music are articulated through clear patterns of pulsation and beat; though completely rational, the objective sound-structures of the new music lack the rhythmic clarity which pulsation and beat provide, and are paralyzed into formlessness through beat suspension.

Adorno states that

> when subjective freedom—an essential condition of all modern art—is exorcised, and when an artificial and tyrannical mania for integration at all costs—not, after all so very different from other forms of totalitarianism—is in complete command, this results in the production of scores which from a technical point of view, are, so to speak, fool-proof: each bar is a demonstration that the composer is fully conscious of what must be done to ensure that his music is immune from any conceivable reproach.[23]

Adorno is not completely right, although he is not wrong for reasons that uphold the aesthetic and practice of the new music he is criticizing. The subjective freedom he refers to, although consciously exorcised, does return. It returns in a subverted form as indeterminacy; but because it is the negative consequence of the rational order imposed and not the expressly desired result of the order, it turns the order into perceptual disorder. Still there is a truth here; for in attempting to escape from the irrationalism of subjectivity by manipulating supremely rational devices and procedures, these composers have fallen into indeterminacy. This negative reflection of what is most characteristic of our time therefore lends a certain validity to the new music. Doing the right thing for the wrong reasons, however, is not nearly as good as doing it for the right reasons.

The problem for contemporary art is to discover what Erich Heller calls "true order": "an order that embodies the incalculable and unpredictable, transcending our rational grasp precisely where it meets the reasons of the heart."[24] It does not follow from this that art must return to earlier practices and visions. On the contrary, the contemporary vision of new dimensions and values floating in a field of uncertainty is precisely what lends excitement and vitality to the art of our time. The meaning of twentieth-century art lies in the full acceptance of subjectivity. We see this most vividly in the style of painting called Abstract Expressionism. These painters, responding to the emergence of subjective freedom in our time, have seized on indeterminacy itself as both the subject matter and the means of their art, and as a result consciously *order chaos*. Thus indeterminacy becomes a positive value in art, consciously sought after for its own sake because it is the condition of existence itself and forms a new basis for creative expression.

This is instructive for the composer, for his essential problem is very similar; only the medium through which he works is different. To rely only on internal systematic order, without finding the way to control the macrostructure, is not compatible with the existential situation confronting the composer. His task is to accept this situation as it is, inimical though it may be to the idea of order as rational process, and to reduce it to order. But how can we order the indeterminate? How can shapelessness be given perceptible shape and defini-tion? How can the tendency to entropy be controlled?

Musical discourse is as dependent on effective recognition of its charac-teristic contents as it is on the interaction of micro- and macrostructure. Effec-tive recognition implies perception of the images and gestures through which pitch and time are formed. The composer who plunges into indeterminacy, then, faces the immediate problem of how to establish a new basis for the continuity of musical discourse, indeed, for the nature of the discourse itself, and the connection between image and gesture. Too much logical continuity of discourse will throw him back into history. On the other hand, unless he can establish a clear profile in both micro- and macrostructure, in image and ges-ture, he will lose control of the situation, and of what he is attempting to do—which is literally to reduce chaos to order and establish differentiation of a new kind while consciously retaining the tendency of his music to entropy. He will have to learn to deal with contraries and contradictions, to shape shapeless-ness, to differentiate sameness. He will have to learn how to project himself in time while shaping the instant, how to make each instant part of a continuum of instants related to one another in the continuum.

It is said that after one has studied Zen Buddhism "then mountains look like mountains again and rivers like rivers." This implies a new simplicity which will undoubtedly come. But now, at a time "when mountains do not look like mountains or rivers like rivers," before we can be certain again, we shall first have to learn to be certain of the uncertain, to feel and to love where there is no apparent reason to feel and love, to live and act because living and acting are all that human beings are capable of. The composer is no more exempt from this than any other creative artist. This is the condition of our subjective freedom—now stripped of the old value forms—and therefore the material of our art and music. Our immediate problem is well stated in these lines from Samuel Beckett's *Waiting for Godot*.

> *Vladimir:* (in anguish) Say anything at all!
> *Estragon:* What do we do now?
> *Vladimir:* Wait for Godot.
> *Estragon:* Ah!
> (silence)
> *Vladimir:* This is awful!
> *Estragon:* Sing something.
> *Vladimir:* No no! (he reflects.) We could start all over again perhaps.
> *Estragon:* That should be easy.
> *Vladimir:* It's the start that's difficult.
> *Estragon:* You can start from anything.
> *Vladimir:* Yes, but you have to decide.
> *Estragon:* True.

NOTES

1. Blaise Pascal, *Pensées* and *The Provincial Letters* (New York: Modern Library, 1941), p. 21.
2. *The Disinherited Mind* (New York: Farrar, Strauss, and Cudahy, 1957), pp. 269–70.
3. Ibid., p. 273.
4. Ibid., p. 292.
5. *The Score* 12 (June, 1955): 65.
6. Ibid.
7. They are the "logical positivists" of music; or we might call them "musico-logical" positivists.
8. *The Human Uses of Human Beings*, 2d rev. ed. (New York: Doubleday Anchor Books, 1954), p. 12.
9. "Modern Music is Dead," *The Score* 18 (December, 1956): 23.
10. Ibid., pp. 23–24.
11. "Anton Webern," in *Die Reihe*, No. 2, *Anton Webern* (Bryn Mawr, Penn.: Theodore Presser Co., 1958), p. 33.
12. Schoenberg says in his essay, "Composition with Twelve Tones (I) 1941" (in *Style and Idea* [New York: St. Martin's Press, 1975]): "The two-or-more dimensional space in which musical ideas are presented is a unit. Though the elements of these ideas appear separate and independent to the eye and the ear, they reveal their true meaning through their co-operation, even as no single word alone can express a thought without relation to other words." To call the interrelation of these "co-operating" elements an *identity* is to misunderstand Schoenberg's statement completely. Things which cooperate to produce meaningful relations are not necessarily the same because of their action on each other.
13. In a piece for piano entitled *Quantitäten*, the Swedish composer, Bo Nilsson, offers the performer this direction regarding the relation between pitch and time:

    The *tempo* of the piece is decided by the smallest note-value: as fast as possible. The effective values thus obtained are modified in accordance with the frequency values to which they are linked. The maximum pitch interval is 1:128 (C_1—c^5=1:128), and any written time-value will accordingly be prolonged or shortened up to four times (or down to a quarter of) its length, as defined above. Whereas the maximum frequency proportion is 1:128, the largest possible time proportion is two octaves (1:4, for example ♪ : ♪); a basic stated value of a note can therefore take on 85 time values in the 85 pitch levels used in the piece. Rising pitch intervals are matched by a prolongation, falling intervals by a shortening of the notated values.

For a discussion of these questions see also Paul Gredinger, "Serial Technique," in *Die Reihe*, No. 1, *Electronic Music* (Bryn Mawr, Penn.: Theodore Presser Co., 1955), pp. 38–44.

14. "Modern Music is Dead," p. 24.

15. Bo Nilsson attempts to establish a numerical scale of degrees of volume from 0,0 to 0,5 to 1,0 to 1,5, etc. In electronic music volume of sound (or intensity) is calculated precisely in degrees.

16. "Anton Webern," p. 32.

17. Ibid., p. 35.

18. Ibid., p. 32.

19. But Webern cannot be understood only in terms of his instrumental music, for he was essentially a vocal composer. A glance at the list of his thirty-one works will show that he composed actually more for the voice than for instruments. In his last two cantatas, and in *Das Augenlicht* and the songs with piano, Op. 23 and Op. 25, we meet a different Webern. Here the objective considerations which dominate his later instrumental works are combined with more traditional ones. The exclusive principles of the proportioned interval and of "the structural spatial dimension" join forces with lyrico-dramatic demands. Melody and accompaniment appear again in the songs with piano and in the first and fourth movements of the Second Cantata, for example. Most important of all, time is liberated from its objectified, mensural identity with pitch, so that it is autonomous once again and the music moves through time, creating a sense of urgent direction and perceptible form.

20. "At the Ends of Fruitful Land," *Die Reihe*, No. 1, *Electronic Music* (Bryn Mawr, Penn.: Theodore Presser Co., 1955), p. 23.

21. "Structures and Experiential Time," in *Die Reihe*, No. 2, *Anton Webern* (Bryn Mawr, Penn.: Theodore Presser Co., 1958), p. 74.

22. Ibid. This late awakening to the possibility of the emergence of a macrocosmic view of form undoubtedly lies at the root of such a work as Stockhausen's *Zeitmasse* and will perhaps bring about important changes in the new music.

23. "Modern Music is Dead," p. 26.

24. *The Disinherited Mind*, p. 295.

The New Image of Music

The break with tradition which resulted from profound changes affecting the sound, structure, and form of music continues to exert its powerful but negative influence on composers, few of whom have been able to accept it without qualm or reservation. This accounts in large measure for the difficulties they have experienced in attempting to solve their problems. Ambivalence, uncertainty, and nostalgia are reflected in the attitudes and works of the masters of the first half of our century—Schoenberg, Stravinsky, and Bartók; although, in the case of Varèse, we see no sign of the vacillation that afflicted his generation. The first generation to accept unreservedly the break with tradition grew to maturity following World War II. Nevertheless, in the ranks of today's advanced composers there is now discernible a growing tension and widening gap between those who proclaim their abandonment of and disengagement from history and those who, reacting against the consequences of this denial, reassert the value and necessity of a sense of historical continuity, a feeling for the continuum of human life and culture. Despite all this—the ambivalence toward the break with tradition, the rejection of or adherence to historical continuity—in the process of casting about for and searching out viable means of composition, certain processes of thought and attitudes of mind, resting on commonly held assumptions, which tend to ameliorate and reconcile differences, have crystallized to create what we may call the new image of music. At first glance this image appears strange, many-faceted, and complex, its features seemingly distorted and disarranged in cubist fashion and, like a cubist image, looking in several directions at once—or in none at all. And, like the cubist image, it is an aggregate with a compelling unity about it, gathering into its field the plurality and diversity of methods and means which have been and are still being devised, transformed, discarded, and replaced in the ceaseless search for solutions to the problem of musical composition. Viewed in this way, the image loses its aspect of immobile complexity and instead acquires that fascination which derives from contemplating the richness of a constantly metamorphosing process which, despite surface changes, retains its basic morphology.

In order to bring the new image of music into clearer focus, it is necessary to show how developments in twentieth-century musical thought came to bear on those processes of thought and attitudes of mind which may be said to be widespread, if not universal, among today's advanced composers. The most significant effect of these radical departures from tradition is that which we can discern in the nature of the musical discourse itself. Traditional processes of thought had assumed tonality as the basis of melodic-harmonic organization and periodicity as the regulator of metric organization and rhythmic flow. When these fundamental direction-producing forces gave way to freely chromatic atonality and an essentially nonperiodic rhythmic structure, a musical discourse based on readily predictable continuity was no longer possible. Since the time the break with tradition occurred, this has remained a virtually insoluble problem.

Schoenberg admitted that "it seemed at first impossible to compose pieces of complicated organization or great length."[1] Later, relying on the structural layout of texts, he found he was able to "construct larger forms," thus differentiating the parts of the musical setting "as clearly as they had formerly been by the tonal and structural functions of harmony."[2] From the doctrine of "the emancipation of the dissonance," it was a logical step for Schoenberg, with his deep-rooted, unshakable belief in the efficacy of traditional structure, to formulate what he chose to call "the method of composing with twelve tones which are related only with one another," a procedure in musical construction "which seemed fitted to replace those structural differentiations provided formerly by tonal harmonies."[3] Schoenberg's efforts to cast his large-scale twelve-tone instrumental works in classical structure and formal design proved no more satisfactory a reconciliation with the structural logic of traditional procedures than Stravinsky's attempt to adapt his musical ideas to the molds of neoclassicism. Both masters suffered a severe reaction to the very crises they were chiefly instrumental in bringing about. On the other hand, the search for precisely structured, self-contained musical organisms led Webern to the production of prismatic shapes, often geometric in structure by virtue of their symmetric ordering. Thus, Webern achieved a unique type of continuity which profoundly affected the direction in which musical discourse was to go.

In the early years of atonality, melodic motion, lacking the organizing factor of a tonal center, became almost completely "disjunct." As a consequence, melodic shape or contour tended to be less predictable, its direction less certain, its topological formation showing the effects of distortion and stretching. In Webern's purely instrumental serial works, melodic shape was unable to withstand the fragmentation into intervallic units to which it was subjected. Points of entry and attack could occur in any register without preparation and be spread over the total pitch range, the range itself being treated as a homogeneous unit. Because of this attenuation of shape, musical discourse, though precisely ordered, stood in danger of perceptual disorder; only Webern's remarkable ear and sense of control held it together, preserving both clarity and coherence. Still, Webern's predilection for condensation, for stripping away nonessential elements, further reinforced the tendency toward unpredictability; for by eliminating all connecting links, he was able to move at will, juxtaposing unprepared though not necessarily unrelated gestures. The resulting sensation was one of discontinuity. A similar tendency may be observed in the early works of Varèse, whose style was characterized by seeming unpredictability of motion in the form of discontinuous gestures. However, it must be pointed out that he sought this effect consciously, whereas it is not certain that this was true of Webern. In Varése's case, the unique forms he created developed their own sense of "rightness"; as he has pointed out, each was "the result of a process."

With Webern's instrumental serial works as their point of departure, the post–World War II generation of Boulez and Stockhausen, deeply involved in both serialism and electronic music, ventured directly into the realm of perceptual disorder. They were unable to keep the precarious balance Webern had maintained. While the stream of events in totally serialized works may be continuous in the sense that sound is always in motion, the discourse has lost its sense of direction, resulting in a type of unplanned indeterminacy. Planned indeterminacy, on the other hand, seeks to be utterly discontinuous and perceptually unpredictable in order to preserve spontaneity, the freshness of the living situation. In "situational" composition, sounds emerge from silence only to sink back again. John Cage likens this to what he considers life to be.

> Something is always starting and stopping, rising and falling. The nothing that goes on is what Feldman speaks of when he speaks of being submerged in silence. . . . So that listening to this music one takes as a springboard the first sound that comes along; the first something springs us into nothing and out of that nothing arises the next something, etc., like an alternating current.[4]

Cage calls this interaction of sound and silence "no-continuity,"[5] which, so far as the basic problem of continuity is concerned, clearly leads to a no-solution.

So far, I have been trying to show how the developments of this century affected the nature of the musical discourse by tracing the emergence of compositional procedures which led to structural and perceptual indeterminacy, unpredictability, and discontinuity. To gain a better insight into the causes of this state of affairs, we turn our attention to an analysis of the underlying assumptions which, I believe, have a direct bearing on the thought processes and mental attitudes these procedures reflect. The new set of assumptions which has evolved in the course of this century may be said to be the common property of today's composers, though perhaps not all swear equal allegiance to them. We must also be prepared to recognize that though these assumptions serve as the source for new points of departure, their influence is not necessarily overriding in all quarters, nor does it rule out divergence of choice or of preference for one procedural method over another, or cancel out the idiosyncrasies of personal vision and style, among other imponderables, which play their not insignificant role in the creation of art.

These new assumptions arrange themselves around two focal points: the nature of the sound material, and the handling of time. They embody a critical revaluation of the nature of music itself, what it is and what it can be. Even in instances in which composers still adhere to principles related, however distantly, to traditional procedures of form building, phrase construction, harmonic progression, and voice leading, the influence of the new assumptions modifies actual results so as to draw them inexorably within their sphere.

Today, the sound material of music enjoys an autonomy never before accorded it. This is due largely, I believe, to its liberation from what Sessions calls "the musical train of thought," the process of establishing logical connections between melodic phrase shapes and the harmonic progressions which support them. This liberation *permits sounds to create their own context*, a reversal of the traditional procedure in which the train of thought largely determined the individual sounds and their succession. The view of sounds as concrete, quantitative entities in themselves is revealed by such current terms as *densities, vertical pitch aggregate, sound structure*, and *sound object*. Since such complexes no longer derive from harmonic functions per se, whatever structural "meaning" they have must be derived from other functions in which they now play a role. Nor can they be meaningfully defined any longer by their interval structure alone.

We can attribute this new view of sound to two sources: atonality's radical consequences for pitch combination and chord construction, and a growing preoccupation with timbral independence. The new chords freed from tonal harmonic functions by the emancipation of the dissonance could include all or some of the twelve discrete chromatic divisions of the tempered system in any order of vertical arrangement. This led to a new range of sonorous densities from the most transparent to the most opaque combination of pitches. The step to the independent sound structure was taken when it was realized that timbre could be an essential means of differentiating and characterizing densities. Although Schoenberg himself did not rigorously pursue this new direction, his concept of *Klangfarbenmelodie* was taken up by Webern as a basic principle, leading to the pointillistic style embodied in serialism. With the invention of electronic means of sound production and the discovery of the noise spectrum as a musically viable sound source, the invention of new timbres became an all-absorbing preoccupation. As a result, sounds today live in a realm of free potentiality. They have no traditional models or prototypes. Newly created each time, they are, especially in the case of composers of profoundly keen aural sensibilities like Webern and Varèse, pure in essence and radiant in their projection.

The motion of sounds structured in this manner requires that it not interfere with their projection but rather enhance it; i.e., the duration assigned them must permit each its fullest opportunity to be heard. Where a series of sounds forms, through its movement in time, an accumulation into a larger aggregate, it becomes essential to be able to control the time of entry of each as well as the time of cutoff, especially if the aggregate is to dissolve in order to make way for the next. Obviously such conditions do not prevail when motion is measured in periodic fashion and where pulsation, through a regularly felt or established beat, ensures and regulates the flow of movement. The projection of the sound object, singly or in series, makes mandatory the suppression of pulsation. The beat may remain as a referential point but has no other function in many traditionally notated contemporary scores. This is precisely the case in Webern's mature works where motion exists for the sake of making clear entry and cutoff; it is also largely true of Varèse's music except for those passages where he resorts to pulsation again in order to drive the music forward. The suppression of pulsation radically affects the perception of time in music. One of its more obvious results is to slow down the passage of events, sometimes to the point of near immobility; and even where the rapidity of the projection of sounds tends to increase the speed of the passage of events, the perceptual sense of the movement remains essentially nondynamic. The most obvious consequence of the suppression of pulsation is the uncertainty which attends the effort to perceive and to predict the motion of the sounds projected. Lacking the presence of a felt or established beat, this becomes virtually impossible.

Given such prevailing beliefs about sound and motion, it follows that the musical discourse must partake of discontinuous motion, unpredictable happenings, etc. It is impossible to say precisely how the problem of continuity can or will be solved. If we take an extreme position, as Cage and others do, there is no problem; "no-continuity" is the logical and inevitable result of twentieth-century musical evolution thus far. But Cage's position leads to the absurdity of silence; to continue to compose, it will be necessary to discover some type of continuity in which unpredictability and indeterminacy may possibly serve as dramatic contrast, as a form of perceptual "dissonance" juxtaposed with clearly defined potentially predictable structural elements. To extend the structure of music to its outermost limits of perceptibility without permitting it to disintegrate into utter chaos will demand enormous powers of skill and imagination. Clearly some means must be discovered to effect adequate control of these tendencies toward chaos if composers wish to create works whose structural characteristics achieve perceptible clarity of function and design. To maintain that there is no meaningful relation between structure and its perception, that it makes no difference what the nature of the structure is and, further, that its perception is no longer a matter of import, is to deny the validity as well as the possibility of music as an art.

Until now I have dealt with those aspects that make up the "cubistic" image of today's music. What I have not yet accounted for—and what has apparently not yet emerged into full general consciousness—is that element whose pervasive presence ensures the "compelling unity" of the image. Unless we can discover what this unifying element is, in what it inheres and how it affects music, our understanding of what has happened in this century cannot go beyond purely descriptive limits; and this is to my mind insufficient if we wish to grasp the significance of the radical changes which music has undergone. We need to understand the larger purpose of these changes in order to apprehend the source of the new assumptions which have arisen in relation to the sound material and the handling of time. This unifying force emerges as the *spatialization* of music. It is this phenomenon of the fundamentally altered character of music which, when grasped in its fullest implication and followed to its furthest ramifications, renders the new image of music with sudden clarity, revealing its profound significance. We can then begin to understand why atonality was necessary to the liberation of the sound material and how it prepared the way for the creation of the sound object as a structural entity moving in a free realm of time; we can then begin to understand why the suppression of pulsation was necessary to the liberation of time and the emergence of a new order of continuity embracing the discontinuous and the unpredictable. It is in the tendency toward the spatialization of music that the larger purpose of the chief developments of this century reveals itself. Of the indications and premonitions which figure in the emergence of the spatialization of music there are four which have special interest.

First, in 1907, Charles Ives sketched but did not complete a work for string quartet and mechanical piano to which he gave the (for that time) startling title, *Space and Duration*. Later, in 1932, he remarked: "seemed far-fetched at the time but doesn't now."

Second, Schoenberg's concept of *Klangfarbenmelodie* found its first, significant realization in "Farben" of his Five Pieces for Orchestra of 1909. A note appended to the 1949 revision states, "The change of chords in this piece is to be executed with the greatest subtlety, avoiding accentuation of entering instruments, so that only the difference in color becomes noticeable. . . . there are no motives in this piece which have to be brought to the fore." The implications of this intentional suppression of accentuation, the stress on timbre for its own sake, the athematic and nonmotivic structure are, in this context, unmistakable.

Third, in Webern's mature works, composed from about 1920 on, geometric, "spatial" configurations assume major importance. The opening and closing sections of his Piano Variations, for example, are based on self-enclosed, athematic phrases organized by means of reflective (or mirror) symmetry. Each phrase returns to its opening sound, suggesting a curve in space, a self-sufficient unit. Lacking timbral differentiation, the emphasis is entirely on structural symmetry. In order to make these bilateral mirror shapes audible, Webern employs the metric unit (3/16) as a frame of reference only; accentuation alone permits the shapes to define themselves. Webern's intuitive affinity for the properties of geometry, the mathematics of space, is clearly evidenced in his symmetric shaping of the musical structure. Temporality is overcome by treating the sound material as "sonorous bodies" which assume, by virtue of their symmetric order, the characteristics of perfectly balanced spatial configurations. Motion is adjusted to the requirements of permitting the shape of these configurations maximum audibility, the inevitable consequence of which is to slow down or arrest movement until it achieves virtual equilibrium, giving at times the impression of immobility.

Finally, in the work of Varèse we discern the essential characteristics of a music which is fully and consciously spatial in its structure and imagery. Varèse's first major works, composed in the 1920s, reveal these characteristics in the full measure of maturity. Though it does not give up the motive, Varèse's music relies heavily on densities, organized by the imaginative control of timbre, among other things. These densities gather themselves into assymmetric spatial configurations by a process in which entry and attack determine motion. Varèse confirms this when he says, of "Intégrales," that it

> was conceived as a spatial projection . . . constructed . . . according to certain acoustical principles which had not existed previously, but which I knew, could be realized and made use of sooner or later. . . . While in our musical system we divide quantities whose values are fixed, in the realization which I sought, the values would be continually changed in relation to a common factor. In other words, it would be like a series of variations, the changes resulting from slight alterations in the form of a function or the transformation of one function into another. In order to make my meaning clear—for the eye is quicker and more disciplined than the ear—let us transfer this conception into the visual field and consider the shifting projection of a geometric figure on a ground with the figure and ground both moving in space, but each with its own individual speeds changed and varied according to position and rotation. The immediate form of the projection is determined by the relative position between the figure and ground at this moment. But in permitting the figure and ground to have their own movement one is capable of representing with the projection a highly complex image seemingly unpredictable. In addition, these qualities can be further developed by letting the forms of the geometric figures vary as well as their speeds.[6]

Eduard Hanslick defined music as "sounding forms in motion," a definition whose intention was to stress the essential temporality of music. As a definition, it is still apt even if our interpretation of it is entirely different, especially in the light of our discussion of the emerging spatialization of music. The temporal aspect, long dominant, is now at the service of the "sounding forms." Whether these forms are differentiated by timbre alone, by reflective symmetry, or by the geometric analogue of the figure-ground relationship, they take on the characteristics of spatial projections and configurations, self-sufficient entities, sonorous bodies with mass and density moving in time. It is the very self-sufficiency of these sounding spatial projections and configurations which requires that the temporal field in which they move be utterly free of an autonomous, self-generating rhythmic structure based on the beat, felt or heard. The sound structures of serialism and the free sounds which occur in "situational" composition based on chance operations and improvisation belong to this same sphere, however random or nondetermined they may be. The motion of all these different musics tends either toward a state of equilibrium bordering on entropy or toward erratic gestures of rapidly changing shapes and speeds. Music can no longer be said to be a purely temporal art when its very temporality, its durational dimension, is at the command, so to say, of its sounding forms. The liberation of sound from tonal harmonic functions (which was the great accomplishment of atonality), the suppression of the beat and pulsation (which parallels the evolution of atonality and its subsequently systematized procedures, twelve-tone method and serialism), and the resultant emergence of unpredictability and discontinuity—these are the paths which have led inexorably to the spatialization of music and to the overthrow of a long-dominant temporal structure. The passage of sounding forms in traditional music is dominated and organized by a flow of measured beats, presenting an image of time in a constant state of flux and movement, of change and becoming. But in the new music it is the image of space which predominates, an image in which the sound substance forms itself as the primary object of perception, its motion secondary, contingent on the structure of the sounding forms themselves.

What, then, is the significance of the new spatial image of music? What is its expressive import, if any? To answer these questions, we must first reaffirm the essentially human source of music; for it is in the condition of man that we discover the tendencies of his art; and as man's view of his present reality alters, so, too, does his view of art and its expressive structure. What has happened in our time that the composer should come to view music as a spatial rather than a temporal image? It seems as though twentieth-century man has, with Blake's sunflower, grown "weary of time" and history, the very time and history adulated by earlier centuries. According to Mircea Éliade, contemporary man is in "terror of history" and its increasingly relentless pressure. He would appear to be rejecting three centuries of a doctrine he can no longer live with because it does not provide him with the means by which he can successfully cope with the reality of his present existence. As Éliade points out: "the new conception of linear progress professed, for example, by a Francis Bacon or a Pascal," set in motion "from the seventeenth century on, linearism and the progressivistic conception of history," which asserted themselves more and more, "inaugurating faith in an infinite progress, a faith already proclaimed by Leibnitz, predominant in the century of 'enlightenment' and popularized in the nineteenth century by the triumph of the ideas of the evolutionists."[7] We shall not dwell on the noteworthy fact that, beginning with the Baroque era, the temporal structure of music, linked to an increasingly strong and expanding sense of tonality, developed ever more complex forms of sonorous continuity which reveal the presence of an implicit assumption of time as irreversible, linear, progressive. Bergson, the philosopher of pure duration, saw in music the embodiment of his ideas of "lived time," the flux of change and becoming. But in 1927 Wyndham Lewis in *Time and Western Man* lashed out at the Bergsonian doctrine of duration and reasserted the archaic values of the "classical man" of Greek culture. "We have seen," he said, "the subjectivism of the 'Faustian' or modern Western man, associated fanatically with a deep sense for the reality of *Time*—as against Space." Lewis cherished classical man because he had "no sense . . . of Time. His love of immediate 'things' found its counterpart in his love of the 'immediate" in 'time.' He was that creature of the Pure Present so admired by Goethe." Lewis's rejection of the time doctrine and his reassertion of the spatialized consciousness of ancient man parallels the turning away from the "terror of history" which Éliade notes, on other grounds, as the emerging state of contemporary man's consciousness.

Music dominated by the temporal image and music dominated by the spatial image reflect completely opposite attitudes or stances toward reality. While they are both supremely human forms of musical expression, the former tends toward the subjective utterance of the individual while the latter leans toward an objectified projection in which the composer's energies are focused beyond himself and the lyrical flow of his inner personal states. Subjective man, "Faustian" man, to use Lewis's terms, views existence as change, himself and his history at the center of a process of becoming. For him, life is an experience, whatever the nature of its content, in which nothing stands still, nothing lasts, and the future beckons. Subjective man cannot transcend time; he is trapped in it. However, when man seizes on the present moment of his existence as the only *real* time, he spatializes his existence; that is, he fills his present with objects of perception which take on solidity and concreteness—a state of permanence. His world is no longer one of time and change alone; it is a world of space in which time and change are modes of motion.

In the new music, time as duration becomes a dimension of musical space. The new spatial image of music seeks to project the permanence of the world as cosmos, the cosmos as the eternal present. It is an image of music which aspires to Being, not Becoming.

NOTES

1. *Style and Idea* (New York: St. Martin's Press, 1975), p. 106.
2. Ibid.
3. Ibid., p. 107.
4. "Lecture on Something," in *Silence* (Middletown, Conn.: Wesleyan University Press, 1961), p. 135.
5. Despite the term's complete denial of the possibility of a meaningful, ordered discourse of musical events, the view it represents is symptomatic of the crisis of contemporary music; and for that reason alone, if for no other, it must be granted a certain degree of authenticity if not in terms of results achieved, then as indicative of current thought processes and mental attitudes.
6. My translation from the original French, published in a record review by Istvan Anhalt, *Canadian Music Journal*, Winter, 1961, pp. 34–35.
7. *Cosmos and History* (New York: Harper Torchbooks, 1959), pp. 145–46.

On Schoenberg and Serialism

- *Tradition and Twelve-Tone Music (ca. 1955)*
- *Reflections on Schoenberg (1972)*

Tradition and Twelve-Tone Music

Schoenberg's discovery of the 12 note series was of fundamental importance from two points of view: firstly, for the new ordering, which had now become a necessity, of the material of sound which had no tonal center, and secondly, for the unity and ordering of the development of non-tonal music in the line of classical and preclassical tradition.
                    —Josef Rufer in *Composition with 12 Notes*

At a time when the method of "composition with 12 tones related only to one another," as Arnold Schoenberg called it, seems at last to have established itself unquestionably as the most positive contribution of general structural significance to music in the twentieth century, it is something of a paradox to hear deprecating voices raised against the very man who discovered and established the method. It is even more of a paradox that the camp of dissenters and detractors does not comprise those sentimental guardians of the Holy Grail of Tonality who have always objected to Schoenberg and twelve-tone music but rather comes from the ranks of those younger composers in Europe and America who have taken Anton Webern, Schoenberg's pupil, as their model and spiritual father, rejecting categorically their spiritual grandfather.

In 1952, Pierre Boulez wrote an article which appeared in *The Score*, a British publication, berating Schoenberg for having explored the twelve-tone technique in the wrong direction. Firstly, he took to task Schoenberg's use of the method of twelve-tone composition as being "nothing more than a severe discipline to be enforced on chromatic composition." Further, he stated that Schoenberg's "ambition" was, apparently, once he had established the new technique, "to construct works of the same kind as those of the tonal world he had only just abandoned, in which the new technique of composition would prove its possibilities." Boulez continues: "But unless some attempt was made to explore the structures *specific* to 12-tone composition, how could this new technique yield any satisfactory results? *By structure, I mean the growth from given material to the form of a composition* [emphasis added]. On the whole Schoenberg was not much preoccupied with the problems of forms that would derive essentially from a 12-tone basis." Boulez sees a fundamental contradiction in Schoenberg's use of preclassic and classical forms, arising from the fact that the twelve-tone "language finds no sanction" in these forms "but something more negative: namely, *that these forms seek out every possibility of organization implicit in the new material* [emphasis added]. The two worlds are incompatible and he has tried to justify one with the other." Boulez next complains that

Schoenberg continued to employ the devices of accompanied melody and of counterpoint based on principal and subsidiary voices (*Hauptstimme* and *Nebenstimme*, as Schoenberg termed it). Rhetorically, Boulez asks: "This, surely, is a most unfortunate inheritance from romanticism?" He concludes that Schoenberg has failed to realize the essential nature of his own discovery and suggests dissociating "Schoenberg's work altogether from the phenomenon of the tone row. The two have been confused with obvious pleasure, sometimes with unconcealed dishonesty, and a certain Webern has been only too easily forgotten. . . . Perhaps, like Webern, we might succeed in writing works whose form arises inevitably from the given material."

Since the views represented by Boulez and similar expressions of dissent appear to be circulating like a virus, and the younger avant-garde is only too ready and eager for this latest infection, I am impelled not only to ally myself with Schoenberg but to reveal these arguments and views for what they are— faulty and specious. This rebuttal, therefore, is aimed specifically at those who have seen fit to make less of Schoenberg in order to make more of Webern. Although I have allied myself unequivocally with Schoenberg and his artistic aims, I will not find it incompatible with my position to offer an appreciation of Webern's unique contribution, focusing at all times on the need for keeping in perspective a situation which has been distorted by these deprecations of Schoenberg.

What is of value for us in Boulez is that he has raised important questions concerning the relation between the method of twelve-tone composition and "traditional" attitudes toward formal and textural procedures, a matter which takes us far beyond internecine factionalism. These questions have as much to do with music *as music* as they have to do with matters twelve-tone. Their solutions shall be my main concern since, as I see it, twelve-tone composition, if it is to win final acceptance not only by musicians but the world at large, must be a way of producing significant art works which will be listened to and performed not as curiosities or strange novelties but *as music.*

Before attempting to answer such questions as "What forms and textures are appropriate to twelve-tone composition?" or "Are there specific forms and textures intrinsic to twelve-tone music alone?" or "What is the relationship between the method of twelve-tone composition and formal-textural procedures inherited from the past?" I wish first to discuss them in relation to tonal music. This is necessary because we now have a historical perspective where tonal music is concerned from which we may learn a great deal about the evolution of form and texture; and because, despite the apparent dichotomy in basic premises, both twelve-tone music and tonal music are in a line of historical progression, a fact which must not be overlooked. Although twelve-tone music as first formulated by Schoenberg "broke" with tonal principles (key center, diatonic scale, harmonic functions), the question is whether it actually constituted a break with psychological and aesthetic principles of form building and texture building which are embodied in the great works of tonal masters. Therefore, a preliminary survey of how these factors of form and texture function in tonal music can and will be of invaluable aid in understanding their function in twelve-tone music.

We have learned to associate with tonal music such "forms" as the sonata-movement form, song form, variation form, rondo, scherzo, minuet, fugue, chorale prelude, and others. It is by now an established belief (because it is taught as such) that these forms had their origins and roots in tonal thinking. Viewed with the short end of the telescope, it would appear to be true that these forms are consistent and simultaneous with the flowering of tonal music. But turn the telescope around and we immediately recognize that we have been confusing the *names of forms* which are historically associated with tonal music with formal principles and ideas of shapes which, while embodied in tonal music, are not at all specific to it. The basic principles from which these forms and shapes arose can be traced into the preclassical period, as far back as the beginnings of monodic lines and the first attempts at polyphony in the ninth and tenth centuries. These principles are both psychological and aesthetic—psychological, because they have to do with creating interest, aesthetic because they determine clarity of design and function.

Let us consider, for example, polyphonic structures such as the fugue and canon, forms which Donald Tovey calls "texture-forms," and William S. Newman refers to as forms based on the "progression of motivic play." With the aid of the musicologists, we have clear evidence that the underlying principles of these forms, repetition and imitation, existed centuries before the tonal system was finally crystallized. Repetition and imitation are the nerve and sinew of the medieval motet, the late Renaissance madrigal, the ricercare, toccata, fantasia, canzone and countless other vocal and instrumental forms which flourished in abundance before the time of Bach. The laws formulated by Rameau in the eighteenth century are the first step toward establishing the harmonic functions of tonal music; and yet the principles of repetition and imitation were practiced by many successive generations of musicians prior to Rameau's historic formulation (as were the very chords he codified). By the middle of the eighteenth century, the tonal system, still to evolve, had made it possible to apply these principles—repetition and imitation—on a larger canvas, giving them dimensions not possible previously. Thus, by the time of the first formulation of tonality and the harmonic functions which became the central core of tonal thinking, the principles of repetition and imitation had been known and practiced with consummate skill and imagination.

When the Florentine Camerata stumbled on the dramatic vocal form we now call "opera," at the turn of the seventeenth century, they brought about the first major upheaval in modern music, for they integrated accompanied melody into an ambitious art-music form. (Accompanied melody had of course existed at least since the trouvères, troubadours, and minnesingers of the Middle Ages.) Leaving behind the complexities of Renaissance polyphony, the early opera composers developed a style whose mode of successive presentation called into play another kind of formal-textural procedure: these forms, which Tovey describes as "shapes" and Newman as "progression by phrase grouping," became the seedbed of practically all later successive-shaped forms. Later, cross-fertilization caused the emergence of forms which combined accompanied melody and polyphony; and out of such beginnings as the early opera *sinfonia* and the Baroque concerto grosso came the sonata form, the solo concerto, and the symphony. The story of emerging forms is too complex to render here without the attendant danger of oversimplification. However, it can be said with safety that tonality crystallized the successive shape-form but did not originate it. Through tonality these forms evolved into the large-scale structures with which we are now familiar, structures capable of conveying many different varieties and kinds of expressive attitudes. Thus the forms which generally employ heterogeneous textures (based on contrasting structures: melody and accompaniment) as well as homogeneous textures (based on noncontrasting structures: the canon, the hymn, and the fugue) did not begin with tonality; rather they achieved their highest historic crystallization in the tonal system.

If, then, the forms associated with tonality cannot be *attributed to* tonality, to what *can* we attribute them? As I suggested earlier, there are two basic factors which create valid art forms: interest (psychological factor) and clarity (aesthetic factor). Music has always been a matter of commanding attention and maintaining interest through clear organization; the stylistic tools at hand must be suitable for this purpose. As the focus of the creative goal changes, the means also undergo change. Music has been changing constantly since its beginnings and this is perfectly consistent with the fact that man too has been changing, for music does not exist (in this world at least) apart from its human creators. Despite this surface alteration, underlying this ceaseless activity and eternal restlessness are constants which exist, however intangibly. Interest and clarity can only be rendered when, as Josef Rufer says in his *Composition with 12 Notes,* a piece of music "explains itself in the coherent presentation" of musical ideas. "In order to communicate themselves, these abstract thoughts must assume a concrete motivic, thematic, or melodic shape. In order to gather its characteristic features firmly together such a shape needs a form, i.e., it needs definition and subdivision." Rufer also points out that Western music has evolved from fundamental principles of presenting "musical thoughts in shapes and forms. . . . These principles have played such a decisive part, both in the creation of the smaller 'thematic' forms and in the development of larger movement-forms out of these, *that one can describe them as antecedents of form-building*" [emphasis added]. To achieve "definition and subdivision," i.e., clarity, Rufer cites repetition and variation as principles affecting the creation of smaller forms and the development of larger forms out of them. Repetition, the coherence factor, is primary since it has a unifying effect and insures (Rufer continues) "that all parts of a work can be related to one another and thus create the necessary conditions for the building of its form." Repetition also aids the function of memory. Through repetition only can an idea be grasped and its content retained. Through repetition the musical idea achieves familiarity and becomes recognizable. Without it, structural comprehensibility is unattainable. However, "as limitation is a characteristic feature of form, exact, unvaried repetitions" are not sufficient to maintain a form. For "every form grows toward a conclusion, a limit," and exact, unvaried repetition produces inconclusive forms leading only to mere cessation. In order to avoid this inconclusiveness, variation of ideas must be combined with the principle of repetition for higher levels of form; "repetition combined with variation allows the unit to create the manifold by procreating new shapes through developing variation." Thus Rufer confirms our principles of interest and clarity: repetition through its unifying effect creates clarity; variation allied to repetition maintains interest. Rufer also disclaims the view that the harmonic functions of tonality were the sole factors in creating the forms associated with tonality and maintaining the necessary tension to keep them alive.

The forms of classical tonality are, therefore, not given by the nature of the harmonic functions of tonality. Stylistically organized around them, *these forms are not attributable to them.* Tonality did permit larger and more complex structures; it did render coherence through its system of harmonic cadence to larger and larger subdivisions. But we must emphasize that tonality broadened and developed but did not create the principles of form building. Therefore, when we deal with the forms of tonal music we must realize that we are apprehending only one way and one general kind of musical thinking. The fact that music is couched in terms of tonal functions in no way alters the priority of the psychological factors of interest and the aesthetic factor of clarity. In the case of tonal music, then, forms have taken on particular characteristics due to the nature of the functions of tonal harmony; but these forms, though modified by tonal functions, cannot be said to stem from them. It is possible then to state that the basic ideas of these forms, resting as they do on statement, repetition, contrast, variation, and development, may also obtain whenever different pitch concepts are at work, and that they will differ from their previous appearance in tonal music to the extent that they will organize their limitations and subdivisions in accord with the new conditions brought about by these different pitch concepts. These forms will exhibit their own variety of unique characteristics, dimensions, and textures as they regroup themselves around the new point of view, but they need not therefore be lacking in kinship with their tonal counterparts, nor is this kinship a stigma to be attached to the newer regrouping.

A form can, under new conditions, regroup itself around coherence factors attributable to the new conditions. To the superficial eye it may then look like a "new" form, but to the perceptive, discerning eye, it will be clearly only a variation on an old, eternal theme: creative form building. It is of no importance at all what name we give to each regrouping, so long as the content and the form are coextensive, convincing, and inevitable.

Boulez's notion that the form of a piece of music is an inevitable growth from given material would appear to have a certain plausibility. Put to the test it becomes not only implausible but untenable as well. We have just discussed briefly the relation of formal and textural procedures to the development of tonality. The evidence arising from our investigation led us to the conclusion that the principles of form building were established long before the crystallization of tonality took place; that these principles emanate from psychological and aesthetic factors, in short, from the creative mind of man.

To accept the notion that form is totally dependent on "given material" is to deny creative will and its dominance over material. In the equation "creative will → material," we posit an active, motivating factor acting out an artistic purpose on neutral, passive matter. This act is of necessity a human one and is the measure of man's creative capacity. Besides the material of pitch vibrations (to which I believe Boulez has incorrectly confined himself), there is another basic musical material which we have not as yet mentioned—rhythm. Musical time or rhythm is the direct means for organizing limitations, "divisions and subdivisions." Rhythm does not arise from sound vibrations but organizes them in temporal patterns in accordance with the composer's inherent grasp of subjective time. We must therefore add to the other form-determining factors indigenous to man's nature—the need for interest and clarity—the subjective-psychological grasp of temporal values. Not only must we recognize that differences in *feeling* rhythm—a living, subjective means of grasping the very essence of formal structure—determine a preference for this or that shape but also that emotional and psychological differences in artistic personality often create wide divergence in how the same pitch material is to be used. If this were not true, Mozart would be the same as Beethoven, as Schoenberg would be the same as Webern.

Any aesthetic of music must therefore base itself on rhythm (residing in man as a psychological-subjective relation to time and proportions of time) and on pitch (or vibrations of sound residing outside of man as physical, potential material). In my view, rhythm is therefore autonomous in its relation to pitch. It is the means of determining and ordering the duration of a melody or a counterpoint of melodies, of a transitional section, or of any other formal device. To understand the nature of form and its relation to the kind of sound it forms, it is essential to grant rhythm its form-giving properties. It is rhythm, autonomous of pitch, which gives plasticity, shape, and life to music, regardless of the nature of the pitch material, whether tonal or nontonal, determinate or indeterminate. Musical time bears a direct relation to a composer's grasp of his subjective experience of time itself. How a composer organizes his pitch material, therefore, depends to a great extent upon his rhythmic, plastic sense of form.

The ordering of musical pitch vibrations, like all neutral, inert, passive material, will offer resistance to the creative will. As we saw in our discussion of tonal music, the harmonic functions of tonality became a coherence factor around which form was built. We also decided that any new coherence factor beside tonality would cause form to group its divisions and subdivisions around itself in order to create a new type of unity, but could not be given credit for forms so built, any more than we could credit tonality with creating forms historically associated with it. The problem of the composer has always been to impose, by an act of creative will, his vision on material while at the same time respecting the properties of his material. There is undoubtedly an awareness of the intractibility or resistance posed by his material on the part of the composer. If he cannot overcome it, he fails creatively. But when emotional fire is wedded to intellectual power, material and resistance are no longer impediments but a pliable means to the realization of artistic purpose.

Boulez's aesthetic assumes that twelve-tone material is different from any other previously used. As material, which poses new problems and new resistances, twelve-tone *is* different. To that extent he is right. But little else has changed. Composers' grasp of psychological time metamorphosed into musical time, their need for creating interest and clarity—these remain the same factors as before with individual differences and manifestations granted. It is in these important matters that we see the incompleteness and arbitrariness of Boulez's view of Schoenberg and the method of twelve-tone composition.

What is the nature of twelve-tone material? The method of "composition with twelve tones related only to one another" was the end result of Schoenberg's creative, not theoretical, search for a unifying, coherent principle around which he could organize shapes and build musical structures. Like tonality, the twelve-tone concept is essentially neutral, in the sense that it tells us nothing about how it must be used while offering the widest potentialities for how it can be used. In the twelve-tone method, harmonic functions have theoretically little or no structural meaning as regards form. It is a method open, however, to all other kinds of musical thinking: contrapuntal, accompanied melody, and monophonic statements (as for example the opening of the third movement of Schoenberg's Fourth String Quartet). It is open to all and any kind of rhythmic treatment in both the minutiae of metric detail and the overall time dimensions required by large forms.

Taking the twelve chromatic tones of the tempered scale as individual but related tones, one may arrange the order of these twelve tones into a basic set (or row). From this original set three other forms are possible: inversion of the original basic set (under special conditions, a mirror inversion), and the retrograde (beginning with the last tone and ending with the first) of both original and inversion. This, then, is the raw pitch material. As Rufer points out, this formulation by Schoenberg of a new principle of ordering tones

> was of a general and fundamental significance which went beyond the works of its creator; for it became clear that the individual style of a composer was not in the least affected by it, and that it could be used in an entirely personal manner, varied only by the quality and degree of the creative imagination.

Not only does this method allow freedom in the creating of a basic set; it also allows the composer freedom to build upon this basic set whatever melodic, harmonic, and rhythmic structures he may require for the expression of his musical ideas. Within the formulation of the method, there are no prescriptions as to how these musical problems may be solved and their solutions presented for aural perception.

One should expect to find in music organized on the twelve-tone basis that every aspect of the texture and form is permeated by one or another manifestation of one or more of the four possible forms of the basic row, just as the texture and form of tonal music is organized by harmonic functions which define tonality. This brings about the cohesion of all aspects so that, despite the varied means employed to articulate texture and form, they derive their unity from the coherence factor of the series or row. Rufer says:

> Inventing themes is identical with giving them shape. Here it means shaping them out of the series, which arises out of the basic conception of the piece as the preliminary formation of the entire thematic material. This shaping takes place through the use of the artistic means which still apply here—those which were used and developed by classical and pre-classical music on the basis of the principles of repetition and of motivic working in polyphonic music, or motivic variation in homophonic music.

On the subject of what forms are attributable to twelve-tone music, Rufer comments that

> composition with 12 notes can, but need not, lead to new forms; this entirely depends on the content. One would naturally expect that the "possibilities of the logical creation of form" which this method produces would also cause the appearance of new forms; but to make this a re-

quirement and to regard the capability of creating new forms as a criterion of the worth or worthlessness of this method of composition only shows a complete misunderstanding of the idea and essence of the method. And it shows mistaken thought; for forms could never arise from a technique of composition—they only arise from ideas.

What should interest us in works based on the twelve-tone method is not whether their forms are "new" but whether their structural lines and groupings are coextensive with their artistic content and create coherent shapes which share a common purpose—the realization of the ideas of each work. Thus for Schoenberg the form of a musical work was created by adherence to the *Grundgestalt,* which was the "law" of that particular work. In each twelve-tone work, then, the functions of the notes given as melodies or harmonies are governed by the "law" of the series, which is the coherence factor operating throughout the musical organism. On a still higher level we may say that, metaphorically speaking, the law is administered by the creative imagination of the composer. The twelve-tone series, the raw pitch material, is the source of all pitch relationships—melodic, harmonic, contrapuntal. Each of the four basic shapes (original, inversion, retrograde original, and retrograde inversion) rotates in a perpetual motion of variation until the larger shape of the work has been realized and fixed. As in tonal music, rhythm is autonomous, determining the profile of the form, its "division and subdivisions," of a composition based on a twelve-tone series.

As a composer, Schoenberg not only achieved a new means of structural unity; he also revitalized traditional contrapuntal techniques and gave a new quality to melody. His concept of texture is unique in music; for the first time, through the twelve-tone method, he found a way of composing melodies and accompaniments which gives them a fundamental relationship to each other which goes far beyond eighteenth- or nineteenth-century practice. Texture in his music is dense, rich in internal relationships, and dramatic; for in creating accompaniments which are no longer mere figuration or arpeggiation of chords but essentially contrapuntal, he intensified the background against which his plastic, arching melodies are projected with maximum contrast and effect. There is no meaningless padding in Schoenberg. His musical space has genuine depth. His preference for this type of heterogeneous textural relationship undoubtedly stems from his essentially dramatic view of music. Dramatic music, without words and mise-en-scène, is more a matter of expressing tensions and conflicting musical relations than of delineating a known human emotion or crisis. It is no use asking what this kind of dramatic music is about, since more often than not it is not about anything except the immediate rendering of intense musical emotions. As a composer of this kind, Schoenberg ranks high.

I can find no better explanation for his sudden juxtapositions, his sharp con-trasting sonorities, his sense of the dramatic pause (expressed in passages of utterly suspended motion only to be followed by some new, unexpected feel-ing expressed in a new quality of timbre or sound), his sense of the angelic and of the diabolical. His feeling for the dramatic is as well expressed in his Fourth String Quartet as in his "Survivor from Warsaw," in his music without words as well as in his music with words, *Sprechstimme'*d or sung. Schoenberg's artistic personality is vibrant, glowing, and eloquent; he proceeds according to a logic of emotions and vivifies everything he touches. Though a great contra-puntist (likened by some to Ockeghem, by others to Bach), he is also a supreme melodist, though by no means a lyrical one. His melodies, only occasionally lyrical, are not poetic structures but possess an eloquent rhetoric we associate with prose or blank verse. It is remarkable that his intensely personal ex-pression is achieved by the most objective use of the twelve-tone technique. For in no other twelve-tone composer does the use of the method lend itself to as completely objective an analysis as in Schoenberg's. The clarity and cease-less inventiveness of his mind is as intense as his purely artistic nature.

From his first twelve-tone piece (Op. 23, No. 5 for piano) to his last completed and published work ("De Profundis," Op. 50b, for six-part a cap-pella chorus), Schoenberg sought to establish the method of twelve-tone on ever more objective grounds. Starting from a kind of primitive use of a con-stantly rotating series, he finally, and only after many years, achieved a refine-ment of the technique which has come to be called the hexachordal principle. Without a comprehension of this principle Schoenberg's maturest works in the twelve-tone method cannot be truly assessed; analysts who do not com-prehend the hexachordal principle are baffled and frustrated and, annoyed, claim that Schoenberg lapsed into inconsistencies. Only a technical discussion could adequately detail the full meaning and development of the principle of the hexachord. Nevertheless, we can describe here its basis in simple terms. Schoenberg discovered that a group of six tones could be constructed in such a way that when mirror-inverted this group could produce six new tones. By using the tones of the mirror as the second group of six to complete the original set of twelve, the mirror of the second group would produce tones identical with the original six-note group. This may be demonstrated by using numbers as symbols:

$$1 \quad 2 \quad 3 \quad 4 \quad 5 \quad 6 \ \| \ 7 \quad 8 \quad 9 \quad 10 \quad 11 \quad 12$$
$$7 \quad 8 \quad 9 \quad 10 \quad 11 \quad 12 \ \| \ 1 \quad 2 \quad 3 \quad 4 \quad 5 \quad 6$$

This, however, is an oversimplification. One qualification is necessary: that the second group need not follow the exact order of tones in the mirror on which it is based. Consequently the mirror of the second group will automatically re-arrange the tones of the original six-note group or hexachord. For example:

1	2	3	4	5	6	‖	11	10	12	8	9	7
7	8	9	10	11	12	‖	5	4	6	2	3	1

The meaning for compositional purposes of this refinement of the first type of twelve-tone series is enormous. For, as Schoenberg demonstrated in his practical application of this principle, each hexachord and its complementary mirror could function as a unit, whether melodic or accompanimental. A new approach to "tonality" is effected: no longer key centers but structures oriented by units of six tones, defining both melody and harmony. Through the hexachordal principle, the twelve-tone method achieves a clarity, breadth, and function not possible previously (and not possible through the consistent fragmentation of a row). Each hexachord, its characteristic features defined by internal relationships, develops a sense of aural orientation which, though not tonal in the old sense, defines an area for clear aural perception—which is, in essence, what the traditional system of tonality also accomplished. Schoenberg's music, beginning with his Op. 30's, developed this principle until his Op. 50b, where he was on the verge of finding a new link between the older system of tonality and the mirror combinations of the hexachordal principle. In his later twelve-tone music, Schoenberg developed the hexachord as a highly refined coherence factor bringing about unity in the context of his textures, the relations between melody and accompaniments.

Rhythm in Schoenberg is autonomous. It is part and parcel of his dramatic urgency. With no apparent feeling for the minute metric detail as evidenced in Webern, or for the motoric energy of Hindemith, or for the physically disruptive meters of Stravinsky, Schoenberg used rhythm in the traditional formal sense—to create proportions. We will not, however, deny him a keen sense of propulsion or the subdivision of metric units into fascinating asymmetrical patterns. These are in his music, but subject to the larger span of structural rhythmic lines. It must be noted, too, that his use of the hexachordal unit is consistent with his large, rhythmic phrases, cadences occurring simultaneously between rhythm and hexachord. This is analogous to the rhythmic cadence in tonal music.

If one has grasped the meaning and extent of the mirrored hexachord, one recognizes immediately that Schoenberg did not exhaust all the possibilities. Much yet remains to be achieved. Yet his works based on this principle—the Fourth String Quartet, String Trio, Violin Concerto, Piano Concerto, Phantasy for Violin and Piano, and "De Profundis"—illustrate his inexhaustible technical inventiveness. Each reveals new applications, new combinations. Each work constructed on this principle defines its own artistic world and personality. Any critical analysis of Schoenberg's work will, in the future, have to take into account his creation of the principle of the mirrored hexachord and his application of it. Such analysis, I am certain, will confirm my belief that in Schoenberg the twelve-tone method reaches its most objective conditions through the hexachordal principle, leaving ample room for differences of artistic purpose. As an extra bonus, it will perhaps also confirm my conviction that Schoenberg's search for a new "tonal" orientation and his continuing use of "traditional" forms was due to his acceptance of what remains valid in the older practice and his wish to revitalize those traditions which antedate tonality.

In the case of Webern we find a point of view totally different from that of Schoenberg. Webern's music seems far more cool and impersonal. Yet he offers a paradox: a music and an aesthetic so unique to himself and a grasp of twelve-tone problems so completely specialized that he left nothing more to be explored in his way. In actuality Webern's art is deeply personal, the quintessence of a distilled view of music in general and composition with twelve tones in particular. Whatever we may think of Webern's accomplishment, we cannot deny him his special qualities of subtlety, brevity, and an amazing feeling for the individualized tone. Characteristic of any Webern score is the sparse texture. There is an exactitude, not only in his choice of placement of the individual tone but also in his choice of the timbre, rhythm, and dynamics of each tone, bordering on a state of perfection which has reached an aesthetic condition of nonaction, a kind of musical Nirvana. And indeed, Webern's music creates a tiny, precious world of thin, wired sounds which spark and crackle occasionally, but which, for the most part, possess a feeling of *already completed action*. This develops an overall feeling of "motionless motion," perfect equilibrium, a static, suspended moment of time. While there is definitely an excitement in some of his music, it is never occasioned by such means as big climaxes, wild rhythms, or impassioned utterance. Everything is in order, always under perfect control; consequently his music develops a limited range of expressivity. Webern proceeds by understatement, by the power of piano and pianissimo. Psychologically his music is easier on the ear than Schoenberg's; but because of the extreme limitations he imposes, it is aurally difficult to find defining melodic ideas. Webern's real strength lay in the realm of the minute, the microscopic. Webern's is a private art as opposed to Schoenberg's public art.

We mentioned the sparseness of actual notes in Webern's scores. This is aurally and visually apparent. His textures are mainly the result of his penchant for canonic imitation and an economical handling of the musical space. Webern constructs his rhythmic details in such a fashion that they become the temporal counterpart of his handling of individual pitches. It is common to find in Webern rhythmic retrograde and rhythmic canon. This is the inevitable result of his concept of organizing *all* aspects of his music by means of a common formulation. By controlling every aspect of the music, Webern hoped to achieve absolute unity. There is no structural tension between his temporal, rhythmic ideas and his pitch concepts. This homogeneity has a corresponding effect on the texture of his music: it too achieves a homogeneity and therefore a corresponding deficiency in tension. For these reasons Webern does not need climax; it would destroy the delicate machinery he has so painstakingly created.

It has been said that twelve-tone music is essentially contrapuntal. In Webern we see this carried out fully; entire movements and sections are based on such technical tours de force as double canons in contrary motion. Yet the aural perception rarely confirms the visual perusal of the score. We can only conclude that the canon was for Webern a structural point of departure rather than a musical idea to be heard as such. Whether canonic or otherwise, Webern's melodies rarely move on a single-dimensioned axis. They are fragmented, moving motive by motive through the various registers of his texture. Despite fragmentation the aural effect is a complete one—the pointillist technique accomplishes a unified effect although one can no longer use the term *melody* in the usual sense of a defined and definable profile. Webern carefully gauges motivic entries so as not to allow them to coincide with other tones which would destroy the effect of the gently ordered rhythmic flow. The effect of this is often an imperceptible swaying or rocking in place. By gauging these rhythmic details with an ear to absolute perfection, Webern develops a sense of total suspended animation. By reducing the potential of differentiation and bringing everything under the aegis of one musical concept, he creates homogeneity of means and result. Thus Webern has been the first to subject rhythm to an absolute order. He has taken from it its autonomous character and has subjected it to a process of refinement which requires control of every beat and subdivision of a beat. This reduction of rhythmic detail to conformity with pitch concept forced Webern to work with the simplest metric elements in order to succeed in his task—and therefore to limit his forms. He has applied one technique of organization to both temporal and spatial disposition. In so doing he has reduced his structures to the simplest, most homogeneous elements in order to refine them and raise them to a new level of subtle construction. And this he has done admirably.

Homogeneity in Webern's music is further enhanced by his rigid control of dynamic levels. For example, in one place in his Symphony Op. 21, we find that the dynamic gradations move from *pp* through *p* to *mp*, *p* being the pivot for *all* parts. Thus in addition to his ordering of pitch and rhythm, Webern carefully controls his levels of volume. One other factor which is significant in bringing about an overall homogeneity is Webern's predilection for short motives in which the interval shape and not the rhythmic shape appears to be more prominent. By restricting much of his music to the traditionally dissonant intervals, whose psychological values are very similar, Webern agains narrows down his materials until homogeneity results. The perpetual shifting through the registers of the musical space of these similar interval values eventually produces an intervallic homogeneity which reinforces the rhythmic and dynamic homogeneity. To achieve his special purposes, Webern has eschewed the large rhythmically autonomous gesture required for large forms built on the principle of phrase succession and instead has confined himself to smaller gestures perfectly compatible with forms based on motivic play—texture-forms. His phrases and motives are minute, self-contained capsules which do not require impetus; therefore, they lack the power to propel themselves forward, lack that urgency which arouses expectancy and alerts interest and attention.

In a short essay, lacking specific musical analysis, it is manifestly impossible to be complete or all-inclusive. I have attempted to present the salient features of the mature musical approach to twelve-tone composition of two masters, Schoenberg and Webern, in the hope that certain broad concepts may be developed which are applicable to the problem of twelve-tone music itself. In comparing these two composers, the first thing that strikes us is that each composer has a different view not only of the twelve-tone method but of music itself, stemming unquestionably from the natural differences in artistic personality. There is no room here for a total investigation of this dichotomy in view or aesthetic, except as we can suggest it through a comparison of their attitudes expressed musically.

Both composers achieve a high degree of clarity and coherence through their particular application of the twelve-tone material. Both succeeded in their individual treatment of the characteristics they found to be inherent in the type of twelve-tone row each devised for compositional use. For Schoenberg, the hexachord produced a flexible, rich potential in forms and textures structured in phrase groupings, melodies, and accompaniments; for Webern, a twelve-tone series became amenable to fragmentation, to motivic building, and to canonic-imitative structures. With the hexachord Schoenberg can work a large canvas and develop a piece over a long period of musical time; Webern restricts himself to short spans of time and telescopes, distills, and condenses his material. In Schoenberg's music, rhythm remains largely autonomous, a force on which he draws in order to build large formal structures in which melodies may be presented, varied, and restated; in Webern, autonomous rhythm is sacrificed in favor of a tightly controlled metric design—we do not find in Webern the large rhythmic gesture. Where Schoenberg organizes his hexachordal phrases according to large-scale rhythm, Webern makes rhythm obey the same principles of construction he applies to individual motives and pitches. It is this which creates in Webern the sense of "motionless motion" as contrasted with Schoenberg's sense of dramatic, urgent power. In Schoenberg, rhythm is a controlling, propelling force shaping the disposition of his hexachords; in Webern it is a controlled factor, another element to be ordered with minute care. Autonomous rhythm allows Schoenberg the latitude he needs to express his dynamic ideas; controlled rhythm aids Webern in his pursuit of static perfection.

We pointed out Webern's preference for homogeneous interval tensions which, through their filling of musical space, lend homogeneity to the musical texture. In fact, in Webern's music "traditional" dissonances lose their sharpness and psychological intensity because there is no contrasting interval structure. The result is a strange kind of concordance: a neutralizing of psychological tension. However, in Schoenberg, the context renders dissonances at their maximum psychological value. In Schoenberg the melodic shapes organize the intervals drawn from individual hexachords (sometimes changing the original order of their notes), where in Webern the intervals of the row organize the motives.

Schoenberg's textures are mainly heterogeneous in character, Webern's homogeneous. This is not to say that Schoenberg does not also use homogeneous textures or Webern heterogeneous ones; but it is significant that Webern's passion for contrapuntal organization leads him constantly toward homogeneity, while Schoenberg's feeling for large form based on melody and accompaniment leads toward heterogeneity. Musical space for both composers is determined largely by their individual handling of texture and rhythm. Schoenberg's musical space is dynamic, fluid, breathing in rhythms of expansion and contraction, increase and decrease of tension filling up and emptying out the space. Webern's musical space is static, fixed, its established limits defining the precision of his treatment of the individual tone, its rhythmic treatment, its volume and its timbre. Schoenberg's musical space is a pulsing architecture of tensions; Webern's is immobilized by the achievement of an almost perfect equilibrium of tensions.

Both Schoenberg and Webern had a feeling for traditional values which goes deeper than external appearance. Each in his own way—Schoenberg by himself, Webern with Schoenberg's example before him—rethought the process of art music. Each wished to reestablish and join the mainstream of the great tradition of the masters of the past. Thus we find them applying traditional basic principles of forming music inherent, not in twelve-tone music per se, but in the creative need to "define and subdivide." That Webern chose the canon, one of the oldest procedures in music, as the cornerstone of his art cannot be claimed as superior to Schoenberg's decision to follow a principle of a later historical epoch, "progression through phrase grouping." Webern's art is one of selectivity, exclusion of anything foreign to his personality; Schoenberg's one of all-inclusiveness. For there are few possibilities of musical thinking which Schoenberg does not employ at one time or another, including the intellectual feats of canonic contrapuntal construction so necessary to Webern.

These two basic attitudes toward potential form result in structures that are either valid or not depending only upon the creative capacity of the composers who elect to use them, not on the nature of the material itself, regardless of what that may be. I have tried to show that twelve-tone music can be produced in either one of these two fundamental ways, and that there is, theoretically, no limit to the potential variety of individual approaches within or cutting across these two distinctly opposite views.

We are now ready to answer a question raised earlier: What textures and forms are appropriate to twelve-tone music? My answer is, as many and of whatever kind genuine composers are capable of inventing. So long as composers invent musical ideas organized by the twelve-tone method, the textures and forms they produce will be valid expressions of the "law" of the series, or the "law" of the hexachord, regardless of individual variations, so long as they administer the "law" creatively. Whether the temporal disposition is autonomous (as in Schoenberg) or coextensive with the organization of pitch (as in Webern) makes little difference where validity is concerned; neither one nor the other attitude belongs to the twelve-tone method per se, despite the fact that the type of control observed in Webern is simultaneous with his exploration of the twelve-tone method. The method itself may have suggested this to him, but it cannot be claimed that twelve-tone music lacking this temporal rigidity is not twelve-tone music but some inferior product by a mind incapable of this "high" order of thinking. Webern's music leaves his followers no new, unexplored territory. He completely exhausted one side of the spectrum of twelve-tone possibilities. His art is unique and individual and offers no general principles which would permit the growth of another personality along the same lines. His road is so clearly marked that his followers can add nothing of importance and, unfortunately, will end up as imitators. Schoenberg, on the other hand, left much yet to be done. In discovering the principle of the mirrored hexachord he opened a vast unexplored area in which creative personalities can yet stake their claims. It is still an uncharted, virgin territory which will succumb only to the hardy ones, the composers who can think for themselves. We do not deny Webern his place; it is already there because he carved it out, single-handedly. But we also accord Schoenberg his rightful honors: a supreme artist and equally supreme thinker-in-tones who opened a new world, to Webern and to us, so vast that he could not in a single lifetime possibly complete the work that is still to be done by our generation and the next. We should not be surprised to find new applications of the twelve-tone method, particularly through the hexachordal principle.

Creative action is unpredictable, obeying laws man may never understand. Out of creative thought emerges the potential of all attitudes and forms; like nature itself, creative thought mothers perfection and imperfection, the fruitful and the unfruitful, incompatability and conformability, mutation and the common species—in short an endless variety of every conceivable kind of idea stemming from man's creative powers. We are rich in spiritual forerunners; we can only repay our inheritance by pursuing art as they did—without fear and without expectation.

Reflections on Schoenberg

I think it best to acknowledge at the outset that these "reflections" on Schoenberg are personal, therefore biased; that they are somewhat random in their
organization, even containing contradictory elements, because I take it as a
rule of reality and of the mental realm (a seemingly separate but no less important "reality" than its physical counterpart) that existence is not logical but, in
fact, full of paradox and contradiction and not reducible to neatly arranged
verbal packages. These reflections, then, comprise a series of related but not
necessarily connected thoughts, observations, and notes whose sole, common
link is the contemplation of the body of work of a master. This work, despite
the many years during which I preoccupied myself with a close study of it and
even carried out in my own work ideas and tendencies directly derived from
and based on it, still puzzles and disturbs me and gives me no complete
satisfaction because I find in it much—though fascinating—that does not con-
vince me. And yet, for all that, the serious lacks or imperfections or, even now,
alien elements (as I see them) of his art do not obscure or overbalance or
diminish the compelling power and beauty of portions of his work and, occasionally, entire compositions. The stance of my particular approach to the
problem of coming to grips with Schoenberg is best conveyed by this journal
entry of Delacroix dated November 1, 1852:

> To write treatises on the arts *ex professo*, to divide, to treat methodically,
> to summarize, to make systems for logical categorical instruction—all
> this is error, loss of time, a false and useless idea. The ablest man cannot
> do for others more than he does for himself, which is to note and ob-
> serve. . . . With such a man, the points of view change at every moment.
> Opinions must necessarily be modified; one never knows a master well
> enough to speak of him absolutely and definitively.

Perhaps it is even more important to confess that I view Schoenberg with all
the limitations of one composer reflecting on the work of another. A historian
or critic potentially has a larger perspective to operate from than a composer
who is locked into his own needs and interests. Moreover a composer is far less
interested ultimately in history or aesthetics; and although I have not avoided
considerations of either in these reflections, it is the work itself which remains
as the center of my thought. Possibly the advantage the composer has over the
historian or critic is that he is closer than they can be to the making of art and

the problems of craft which are the very substance of his existence, the *materia* of his mental life. Having said this, I also point out that the judgments, evaluations, and opinions which appear here remain subjective and incomplete.

Schoenberg as a Steppenwolf

Schoenberg seems to me a "Harry Haller," a kind of cultural "Steppenwolf," unable to relate any longer to the traditions from which he came, compelled to leave behind whatever security those traditions offered—yet always longing for them. He was, as Hesse described the Steppenwolf in his 1926 novel, "a genius of suffering" who took to himself and lived out the spiritual torments of a transitional period. The parallelism between Schoenberg and Haller is best inferred from Hesse's own words.

> . . . for Haller's sickness of the soul . . . is not the eccentricity of a single individual, but the sickness of the times themselves, the neurosis of that generation to which Haller belongs, a sickness, it seems, that by no means attacks the weak and worthless only but, rather, precisely those who are strongest in spirit and richest in gifts.

Referring to Haller's manuscript, a fantastic record of his inner experience which leads to the soul-transforming "rites" of the *Magic Theater*, Hesse remarks that

> these records . . . are not an attempt to disguise or to palliate this widespread sickness of our times. They are an attempt to present the sickness itself in its actual manifestation. They mean, literally, a journey through hell, a sometimes courageous journey through the chaos of a world whose souls dwell in darkness, undertaken with the determination to go through hell from one end to the other, to give battle to chaos, and to suffer torture to the full.

Schoenberg's internal experiences, particularly those recorded in his works from 1908–09 on, present us with an almost precise parallel to Haller's spiritual journey into hell, his battle with chaos. The historical figure of Schoenberg and the fictional character of the Steppenwolf are literally contemporaries, members of the same generation. They lived in (again Hesse) a time "when a whole generation is caught . . . between two ages, two modes of life, with the consequence that it loses all power to understand itself and has no standard, no security, no simple acquiescence." Schoenberg, like his fictional counterpart, was similarly "caught between two ages," "outside of all security and simple acquiescence." Like Haller, it was his fate "to live the whole riddle of human destiny heightened to the pitch of a personal torture, a personal hell" through his music, through the trials of his early atonal works, his invention of the twelve-tone method and the works which followed from it, his ambivalence in regard to "tonality." His whole fight was for a new standard, a new security, and above all, acceptance—"simple acquiescence."

Schoenberg's consciousness, like Hesse's (and, therefore, the Steppenwolf's) was entirely European. There is no parallel, to my knowledge, of this inner journey in the American consciousness of the same period, neither in music nor in literature. Certainly none of the American novelists or poets of the early decades of the twentieth century seem to have been caught in the same spiritual dilemma confronting their European counterparts: Kafka, Mann, Hesse, or Rilke. At least that is not the impression I get from reading the works of our leading expatriates: Henry James, Eliot, and Pound. Physical transplantation did not alter their psychic orientation or erase the layers of their early memories. Europe may have been the longed-for, imagined roots of their souls; but in truth, they could not get America out of their systems. If anything, their particular conflict lay precisely in their divided loyalties. They could no more enter into the real consciousness explosion rocking Europe than could their younger compatriots, Hemingway and Fitzgerald, those spokesmen of the "lost generation" who used Europe as a backdrop for personal adventure, as painted scenery for fictional settings. As for composers, who was there in those days to be taken seriously, except perhaps the young Americans who went to Europe to study composition? Charles Ives, batting his brains out every night, trying to set New England Transcendentalism to music? In fact, Ives seems to have rejected Europe completely. Yet, paradoxically, he was spiritually related to Mahler and (though he evolved his own peculiar brand of atonalism) never to Schoenberg. The problems of Europe were too unreal perhaps, certainly too distant, to have made a dent in the more naive, sometimes brasher, souls of American writers or composers. The Atlantic, which divided the two continents physically, also kept the cultures apart spiritually. This may or may not explain, in part at least, why the American composers of the early twenties and thirties looked on Schoenberg as something of an aberration. Certainly they rejected both his approach to composition and its emotional, psychological base and impulses. It was not until the late forties and early fifties, not till after Americans had been deeply involved physically and emotionally themselves with the European cataclysm of World War II, that a new generation of American musicians allowed themselves to be influenced and affected by Schoenberg. And even here the majority of them showed an abhorrence for Schoenberg's spiritual strivings and probings, preferring instead to elaborate the theoretical side of his music and avoiding the plunge into the torments and hells of an expressionistic art. The greater part of American twelve-tone music retains only the outward manner and facade of expressionism.

Schoenberg and Fatal Gifts

It was Schoenberg's destiny to be possessed of what Delacroix called "fatal gifts." In his journal, dated Wednesday, May 1, 1850, Delacroix, commenting on the perennial conflict between man's urge to express himself and nature's indifference, even antagonism toward the works of man, remarks

> A fatal gift, did I say? Beyond a doubt; amidst this universal conspiracy against the fruits of invention, of genius, and of the spirit which com-poses, does man have at least the consolation of wondering greatly at himself for his constancy, or of a rich and continued enjoyment of the various fruits which have issued from him? The contrary is most often the case. Not only must the man who is greatest through talent, through audacity, through constancy, be also the most persecuted, as he usually is, but he is himself fatigued and tormented by his burden of talent and imagination. He is as ingenious in tormenting himself as in enlightening others. Almost all the great men have had a life more thwarted, more miserable than that of other men.

Forgettable Music

The broad, identifiable changes in music as we move from the eighteenth and nineteenth centuries into the early decades of the twentieth century and then to the music of the fifties and sixties can be characterized in innumerable ways. The one which interests me here, because it allows me to comment on Schoen-berg's music in a particular way, has to do with the decreasing profile of identity of thematic and harmonic content. This decreasing profile of identity could be graphed in a rough sort of way, moving from a music with precise identities (Bach, Haydn, Mozart, Beethoven, Schubert, Schumann, Brahms, Wagner, Bruckner, Verdi, Strauss, Mahler, early Schoenberg) to a music with a marked decline in its profile of identity (the atonal and twelve-tone works of Schoenberg, Webern, Berg, late Scriabin, Ives) to a music entirely lacking in any aurally meaningful, identifiable characteristics (e.g., post-Webern serialist works of Boulez and Stockhausen among others; works of Cage, Feldman, Brown, based on a variety of aleatory approaches; recent works of Elliott Car-ter, who in an interview, expressed concern that his music cannot be remem-bered). In short, from a music that can be remembered, to a music which can be remembered but with varying degrees of difficulty, and finally to a music which utterly (or almost) defies memory.

   The motion over several hundred years from a high, to a low, and finally to a virtually nonexistent profile of identity can be traced as well in painting and literature: from Giotto to Kandinsky to Pollock; from Dickens to Joyce to Robbe-Grillet, etc. I used to think it was pure nostalgia, a longing for a past

Golden Age which always brought me back to the supremely wrought clarities and identities of the old music. Now I realize it was not nostalgia at all but a deep, abiding personal need for clear ideas, for vitality and power expressed without impediments, for grace and beauty of line, for convincing harmonic motion, for transcendent feeling—all qualities which have no specific historical location or inherent stylistic limitations but which supersede theory and aesthetics or the parochialisms of cultish attitudes ("musics of the future," avant-gardisms, etc.). All of which brings me back to the problem of Schoenberg's atonal and twelve-tone works. Dissonant chromaticism—lacking the force of tonal directedness and the availability of its great, open spaces and cadential points of rest and emphasis—necessarily leads to blurring of audible outlines, because one cannot readily grasp the sense of its tendency or of its ultimate shape. Intervals do not melodies make, nor does a preexistent referential order, like a set or matrix of pitches, clarify for the ear what is the main business of a piece of music: to define itself precisely to the ear as it unfolds in time in the air. The problem is identical whether we are speaking of unordered dissonant chromaticism (atonality) or ordered dissonant chromaticism (serialism). Charles Rosen remarks parenthetically in *The Classical Style* that "every composer before serialism played with the shapes of his themes, abstracting them from the exact pitches; only during the first three decades of twelve-tone music did pitch exert so absolute a tyranny that it deprived shape of its importance."

Where Schoenberg's musical genius was able to overcome this built-in deterrent to clear perception of shape and direction, quite obviously he demonstrated his gifts and superiority as a composer. The conflict was intensified, however, whenever his exacerbated emotional tendencies took over and clarity lost out. The cadential problem—the need to articulate the commas, semicolons, colons, and periods of musical phrases and statements—brought about by an imbalance of pitch organization, which leaned entirely on a one-color palette of dissonant chromaticism, illustrates still further the difficulties Schoenberg faced in producing structural order. A phrase requires a clear point of departure and a clear point of arrival, which in turn may become a new point of departure from which it moves to a new point of arrival, etc. Each such point requires articulation of inflection, and, if the phrase is to be accompanied or supported in any way by other pitches, those pitches must comprise some kind of analogous set of confirming tendencies of departure and arrival. After all, this is what "harmony" is about. For Schoenberg the principle of the "nearest way" tended to homogenize all motions, thereby tending to equalize all harmonic values. This process of equalization, finally institutionalized in the twelve-tone method, was precisely the internal pressure which reduced identity of profile to the lowest ebb it had reached since the Baroque era and eventually opened the way to the total disintegration of identity and profile, producing a kind of music which can only be described as "forgettable."

Schoenberg's music hardly falls into that category, but it *is* hard to remember; and it is this characteristic which has, despite the evident power of his work, endangered its position in the repertoire—or, put another way, made it so difficult for it to establish itself there.

Happiest Motifs

Delacroix journal entry, Sunday, February 15, 1852:

> There are few musicians who have not found a certain number of striking motifs. The appearance of these motifs in the first works of the composer gives an advantageous idea of his imagination; but these fleeting impulses are too often followed by a mortal languor. We are not in the presence of that happy facility of the great masters who are prodigal of the happiest motifs, often in mere accompaniments; here is no longer that wealth of substance, always inexhaustible, always ready to burst forth, and offering to the artist everything he needs, so that he has it ready to his hand and does not spend his time over an endless search for the best, or with hesitations later on as to a choice amongst several forms of the same idea. This frankness, this abundance, is the surest stamp of superiority in all the arts. Raphael and Rubens did not search for ideas— which came of themselves, and even in too great number. Their effort was scarcely to bring ideas to birth, but to render them in the best possible way, through the execution.

Without reference to scores or recordings, noting them as they occur to me, the works which contain Schoenberg's "happiest motifs" are: *Verklärte Nacht;* Second String Quartet (with voice); *Book of the Hanging Gardens;* Fourth String Quartet; Violin Concerto; Op. 23, No. 1 for piano solo; Op. 11, Nos. 1 and 3 for piano solo. These contain that which makes them worth preserving, studying, transmitting. They are living proof that, whatever contribution to "style" and/or method Schoenberg may have made which can be viewed and discussed from the abstract point of view of history and/or theory, he was, above all, an artist (as he himself knew he was and insisted on being taken for). Even this short list is sufficient indication that, language aside—whether tonally oriented chromaticism, free-floating dissonant chromaticism, or ordered dissonant chromaticism—Schoenberg's musical ideas were sufficiently indelible to leave their trace on the ear to be restored to reflective consciousness by a simple act of memory. (Which recalls that other delightful entry of Delacroix in his journal dated April 3, 1853: "Returned to the Italians: *The Barber.* All those charming motifs, those from *Semiramis* and from the *Barber* are with me continually.")

Schoenberg and History

The nineteenth century saw the emergence of scientific materialism, the theory of evolution, a new historical consciousness, and the notion of progress, especially economic but technological and cultural as well. If one were living in those days, it would have been well-nigh impossible to escape from the impact of such ideas, all of which contributed their share to the general European euphoria which saw civilization advancing on all fronts toward supermen and supersocieties. Certainly, it appeared that history was on the Western side. Didn't all the events of the day prove and support this? Who heard Edvard Munch's woman screaming on the bridge? Who believed Ivan Karamazov's vision of the second coming of Christ? Who recognized the heartbreak of Mahler's music and wondered what it all signified? Who cared to follow Rimbaud on his journey to hell? Why should they, when optimism was the rule of the day, and the waves of History would carry men over the small setbacks of daily life to a bright and shining future? The artist and composer began to view History as a living reality. They could look back and see how changes in style had occurred, how each significant change had opened still further the avenues of expression. There appeared to be no limit to the reach of nineteenth-century man and the capacity of art.

Schoenberg, as much as any other artist of his generation, must have found all this irresistible. In his essay, "Brahms, the Progressive," one senses how intensely devoted he is to the idea of linear change, how much value he attached to it. He undoubtedly saw his own work as a necessary extension of the past, an inevitable motion in the historical development of music and its materials. So did his followers and his latter-day apologists.

With the idea of history came the notion of cultural conditioning and behaviorism. If what history proclaimed was good, i.e., necessary, why then men would have to learn to adjust since it promised only good for them. This notion found its way into music too. If atonal or twelve-tone music initially eluded the perceptions, even of the most sympathetic and interested, then it was only a matter of comprehending its premises, its rational principles of structuring, its special ways of handling pitch and other parameters and all would be clarified. Progress was not to be denied by such infantilisms as the primitive judgment of the ear; the eye and the brain were now central. One had to study the score and the analyses of the score, and listen to endless repetitions, until one grasped not the beauties of the musical sound, but the beauties of organization. So went (and still goes) the litany.

I do not accuse Schoenberg of these latter-day aberrations which are the inevitable concomitant of attaching oneself to history; but I do suggest that he became too self-conscious about the historical value of his work and lost touch with the primitive instinct of the musician's ear which had guided him through his early tonal works and even during the works of the atonal period. Once embarked on the twelve-tone works he succumbed to abstraction and rational-ization. It may be true that when note "errors" in row dispositions were pointed out to him by friends and students and he was asked why it should be so, his usual response was, "It sounds better." But the fact remains that he had given up the precious gift of his ear in favor of decisions which had little to do, ultimately, with his ear. His twelve-tone music often comes out conflicted—crabbed and strained—where the early tonal and atonal music is large-ges-tured, without strain in its realization, although intense in projection. It is ultimately in his twelve-tone music that Schoenberg reveals the conflict be-tween his brain and his ear—a deadly struggle brought on by the pressure of historical self-consciousness. It is in those works that he paid the price of accepting the false legacy of his time. His rejection of music based on folk material (Stravinsky? Bartók?) was one of the signs of his subjection to a purist idea of art for its own sake guided by its historical necessity. And yet there are the tonal works of his American period. Was this nostalgia? Or was it uncer-tainty about a self-enclosed system based solely on twelve tones relating only to each other? Or was it, even, some dimly sensed suspicion that, in the end, history was a dead hand placed on the mind and spirit of man, while tradition was, indeed, the living force which tied artists and generations and times together through a commonality of memory? This must have been what Schoenberg had in mind when he wrote in his 1948 essay "On Revient Tou-jours": "But a longing to return to the older style was always vigorous in me, and from time to time I had to yield to that urge. This is how and why I sometimes write tonal music."

Schoenberg and Post-Romanticism

The story of Schoenberg's journey, of his "battle with chaos," is truly the story of a man "caught between two ages." Behind him lay the Classical and Roman-tic ages. The elegance and charm of Mozart, the wit and healthy exuberance of Haydn, the nobility and metaphysical transcendence of Beethoven, the bal-anced energies and tensions of Brahms—these were like the sweet, remem-bered dreams of a world long since gone. The mythic serenity of an established culture and order, in which the language of music was still safe from the exaggerated emotional demands and pressures of the Post-Romantic period, was blasted by it into oblivion, seemingly forever. In its place arose the neu-roses of modern consciousness with its discontents, its world wars, political and social diastrophies, its scientifically based technologies and barbarisms, its concentration camps and displaced persons and refugees, its pollution and earth destruction, its public hypocrisies and rationalized political dishonesties.

    The period of overlap between the denouement of the old world and the arrival of the new age which began after Schoenberg's death was a descent into the maelstrom, a wandering in the desert—a time "outside of all security and simple acquiescence." Schoenberg could not have foreseen the new age (which, I believe, began somewhere around 1965–70). He had to survive though he suffered hell from one end to the other, and in order to survive he had to proceed on his own with "no standard, no security, no simple acquiescence." He could take nothing for granted. He was forced to challenge all recognized values and to single out for condemnation what he thought were the spurious values—even at the risk of being wrong. By the time he came on the scene, in fact, there was nothing left which could be taken for granted. His own exacerbated temperament, which characterizes his music from the very beginning, left him no room for the nobler, more serene gestures of an earlier epoch. His intense, taut nature was attuned to the emotionally heightened vibrations of the Post-Romantic generation into which he was born. The examples of Mahler's soul-sickness and world-weariness and Richard Strauss's hysterical heroism were his aesthetic and psychological points of departure. Although he greatly admired and loved Mahler, he lacked Mahler's saving grace: irony and wit. Curiously, he was more like Wagner, Bruckner, and Strauss—all Germanically taking themselves much too seriously. (André Gide, writing on Hermann Hesse's style, comments that it is tempered "by a certain indefinable latent irony, of which so few Germans seem to be capable and the total absence of which often ruins so many works of so many of their authors, who take themselves frightfully seriously.") The occasional bits of wryness which flavor Schoenberg's music are hardly typical of the hard-hitting, aggressively morose intensity of his style. Unfortunately, like Harry Haller (the very epitome of the German intellectual of that epoch), Schoenberg seems to have forgotten how to laugh at himself or life. He never gained enough distance from his own sensations and yearnings and agonies to balance them off against that sense of intellectual irony or that play of the senses which characterizes the work of Debussy and Stravinsky and provided them with the safety valve of a kind of objectivized perspective on, plus a curious psychological detachment from, the world around them.

Not that Schoenberg was insensible to this loss of laughter or unaware of its tremendous importance in life as well as in art. "The Prayer to Pierrot," number 9 of *Pierrot Lunaire,* tells us this.

Pierrot! Mein Lachen   [Pierrot! I have forgotten how to laugh!
Hab ich verlernt!   The image of splendor has melted away!]
Das Bild des Glanzes
Zerfloss—Zerfloss!

Schwarz weht die Flagge   [Now my black flag waves from the mast.
Mir nun vom Mast.   Pierrot! I have forgotten how to laugh.]
Pierrot! Mein Lachen
Hab ich verlernt!

O gieb mir wieder	[Oh, horse-doctor of the soul, snowman
Rossarzt der Seele	of the lyric, Serene Highness of the
Schneemann der Lyrik,	Moon, Pierrot, give me back my
Durchlaucht vom Monde,	laughter!]
Pierrot—mein Lachen!	

If Mahler's music is a neurotic's autobiography, full of private dreams and fears and soul searchings—visions of another world intruding on this one—and Strauss's exhibitionistic music a magician's simulation of profound emotional states made for the bourgeoisie's need for excitement and over-stimulation to fill the vacuum of their daily lives without destroying their sense of self or illusion of controlling the destiny of the world, then Schoenberg, who went through both stages (in works like *Verklärte Nacht, Pelleas und Melisande,* and *Gurrelieder*), emerges from his long artistic apprenticeship as the consummate musical expressionist of the period who acted out with terrible personal intensity the dilemma of a world gone haywire. Unfortunately for Schoenberg, the sensations he gave the public of his day did not fit that society's image of itself. Works bordering on forms of pathology (e.g., *Erwartung,* which approaches a musical equivalent of Edvard Munch's *Scream*) and conveying terror, violence, and catastrophe (e.g., Five Pieces for Orchestra, Op. 16) typify the struggle in which Schoenberg engaged.

After his terrifying intuition of the state of the cultural chaos of the early decades of the twentieth century was captured and embodied in *Pierrot Lunaire,* Schoenberg attempted to reformulate the language of music in an effort to regain faith in existence—his own and the world's. His mistake, as I see it, was to seek salvation in methodology and the rational controls methodology demands of its user(s) by asserting itself as a studiously defined and closed system, separated from and kept apart from the very works based on it, which can then only be explained or justified by reference to the operations of that system.

The end result was an aesthetic and methodological tautology, which Schoenberg surely resisted, but which the next generation accepted (granting a few exceptions) fully and completely and without qualms, defending their theories of the system just as surely as Schoenberg resisted. The last remark of a lecture Schoenberg once gave in the late forties is characteristic: "My friends, let me warn you about orthodoxy." Unhappily, by then the damage was done.

Schoenberg's Search for Faith

There is something profoundly moving about Schoenberg's search for faith, his struggle to regain his roots in Judaism, his deep need to raise a protective barrier against the godlessness and loss of values of his generation. God may have been declared dead by Nietzsche, but Schoenberg wished again to pro-

claim His presence. Being Jewish had its distinct social and professional draw-
backs in the Austro-Hungarian empire into which Mahler, Schoenberg, and
Sigmund Freud were born. By the time Hitler came to power anti-Semitism
had passed beyond the stage of simplistic discrimination, fed by ignorance and
prejudice, into an implacable official policy of genocide pronounced by a gov-
ernment and supported by a people. Mahler presumably died a Catholic, but
Schoenberg reconverted to Judaism in Paris before he left Europe behind forever in 1933, while Freud stubbornly held to the faith of his fathers all his life
even though he did not observe its rituals.

It is worth examining the obsession of both Schoenberg and Freud with
the figure of Moses. Freud's *Moses and Monotheism* can be seen as an old man's
effort to bridge the gap a lifetime of scientific thinking and probing had created
between himself and the traditional values of an ancient religion based on
revelation and prophecy and endowed with moral and ethical power. Schoenberg composed his opera *Moses und Aron* in 1931, leaving the third act incomplete. Whatever surface reasons there may have been for not composing
the music to the third act libretto, Schoenberg's instincts are, in the end,
validated: I cannot imagine a more potent, metaphysically satisfying end than
the present one. No single work conveys better than *Moses und Aron* Schoenberg's passionate belief in an unknowable and invisible God, his sense that
before such a God man must ultimately pass from awkward articulateness to
utter silence, his hatred for all false gods and false idols. In his search for
ultimate spiritual truths, Schoenberg regained a cosmic view of man's place in
the universe. Is it possible that he identified with Moses, seeing himself as the
God-obsessed man of his time who had to keep music alive and pure, metaphorically uncontaminated by the lewd dancing and sensual abandon evoked
by the worship of the Golden Calf, of Baal? If this is true, then who is Aron? Is
he a collective or individual personification and symbol of that which endangered the spiritual and musical purity Schoenberg envisioned and wanted
so desperately to pass on to others?

Twelve-Tone as Device

One of the most fascinating and simultaneously puzzling tendencies of early-
twentieth-century music and art was the shedding, stripping down, and almost dismantling of the various technical modes and apparatuses used by
artists heretofore. The reaction to the overblown and the excessive was accompanied by a narrowing-down of the range of gesture. One recalls Giacometti's
stick figures, Klee's miniature world of forms, and the guitar-and-newspaper
cubism of Picasso and Braque, all of which accord so well with Schoenberg's
epigrammatic Op. 19. With the major exceptions of Picasso (who bequeathed
his guitar to Braque quite early in order to move on to other things) and
Stravinsky, the overall impression, as the century moves on, is that the single-

minded gesture and technical approach became entrenched and well established. Whether short or long in duration, Edgard Varèse's music explores only one basic gestural tendency; Anton Webern's music becomes a series of aphoristic prisms of sound. Each of the major painters of the New York school of Abstract Expressionism ("action" painters) pursues one image essentially, replicating themselves endlessly, just as Kandinsky and Mondrian seemed to say the same thing over and over again. (The "one-idea" artist and "one-idea" art are beautifully delineated by Harold Rosenberg in his recent book, *The De-definition of Art*, particularly in his essay on Mark Rothko.) Thus the compression of means and gesture which began in the first decade of the century was complete by 1960.

It is in this context, oversimplified perhaps, but nonetheless descriptive of essential tendencies and proclivities, that one begins to recognize a peculiarity inherent in the twelve-tone method as a method that, even now, those who are still dedicated to it seem not to see for what it is: merely a large-scale device for organizing dissonant chromaticism rather than a method of composition. I am not denying that what Schoenberg discovered or invented can be construed as a "method," but two things must be remarked about calling it a "method." First, it is not a method of composition but rather a method *for* composition, i.e., a rigorously consistent means applied to one or more parameters of composition seen from the (again) internally consistent limitations of the method as imposed on structural order and organization. As such one is dealing always with exclusivities and of necessity circumventing, denying, resisting, paralyzing, neutralizing a host of other possibilities which, by the interior logic of the method, are beyond the pale—shut out, anathema, forbidden. Second, as a method *for* composition, by definition, it remains incomplete and one-sided, not least of all for its insistence on the organization of only dissonant chromaticism, with its concomitant insistence on those moods and modes of expression appropriate only to that small range of pitch possibilities. Hence the basic "expressionistic" tendencies and characteristics of all serial music—whether realized successfully or not.

It was to begin with and remains, I believe, a serious error to take the twelve-tone method for a complete system of composition. The error stems, in part at least, from the urge—so typical of twentieth-century artists—to find the one, single-minded, exclusive way to say what they have to say. In this sense Schoenberg's invention takes its place along with all the other one-sided and unbalanced aesthetics or systematizations in the story of the twentieth century's search for standard and security, however mistaken or misguided that search has often proven to be. Later, notions similar to those brought forth to make a case for serialism would inform the aesthetics of aleatoricism ("chance" music) and the technological application of electronics. Aleatoricism, like serialism, is generally assumed by its adherents to be a complete method of composition; electronic music (which was, according to its proponents, going to replace "live" music) would also come to be viewed as a self-contained, complete approach to the problems of composition. Thus the error, first begun with twelve-tone music, came to extend to "chance" and electronic music. (As it turned out, the application of electronics to music has stimulated the development of new instruments rather than of a method of composition; and as such it understandably has its own inherent, idiomatic ways of making sound and, hopefully, music.) Serialism and aleatoricism—often juxtaposed as opposites, but paradoxically producing remarkably similar effects under certain conditions—are in reality devices, not methods and, as possible devices of order or disorder, have the same kind of useful but neutral value as do strict canons and invertible counterpoint. I say "neutral" because no device can guarantee its user anything except the skill and invention and conviction with which he informs it. This is perhaps why all compositional devices used by the unimaginative turn out to be academic, dull, and routine. So it is with serialism. The difficulty all along has been, as I see it, an insufficient grasp by many composers of what music is and what composition involves. The point here is that if Schoenberg chose to raise a new device to the status of a method and was willing to accept the consequences of his decision, that decision was and remains personal; its consequences also remain personal and artistic. Nearly everyone else who adopted the twelve-tone method, however, lost sight of the broad spectrum of composition—which can be seen as a great palette along which are ranged all the devices, old and new, which are the tools and materials without which a composer cannot function. If Varèse decided to pass up the twelve-tone method and Bartók, after studying Schoenberg closely, also decided not to avail himself of its use, can it be said, as some have, that they were "wrong"? And if Stravinsky chose to adopt serialism after 1952, did this now make him "right"? In fact, the strange spectacle of people falling in line with the twelve-tone method, after Stravinsky adopted it and seemingly conferred on it a new respectability, says not so much about Stravinsky as it does about the lack of independence among countless composers trying desperately to latch on to something solid, something given and seemingly dependable. But devices are neutral; they guarantee nothing. Everything in art is uncertain and it is this very uncertainty, this very open-endedness, which is the real spur to invention and the creation of order, clarity, and inevitability. The mistake would be to believe, and continue to believe, that a prescriptive approach can remove the uncertainty of composing or that, given the security of preconceived abstract order, invention, clarity, and musical inevitability will automatically follow. Schoenberg was the first to fall into this trap of his own devising.

The Function of the Accompaniment

The design of Schoenberg's accompaniments is always imaginative, rich in character and interior detail. In this area of compositional technique he is the peer of every great composer before him; in his own time, he is matched only by two others, Stravinsky and Bartók. The function of the accompaniment, whose importance Webern undoubtedly learned from Schoenberg (and rightly noted as one of Mahler's special attributes as a craftsman and master composer in Webern's 1930s lectures, *The Path to the New Music*), implies at least two irreducible conditions: (1) nonmonophonic melodies whose inflection and shape as well as metric pattern require reasonably sophisticated accompanimental designs, in order that their phrase structure and inflective tendencies (up, down, and around) be perceptually clear, leaving the ear in no doubt as to what is being projected or how it is taking place; and (2) a complete agreement between the harmonic implications contained in the unfolding pitches of the melodic lines and the supporting pitches contained in the accompanimental designs. The first governs the rhythmic support of the melody; the second governs the pitch accord between melody and accompaniment. Schoenberg succeeds brilliantly in his special way in the first, but fails singularly in the second from the moment he applies to the function of the accompaniment the idea of complementary hexachords; for it is obvious that there is no intrinsic harmonic agreement between a melody based on one group of six notes and an accompaniment built out of a second group of six notes. Quite apart from the very important theoretical question concerning the general problem of "harmony" in Schoenberg's serial method (to which there is still no satisfactory answer), the point is that when harmonic support contradicts—has no common tones with—the melody it is designed to project and carry, it is not the accompaniment which suffers but the melody itself. The reasons for this, though obvious enough, are worth noting, chiefly because this remains one of the undiscussed aspects of musical composition.

The intuitive understanding that a given melodic line had an implied harmonic content was never questioned prior to the twentieth century; it helped form the basis of the development of harmony, and the growing subtleties and sophistications of accompanimental design (which fleshed out harmony), gave aural reality to those contextual implications. One of the chief devices of early modernity, when irony, humor, parody, or satire were perhaps the chief psychological impulses of the music, was displacement of harmony (or random substitution), the result being "wrong" harmony. As long as the ear understood the harmony as "wrong," tonality was preserved despite the distortion and disorientation. (Harmonic displacement is especially characteristic of Stravinsky, e.g., *Rake's Progress*, and is at least as old as "The Musical Joke" of Mozart.) But it is obvious that Schoenberg does not intend irony or parody or humor or satire when he combines two mutually exclusive hexachords. To argue that the resulting contradiction between the pitch-content of the melody and the pitch-content of the accompaniment is justified by the theory of combinatoriality or the serial method itself is simply to reinforce the arbitrariness of the whole idea of serial harmony. The ear remains the best judge of music, however composed, but this intuitive perceiver of sound is not susceptible to outside numerical or verbal logic. That is what serial harmony rests on, theoretically speaking: verbal and/or numerical logic rather than aural perception. For all these reasons I find Schoenberg's melodies often beautiful in shape and form, sometimes eminently memorable and singable—but the sheen of their musical virtues is immediately tarnished and diminished by the harmonic contradictions inherent in the accompaniments he designed for them. In this sense, then, it is those rare moments only, as in the opening unison monophony of the slow movement of the Fourth String Quartet when the music contained in the melodic shape of that opening shines forth in all its glory, that I am convinced again of the power of the man who wrote it, and conversely given cause to regret that he gave up his intuitive grasp of the function of the accompaniment, replacing it with the rationalized distortions of the twelve-tone method.

On Being Mozart's Pupil

It has always puzzled me that Schoenberg considered himself a "pupil of Mozart." Why Mozart rather than, say, Beethoven with whom he seems to have had certain affinities (e.g., Schoenberg apparently viewed the Grand Fugue as a work very close in style and spirit to his own, as something he could have written himself), or Brahms whom he admired greatly? To answer the question of why Mozart, we would need to know more specifically what Mozart meant to Schoenberg, how he heard Mozart's music, what he got from it, what precisely he felt he learned from Mozart. Not having the answers from Schoenberg himself, we are forced to speculate; in this particular instance our speculations lead down curious paths and allow us to remark on Schoenberg's approach to composition in a special way. It is well known that Mozart wrote rapidly, with incredible ease and facility, and most important of all, thought in totalities. Quite possibly Mozart served as a model for Schoenberg in this respect. Schoenberg, undoubtedly wishing to counteract the spreading notion that his method of working was exclusively cerebral, pointedly informed the world that he worked rapidly, easily, and from an inspired condition. The impression he wished to convey, of course, was that the twelve-tone method was no impediment to the act of composing despite its seeming complexities. It is especially striking, according to Schoenberg's own statement, that he wrote down the violin part of the Phantasy Op. 47, *first* and then added the piano part. This corresponds directly with Mozart's way of working: melodies and supporting bass lines were often put down first, inner voices and other details followed after the grand outline had been established. To work this way requires absolute mental clarity and control, a sense of the whole carried in the mind to which all details are subordinate and belong only to the final stage of the act of composition: fixing the totality in its final form. This helps to explain

Schoenberg's spatial analogy, the intent of which is to emphasize not only the *totalness* of a specific musical conception but the fact that, once held in the mind as a spatial object which could be viewed from any and all sides, it is easy enough to examine it part by part, moving them around freely if need be, for purposes of mental examination, inspection, or comparison (like so many pieces of furniture arranged and rearranged in a room until one is satisfied with the appearance), as well as keeping the whole in undisturbed, recollected equilibrium while working out the details of any given part or area. The paradox of a spatial, mental image held in a static, steady state of conceptual memory as the invisible precursor of a temporally unfolding, now-turned-physical, sounding phenomenon of interrelated strata of parts is now clear; and it is my guess that Schoenberg gloried in it because it brought him close to one of his imagined ideals, if not idols—Mozart. All this tells nothing of *how* Mozart or Schoenberg actually did what they did. That cannot be described; it can only be experienced. However, it says everything about the peculiar neutrality of language which offers only possibilities, not actualities, and particularly about the true nature of composition. From a certain point of view tonality and its conventions guaranteed Mozart no more than the twelve-tone method guaranteed Schoenberg—simply a frame of reference. Schoenberg's remark that he was a "pupil of Mozart's" is a piece of what Hesse called "magical thinking."

On Schoolchildren Singing Twelve-Tone Melodies

It was apparently a fancy of Schoenberg's that someday schoolchildren would be taught to sing twelve-tone melodies. This raises some enormous questions and problems. First, from where would such a repertoire of singable tunes be drawn? The only composers whose twelve-tone works could even now, if such a program were to be initiated and carried out in an ideal sense (granting an enlightened corps of music teachers whose training and level of musicianship were up to the task, and granting an overall educational setup which considered such a program desirable and worthy of its bureaucratic support), be considered as source material would be Schoenberg himself, possibly Alban Berg, Webern, and Luigi Dallapiccola. Serial music as a rule, especially of the generations after Schoenberg, cannot be characterized as "lyric," even when vocal. The handful of singable melodies (or portions of melodies) that can be garnered hardly comprise a repertoire. Second, I know few professionally trained musicians who can sing, i.e., literally vocalize, a twelve-tone melody. Pitches become mechanized into intervals and inflection of phrasal curvature tends to be generalized even among professionals. Granting that children under special guidance can be taught skills and subject matter far in advance of what they are generally considered capable of learning, it remains highly questionable whether such a program could be carried out on a broad, universal scale. Third, the dynamics of our present culture tend to separate "high" forms from "low" forms. In order for twelve-tone music to be widely taught in schools, the aesthetic and corpus of works already in existence would have had to spread themselves throughout the culture, to spill over, so to speak, into the broader base of the musical tastes and needs of the larger community far beyond the limits of the concert and chamber hall. There is no evidence that this either has happened or is in the process of happening. On the contrary, outside of the university community—and even there, not necessarily universally—serialism has yet to make its way into the regularly scheduled repertoire of orchestras, string quartets, pianists, and singers. Fourth, Schoenberg could not possibly have foreseen the disintegration of our society as a whole or the problems afflicting our schools stemming from the surrounding, ubiquitous societal dilemmas. For example, black children in the American inner city reject white culture (of what value to them the "great" music of the past or present when their music is "rock"—hard, acid, or Motown?), and white children (who, as much as black children, are the innocent victims of corrupt and corrupting side effects of a morally and spiritually diseased society) are, through ignorance or complicity, adopting attitudes and habits of mind which tend increasingly toward forms of barbarism, undoubtedly in direct imitation of their elders. I am afraid that the time in which schoolchildren might have grown up singing twelve-tone tunes is long past and, perhaps, never could have been.

Claude Lévi-Strauss on Serialism

In what he terms the "overture" to his book, *The Raw and the Cooked* (New York: Harper Torchbooks, 1970), Claude Lévi-Strauss, writing of the "surprising affinity between music and myths," finds it important to his purpose to take up the question of "contemporary musical thought" because, in his view, "either formally or tacitly," it

> rejects the hypothesis of the existence of some natural foundation that would objectively justify the stipulated system of relations among the notes of the scale. According to Schoenberg's significant formula, these notes are to be defined solely by "the total system of relations of the sounds with one another". . . . The serial approach, by taking as its logical conclusion that whittling down of the individual particularities of tones, which begins with the adoption of the tempered scale, seems to tolerate only a very slight degree of organization of the tones.

Lévi-Strauss comes finally to his basic point: "Above all, one must ask oneself . . . what has happened to the first level of articulation, which is as indispensable in musical language as in any other, and which consists precisely of general structures whose universality allows the encoding and decoding of individual messages." Lévi-Strauss maintains that serialism is trying "to construct a system of signs on a single level of articulation." For him the first level of articulation, that which relates to general structures which allow for individual diversity of usage, is "immovable, except within very narrow limits." He absolutely denies that this level is interchangeable with the second level of articulation which becomes the individual, culturally determined in time and space, mode of usage.

> The respective functions of the two forms of articulation cannot be defined in the abstract and in relation to each other. The elements raised to the level of a meaningful function of a new order by the second articulation must arrive at this point already endowed with the required properties: i.e., they must be already stamped with, and for, meaning. This is only possible because the elements, in addition to being drawn from nature, have already been systematized at the first level of articulation: the hypothesis is faulty, unless it is accepted that the system takes into account certain properties of a natural system which creates *a priori* conditions of communication among beings similar in nature. In other words, the first level consists of real but unconscious relations which, because of these two attributes, are able to function without being known or correctly interpreted.
>   . . . in the case of serial music, however, such rootedness in nature is uncertain and perhaps non-existent. Only ideologically can the system be compared to a language, since unlike articulate speech, which is inseparable from its physiological or even physical foundation, it is a system adrift, after cutting the cable by which it was attached.

Lévi-Strauss's formulation, while not historical, points up the real consequences of Schoenberg's act of wrenching himself loose from, but not free of, that general structure which defines tradition—that slow, invisible process of accretion through which "real but unconscious relations" work their way up and through generations of human beings. In the case of the traditions of music, which involves far more than simply pitch-relation (on this point it is worth rereading Donald Francis Tovey's book on Beethoven, especially the section on rhythm and movement), countless efforts produced a language with general characteristics adapted to individual usage of the most diverse tendencies. The incredible facility of composers of the Baroque, Classical, and Romantic periods is predicated on the unconscious acceptance of that language which grew and changed but did not give up its fundamental characteristics. Beethoven's labor, for example, was with the shape of his ideas, not with language. Chopin's endless repetition of the same passage as he composed (as reported by George Sand) was a search for the precise way to say what he wanted to say;

his struggle was to shape the language his way, not to change its premises. In fact, the astonishing thing about the language of music we call "tonality" is its capacity to sustain the most diverse as well as the most extreme usage while remaining stable. Perhaps the greatest error of all which developed out of serialism was the notion that the "forms" associated with tonality had to be abandoned (Boulez's notion, as I recall) and that only "forms" indigenous to serial thought (what these are remains a complete mystery to me) were to be legitimated. The assumption underlying this idea has long been due for close examination and revision, for it is based on a mistaken reading of how form arises in the first place. If we consider the history of music carefully we discover that the impulse toward the phrase, toward imitation, toward contrasting statements, toward texture, toward timbre, toward metrics, toward closed and open shapes is not a property or attribute of pitch per se but an underlying, natural function or set of functions of the articulating mind. As the language develops, articulation becomes more precise, richer in design—or is it the other way around, or both together? One thing is certain: the musical phrase does not owe its articulative urge to tonality or any other pitch system, nor does the basic association between melody and accompaniment.

Schoenberg's solution to the problem of music, as he saw it, was undoubtedly a brilliant one in its day and for its time. But the self-consciousness that the invention of a new language produced served only to intensify his difficulties. The labor of composition was no longer just to find the right shape but to speak the new language he had invented, to make it work convincingly. Miraculously he succeeded more than he failed—but only because he was already a master composer and had come through a long apprenticeship with tradition.

Filling Beats

In liner notes I wrote for a Columbia record release (The Music of Arnold Schoenberg, vol. 7) of Schoenberg's Variations on a Recitative, Op. 40, I commented on a phenomenon of Schoenberg's style which I had never noticed before but which turned out, on subsequent examination and study of works from all of his periods, to be basic, as identifiably characteristic as a fingerprint. What I said in effect was that the work was saturated by an unceasing succession of local harmonic events, or progressions, if you will, one after the other without letup, resolving "from the nearest half steps available (forming mostly fourth chords) to major or minor triads" and that these chords and their resolutions filled the metrical space so completely that "no single beat, main or subdivided," escaped harmonic change. It is, indeed, rare to find Schoenberg dwelling for long on any harmonic point rhythmically. The effect on the ear is ultimately wearing and wearying. One needs not only cadential points of rest to absorb what has just preceded—to catch one's breath aurally—but also to get ready for what follows, to keep up with the flow of the music. In the case of larger structural areas one also needs, I believe, the contrast and foil of longer harmonic spreads with little change, certainly not too much change, and shorter harmonic stretches, more active internally, richer in motion. One cannot set up rules of speed of harmonic change in advance, obviously; style, taste, and temperament combine and determine any given composer's way of treating such matters. That being the case, it seems to me clear that the fire and intensity of Schoenberg's style generally, from first to last, produced in him a kind of harmonic breathlessness. The music pushes on harmonically in relentless, compulsive fashion. Since the gestures themselves are rarely tranquil or serene (there are, I find, no genuine "adagios" in Schoenberg's music) but, on the contrary, demonic, fraught with tension, often exacerbated, it seems inevitable that Schoenberg's treatment of harmony, whether tonal, atonal, or serial, should have been as I described. No rhythmic spaces are left unfilled. One imagines Schoenberg obsessed with the possible multiple harmonic meanings of the notes of a given melody or the possible multiple ways of supporting a given note of a melody harmonically.

Certainly if one refers to the exercises in his 1911 *Harmony Book,* one observes immediately that Schoenberg was trying to demonstrate not the making of satisfying harmonic phrases (with or without melodies) but the rapid ways in which one could move from one harmonic point to another. This habit of mind would necessarily have taken advantage of every metric space available in a given context in order to fill it out with rich local detail, forgetting the total harmonic meaning and effect of the passage. That so many passages of his early music, his atonal music, and more rarely his twelve-tone music turn out to be convincing harmonically becomes one of the minor miracles he performed. One of his most stable, harmonically satisfying passages occurs in the opening scene of *Moses und Aron.*

The Face of Schoenberg

Hanging side by side in the Rijksmuseum in Amsterdam are two self-portraits of Rembrandt which tell the story of the man who painted them more powerfully than any biography could. Just as the history of the earth is recorded in the changing appearances of our planet's surface features, character, and quality, so the face of a human being can be read as a record of his brief and painful experience of life and consciousness, the victories and defeats, the stages (and even nonstages) of his inner evolution. These two portraits which I first saw many years ago remain indelibly fixed in my memory. The young Rembrandt pictured himself as he undoubtedly was at the height of his public career and in the fullness of his early powers: self-confident, self-assured, roundfaced, with a healthy bloom on his cheeks and an easy, relaxed look in his eyes— surely a portrait of success and the pleasure the young artist's ego took in that doubtful state. The ensuing twenty years or more clearly changed all that. In the old face of Rembrandt one finds deep and profound suffering. The ego of the man is burnt out; what is left is a look of such sadness, such a sense of the impersonal wisdom of old age that it catches at the throat.

Perhaps it is merely a fancy and there is no "reality" to be read on the faces of men. But I am so frequently reminded of the incredibly similar look of living in the full consciousness of position and power between busts of Roman emperors and senators, and photographs of American politicians and businessmen. And what can one say when one looks at photos from the 1860s onward of American Indians but that these were remarkable human beings in many cases possessed of a sense of nobility and life-awareness not often to be seen on the faces of their contemporary white "brothers"? Life is to be read on all of those faces as clearly as though written in words—perhaps even clearer. I remember Camus's line in *The Fall* that "after the age of forty, a man is responsible for his own face."

On the retinal tissue of my visual memory there are two images of Schoenberg which always dominate and accompany my sense of the man, his mission, his achievement. They are in themselves a potent record of the human price he paid for his accomplishment. They speak louder than any words of the inner transformation of the man from the famous though feared and hated composer who landed in America in 1933 to the driven prophet who died in 1951—a cultural persona non grata, a human welding torch possessed of and by terrible fires and energies which cut through the subcutaneous fat of complacency, timidity, and mediocrity with which society frequently protects itself in order to ward off the uncontrollable demons of human consciousness.

The two images I see in my mind's eye are a photo and a sculpted bust. In the photo Schoenberg is standing on the dock with his wife and daughter just after he has landed in America: full-face, concentrated, with lively but slightly apprehensive eyes, a sense of himself which reveals that he has battled courageously and is still on his feet despite thirty or more years of critics, enemies, and (more recently) Nazis. This man of fifty-nine, certainly not "young" any longer, is self-contained, in full possession of himself. I don't know in what year the bust of Schoenberg was made nor do I remember by whom, but I first saw it in an art annual of the Pennsylvania Academy of Fine Arts in 1948–49. Unlike the self-portraits of Rembrandt where the essential physical features of the two stages of inner transformation remain clearly recognizable as belonging to the same individual, the bust of Schoenberg reveals a face so ravaged and destroyed by the passage of time and so scourged by the intensity of his inner life as to make one marvel that it is the same man. This is the image that haunts me: its burning eyes, protruding cheek bones, sunken, hollow cheeks—the look of a man who has lived and suffered more than he can tell in music or in words, like an ancient of prehistory or an old Plains Indian who has seen great visions and lives them as the medicine man Black Elk did. There is a power in such a face which is not attached to earthly things but belongs to "the other world." This power that reveals itself on the agonized face also reveals itself in the music—sometimes terrible in its fiery release, its searing heat, oftentimes painful in its tenderness; always intense, electrically charged, demonic in its sound and gesture; but neither is it always "human" in the sense of offering serenity, solace, comfort, charm, wit, grace, playfulness. This power is either one of possession or of being possessed—which, I am not sure. But in its manifestations in human culture—and they are rare indeed—they are not to be understood by the hedged-in capacities of ordinary cognition, because the necessarily technical means which encase and encapsulate these demonic streams of energy, emanating from and passing through the human mind and psyche, do not belong to the energy itself but to the forms, languages, and conventions which are historical accidents of time and place.

More often than not, it is the means and craft (summed up as "style")—without which the artwork cannot be made—that are given priority in efforts at understanding them. As a consequence, History and its accidents of time and place are made to act as a surrogate for Cosmos; and our perceptions of cultural phenomena become misunderstandings and misreadings. Mostly we forget that the energy which produces life, consciousness, and human passions is always outside of cultural forms both before and after they appear; and if the artwork manages somehow to partake of it during its making, it is only because there are those rare occasions when a Beethoven or Blake or Goya or Van Gogh or Dostoevski or Mahler or Nietzsche or Schoenberg is able to break through and tap it at the source (at grave personal risk) and give us works which transcend the ordinary exercise of talent—works which belong to "the other world" of visions which remove themselves from History and enter Cosmos. To speak of artworks *only* as cultural forms and phenomena is to reduce them to mere cultural mechanisms, in which case our perceptions of them follow suit. The prophetic poems of Blake, the Black paintings of Goya, the late quartets of Beethoven, the architectural vision of Antonio Gaudi, the novels of Dostoevski, the poems of Rimbaud, the later works of Schoenberg—these are not for Everyman. It is not, as is widely believed and often stated in these days of wordy analytic comprehension, because the means employed in these works are so complex and difficult to comprehend, let alone approach, but rather because what they contain, channel, and embody, the very stuff of which they are projections and manifestations, is quite literally dangerous to the unprepared and unwary human spirit, destructive of the unstrong, unwary, and unwise—like radioactivity to the unprotected physical cell. When this stuff appears in the undirected, raw form of uncontrolled, ego-driven human passions and is let loose on the world in the "clockwork-orange" forms of war, murder, destruction, brutality, sadism, oppression—violence in all its multifarious forms—no one has difficulty in recognizing what is happening except for those who perpetrate them. But in matters affecting the spirit and art, fools still rush in where angels fear to tread; and for reasons only dimly known to me, it still appears to be generally assumed (even by those who should know better) that the transformed and sublimated manifestations of these terrible energies couched in artistic forms are either innocuous toys made for the sometime pleasure of those who like to look, listen, and read; or complex symbolic codes, whose main purpose, once having sprung to life, is to provide critics and scholars with the material of their professions. Either way, eventually these strange phenomena become tamed and domesticated, made fit for the ordinary round of human consumption and use. Yet something of their nature persists and continues to arouse fear and anxiety or wonder and awe in the midst of the social game. This may provide us with a clue to Schoenberg and his fate.

What was the intuition of the reality of the unpredictable entrance into human life and culture of these terrible and awesome nonhuman powers which, in the case of Schoenberg the composer, led him to be so hated and feared during his struggles to define his personal vision of music? What vague sense of dread and terror led the denizens of culture to shun and despise him—to cast him in the role of a "diabolus in musica"? Was it the invention of the twelve-tone method of composition which caused Schoenberg to become the storm center of early-twentieth-century musical culture? Or was it the specter of a dangerously potent, radioactive spirit come to life in the midst of the musical world which produced the revulsion and resistance whose effects were ultimately recorded on the embattled, haunted, and haunting old face of Schoenberg?

On Musical Time and Space

- *Duration in Music (1960)*
- *The Concepts of Musical Time and Space (1963)*
- *The Structure of Time in Music (1973)*

Duration in Music

Any discussion of duration in music must necessarily probe the nature of duration itself, particularly as it relates to human experience.[1] Without even the most limited understanding of the relationship between duration and existence, it becomes virtually impossible to comprehend how music becomes the living, dynamic, artistic embodiment of time; for music's great power over all men fundamentally derives from the engagement of the sense of duration in the listener, perceived as motion, as movement, as the occurrence of successive events which culminate in a sense of fullness of experience, of a sonorous content whose passage in time is rich and meaningful.

How do we perceive duration in life? As sentient beings for whom the external world provides a multitude of changing visual and aural stimuli, we come to learn that nothing stays for us, nothing remains the same; we and the world around us move on in a continuous chain of events. As Rilke says in his *Duino Elegies*, "Once for everything, once only. / Once no more. / And we, too, once. / And never again." The present, the only moment in which we know we exist, is burdened by the weight of accumulated past experience, and the future is always one moment ahead of us—the next "present" moment in which we hope to exist. So we live between memory and anticipation, between the past and the future, treading the bridge of the present that, we hope, will carry us across the inexorable passage of time which nothing can hold back. We live in time and through time. We are both of it and immersed in it. The present is therefore more than the moment of physical existence in which we feel pain or joy, in which we experience our lives as something or nothing. The present is destined to join the vast accumulation of all the other lived moments of life, all the other somethings or nothings. It will soon become the past just as it is already eroding the future.

The dynamic of duration is not only change but growth through change; for in this procession of ephemeral moments nothing is lost or left behind because everything, consciously or unconsciously, becomes a part of memory. The past is reclaimed by memory; it is only by means of this act of reclamation or conservation of lived experience that a human being can come to know himself. Without memory he has no history, his life no form. He would live only in the sensation of each passing moment, remembering nothing of what has occurred, unable to anticipate anything ahead. Life as we know it would be lost to such a being, condemned to exist in such a void, without memory of his former inner states and without the power to project their continuance into an anticipated future. His existence would be lost in the meaninglessness of each sensation. A mental life, affective and reflective in nature, must know the modes of duration—past, present, and future—in order to retain its identity and uniqueness.

There is no apparent form to the succession of our lived moments. As duration flows in an unbroken stream, events occur without plan, unforeseeable and unpredictable. If they are to have any pattern of meaning for us we must mentally sort and arrange them according to our ideas of order. Affective memory alone, reliving or refeeling the past, cannot do this for us. We need the power of critical reflection in order to shape to our purpose what has taken place. We literally must impose an order of some kind on our affective memory if we are to see meaning in our existence. It is in the power of forming the data of our existence that we shape ourselves and the world around us; and it is out of this power, this urge to meaning through form and order, that art arises. All our arts derive, then, from the interpenetration of the modes in which we experience life in the phenomenal world; all forms of art correspond in some way to our need for ordering, through sensuous material, the modes of our existence in forms we can comprehend. Through music we experience, outside of ourselves and outside of those events in life which have a purely personal connotation, duration itself—but not in an absolutely pure sense. Just as in ordinary existence the sense of the passage of time comes to us through the perpetually shifting phenomena of the external life which surrounds us, so in music we sense the passage of time through the sensuous data of sound, formed as sonorities, melodies, and harmonies, constantly moving from shape to shape and point to point. In the listener is evoked a direct intuitive response because he knows by his intuition that this is the way life is too—with the important exception that music comes to him as form, while life does not. Music engages his sense of duration because duration is the primary condition of music.

The engagement of the listener's sense of duration calls his faculty of memory into direct play. Just as memory preserves his personal, unique past, it now makes possible the recognition and remembrance of musical ideas which he has already heard as the music unfolds itself to his mind and ears. Even though the music to which he is listening is already formed, the listener must recreate this form in his own mind in order to grasp it. Repetition and return in music therefore function as important and fundamental formal aspects of composition. If like the existence Rilke describes—"Once for everything, only once. / Once no more. / And we, too, once. / And never again"—music too should go on offering nothing but one new idea after another, aural sensation after aural sensation without repetition or return, it would lose itself in its own moments and therefore lose its form. Though "return" in music is seemingly like the recall of memory of lived human experience, it is not precisely analogous. Life is never a closed form because we do not know what death is; but music is necessarily a closed form. Ideas do come back in music to be heard again. In life only our memory of past moments can bring back their flavor and quality. Memory is affective, mental. The past may be recalled or refelt but only internally. It cannot be physically experienced a second time. Return or recall in music is actual, that is, like the idea of which it is either a literal repetition or varied recall, it is *there*, physically present as sound. Nevertheless we can see powerful connections between the phenomenon of human memory of lived experience and return in music. In life, memory centers on those moments and events which have meaning in terms of the uniqueness of our existence. These memories are the substance of our life. (Without them, as we have noted, we would have no mental or affective life other than what passed through us as feeling each moment of our existence.) Analogously, recall or return in music establishes the necessary condition for the meaning of the music experienced as formal order in and through duration. What the composer repeats or recalls must necessarily have meaning. The listener corroborates this by the degree to which he is able to recreate the form of the music.

Return in music then must have the same power to affect as does memory in life. It must be sharply evocative and yet quite literally occur in the present tense as though what is experienced in memory is again experienced in the present moment of life. The power of return in music serves much more than a purely formal function about which we have heard so much in the past from theorists and aestheticians: ideas of unity in variety, variety in unity, repetition and return creating formal unity, etc. This is merely a mechanical description of how perceived repetition and return affect a musical form. It does not account for the sheer power of return, nor does it account for the enormous satisfaction gained when the meaning of a work is suddenly crystallized by the arrival at ideas, stated earlier in a work, emerging on a new plane. Return in music has something of the force of the past suddenly illuminating the felt present as a real element in the present. This suggests the possibility that music is an attempt—limited by human finitude but a valid attempt nevertheless—to create through sound the totality of time, the ground bass of duration in human life; present tense here becomes the predominant mode of occurrence, return suggests the past tense imposed on the felt present, and future tense is the goal toward which everything strives for completion and final resolution. The three dimensions of the human experience of time—past, present, and future—are potentially inherent in the durational process of music perceived as organized sounding pitches. Hence its unfailing power, particularly in Western music, where duration as time span has developed forms which are capable of embodying the durational process in artistically meaningful orders.

I should like now to examine two of the major tendencies prevailing in advanced compositional circles today—chance, or aleatoric, music and total serial music. These two kinds of music define the polar extremities within which composition is now taking place: chance music which operates with situations based on the unpredictability of happenings; and total serial music which purports to operate with situations which are completely predictable. Despite this fundamental difference in approach, both operational systems have a great deal in common, and not least a tacit withdrawal from the three-dimensioned durational process already described.

Before going on, I should like first to elucidate one more idea which you may already have inferred from my previous comments. Though the durational process of existence may be uniform for all men in all cultures, it does not follow that existence is viewed in the same way in every culture. Each culture stresses one or another aspect of its durational experience according to the prevailing philosophical, scientific, or religious modes and beliefs. For a culture in which tradition and conservatism are particularly strong, the past undoubtedly has greater importance than the present and future; in such a society the present exists to conserve the past and to transmit its experience to the future. In a society where the ties with history have been loosened or abandoned and the weight of the past thrown off, the present and future suddenly assume the greatest importance because these are the true moments, actual and anticipated, in which life is lived and is to be continued for its own sake.

The predominant philosophical mode of our time is acknowledged to be existentialism, a view of life which holds that the present moment is the nodal point of existence. It is in the present that existence is actual, most vital; before there can be being, there must be existence. One's sense of being derives from one's sense of existence, and the way to sense one's existence is to charge each present moment with content and meaning. The present is reality. This view, though distinctly Western in origin, stemming from the thought of Nietzsche, Kierkegaard, Heidegger, Jaspers, and others, finds strong reverberations in Eastern Zen Buddhism, which also holds that the present moment is supreme reality.

It is not at all strange, therefore, that composers of chance music, particularly, are drawn to Zen and imply in their attitude toward music an existential tendency; that is, they see music as the occurrence of unpredictable events, each moment of sound or silence freed of formal connection with the moment before or after, audible only as a present sensation, an ensemble of musical happenings of undetermined form or length. The same work may be as long or as short as the performance situation requires. Nothing, theoretically speaking, is known in advance of its occurrence except the frame within which sounds are to occur. The performance is the realization. In this form of existential music, the present erases the past (by allowing no recall or return) and promises no future since the present happening is sufficient to itself, requiring no future event for its understanding. This music (or ensemble of sounds and silences) is ever-present to itself at each instant of its occurrence—we cannot speak of an unfolding here. Because this is so, no contextual preparation is required for any event.

But just for this reason there can be no surprise because everything is surprise. Duration, in the sense of a process incorporating a human past, present, and future in its stream of movement, is no longer possible in this music. It is confined to the sound sensation of the moment, leaving no visible trace behind. As music it is like the individual who lives without a personal history, without a sense of his past or hope of his future and therefore with no sense of the continuity of his unique identity. All he knows are immediate sensations; their nature or order of sequence have no meaning for him beyond their immediate pleasure or pain.

The proponents of chance music relegate history and tradition to the realm of meaninglessness. The sound of this music is to have no associations with anything tainted by history and tradition; it is to be self-sufficient, unique in its occurrence, divorced from the human situation because it is "free" of cultural contingency. Chance music is the epitome of the unpredictable itself, like life. Caged within the present moment, chance music cannot articulate the totality of duration, only the existential point from which the totality could stretch back and forth but in this case refuses to do so. This declared descent into irrationality erases any possibility of the creation of forms which can engage the listener's innate sense of duration. All the listener can hope to do in such music is grasp at each occurrence, just as he grasps at life's formless succession of events, hoping to derive some meaningful order. In the case of chance music this is hardly likely; and, from the point of view of the composers of such music, highly undesirable. Thus duration, in the sense we have described it, cannot be said to exist in this music since it is contradictory to its fundamental premise. The antiorder of chance music has no need for memory and its powers of recall; therefore it deprives the listener of his most powerful affective and mental apparatus for seeking order in himself and his experiences, including that of listening to music. Chance music would reduce its listeners to creatures subsisting wholly on stimulus-response situations, creatures who bring nothing to the moment of stimulus and take nothing away from it. Culture and its transmission are no longer possible under these conditions. It makes one wonder whether chance composers recognize the extent to which they have stripped themselves of the hard-won human characteristic of being able to transcend mere sensation, in order to form it in ways that communicate to other human beings the transcendent quality of human experience.

When we consider duration in relation to total serialism, we are faced with a completely different set of problems because, while chance music operates with wholly irrational situations, total serialism is suprarational, that is, it applies to all aspects of musical composition a controlled program of action based on predetermined relationships derived from number and mathematics. In such a program the irrational is theoretically inadmissible. However inadmissible it may be to its practitioners, I have tried to show recently in a discussion of indeterminacy in the new music that, practically speaking, irrationality is ultimately the victor.[2] But my main concern here is duration as we find it in the music composed according to the program of total serialism.

Duration viewed as clock time, i.e., precise lengths of sounds in "real" time, is one of the so-called parameters upon which a serial composer can project a prearranged order. This order of occurrence of durational lengths is organized (usually in series) according to the particular and specific rationalization required for carrying out these operations in relation to the parameters of pitch, dynamic, timbre, and register. It is significant to observe that these other parameters belong to the realm of musical space. Total serialism thus accords an equivalent status to musical time and musical space, the necessary assumption being that duration as musical time must be equally susceptible to precise ordering as are the elements of musical space; otherwise rational control over the compositional situation is lost. The consequences of this assumption are many. I shall mention only those I consider the most pertinent to this discussion.

First of all, duration is no longer a process. Duration now becomes objectified in series of concretized segments or lengths of either clock time, as in electronic music, or metronomic time, as in serial instrumental music. Duration as process in musical time is cast aside in favor of controlled lengths of microcosmic time, which are considered as discrete elements, as are pitches, dynamics, and so on. We have known all along that pitches are discrete, specific, identifiable entities. But until total serialism, duration has never been characterized as a series of discrete, specific, identifiable segments of time. True, musicians have always concerned themselves with rhythmic and metrical problems, and the conventions of our notation have built up a system of the smallest to the largest possible notational lengths. However, these lengths were never intended as objective, discrete elements but rather as symbols created for the purpose of guiding the flow of musical time in a meaningful way—in short, to make possible the notation of musical time and therefore its performance.

However, duration and pitch stem from two different sources of perception, making their equivalence status in total serialism thoroughly arbitrary and suspect. Pitch, as a discrete element comprising measurable vibrations of a sounding body, is external to man even though man is able to produce it vocally. Pitch exists in the phenomenal world as determinate or indeterminate musical sound (or noise), depending on whether it is regular or irregular in its vibration. Even though man may produce it in his inner ear as internal, imagined sound, the fact remains that his greatest joy is in producing it physically as actual sound. Duration, on the other hand, is an internalized process, its passage noted by discrete events occurring externally but, in itself, an unmeasurable flow insusceptible to limits or demarcation, except as (in music) in the symbolic use of notated time lengths or (in life) by the general terms with which we refer to the durational process—past, present, and future, terms provided us by language. To equate a nondiscrete durational process with discrete pitch elements is to lack all understanding of their separate natures. In other words, pitch is real and phenomenal material, susceptible to objectivization and rational discipline. Duration is nonmaterial; it can only be felt. To objectify duration in the rationalized, arbitrary fashion of total serialism is to deprive it of its dynamic power to accumulate itself in motion and movement and culminate in a perceptible form.

Finally, in serial music in which duration is equated with musical space and its constituents, durational proportions (or time lengths) are coextensive with spatial proportions. They share equally in the sound structures of which they form the integral parts. Sounds thus ordered, though occurring in succession, do not necessarily produce direction. Duration, whose natural tendency is to create a sense of direction in time (and therefore in form), thus becomes antidynamic and loses its form-giving properties. The articulation of time as process, not just of durational segments, is what creates form. If total serialism thus deprives itself of the natural power of the temporal process to create direction and form, in what then does the form of total serial music subsist? Essentially in the carrying out of the prerationalized program. When all the possibilities of a rational plan of action have been carried out, the composition is completed. Time is spanned, not as an organic process in which a form becomes perceptible growth, but in the same way a clock ticks off seconds, minutes, and hours, mechanically marking measured distances with structured sound events but never realizing time as a dimension of human experience.

Serialism of this type is, therefore (like chance music, but for different reasons), another kind of "existential" music. Antidynamic, its structures exist in the moment they are sounding. Perceptually, it is bounded by each moment. By equating duration with space the former is robbed of its dynamic, autonomous energy. Duration takes on the qualities of the spatial constituents of music: it becomes static, arrested, incapable of directed flow. The suprarationalism of total serial music defeats the durational process in the end; that is to say, it does not engage the listener in his most profound intuitive relation to life and experience, through his grasp of duration by means of which he creates and recreates the order of his personal identity and therein finds his being.

NOTES

1. The word *duration* in this essay is used in a special sense: time as experienced in music (or in theater), i.e., felt time, the flow of the passage of events. This is to distinguish it from "real" or clock time.
2. See the first essay, "Indeterminacy in the New Music," pp. 3–15.

The Concepts of Musical Time and Space

I. The Time-Space Conjunction

Musical composition involves complex, simultaneous operations which I shall call, in the broadest sense, articulations of the conjunction of musical time and musical space. These articulations are infinitely variable, determining both external and internal structure and therefore the potentially expressive qualities of music. They are not only the means by which the aural image is shaped but also the means by which musical gesture is made manifest. While all music, regardless of its ethnic source, issues from this conjunction of musical time and space and is sustained by it, Western music in particular has raised this conjunction to ever increasing degrees of intensity of integration. The evolution of art music in the West has produced an unending series of different musics, each characterized by its own unique techniques or modes of articulating the conjunction of musical time and musical space.

The techniques of articulating the time-space conjunction form the compositional practice generally common in any given period. Practice itself reflects the underlying, prevalent concepts of time and space and their simultaneous articulation. Shifts in concept, however great or small, automatically produce changes in practice, determining the direction music will take. Nor need such shifts be the result of "taking thought," i.e., conscious decisions. They may come about as extensions of or reactions to previous practice— entirely irrational and intuitive in nature. The process of change may be sudden and abrupt or it may be gradual. This will depend to a large extent on the depth of the shift in concept. The more conscious the shift, the sharper the break with the past will be. This has already happened twice in the twentieth century, first with the emergence of the twelve-tone method, and second with the radical development of total serialism. When the shift is intuitive, the change is more likely to be gradual. (Consider, for example, the development of instrumental music during the Baroque era.) Thus, stylistic transformations register these sudden or gradual changes in practice in relation to the intensity of shifts of concept. Any change, however minor, in articulating either the temporal or spatial aspect of music ultimately affects the other. A discussion of these tendencies will occupy our attention later.

Needless to say, the concepts of musical time and space are hardly obvious ones. As they form the twin pillars which support this study, it is essential to clarify what I mean by them. Instead of taking the direct explicative approach, I prefer to examine first existing statements which deal with the same concepts; and, by weighing and comparing their similarities and differences, I hope to prepare the way for a presentation of my own views. There are two statements dealing with the problems of musical time and musical space, one by Susanne K. Langer and another by Arnold Schoenberg, which provide the kind of starting point we need.

In her book *Feeling and Form* (New York: Charles Scribner's Sons, 1953), Langer discusses at length the relation of time (or duration) to music. As she says, "Music makes time audible, and its form and continuity sensible" (p. 110). Drawing the necessary distinction between clock time and duration, she points out that duration is

> something radically different from the time in which our public and practical life proceeds. It is completely incommensurable with the progress of common affairs. Musical duration is an image of what might be termed "lived" or "experienced" time—the passage of life that we feel as expectations become "now," and "now" turns into unalterable fact. Such passage is measurable only in terms of sensibilities, tensions, and emotions; and it has not merely a different measure, but an altogether different structure from practical or scientific time. . . . Vital, experiential time is the primary illusion of music. (P. 109)

By separating experiential time from scientifically measured clock time, we are able to make the subtle distinction between time as pure sequence which is the main attribute of clock time, a "one-dimensional continuum" (p. 111) and that "image of time measured by the motion of forms that seem to give it substance, yet a substance that consists entirely of sound, so it is transitoriness itself" (p. 110). Thus, "music spreads out time for our direct and complete apprehension, by letting our hearing monopolize it—organize, fill and shape it, all alone" (p. 110). In this way, Langer establishes musical time as dynamic, duration in the Bergsonian sense, calling its symbolic presentation in music the *primary illusion* of music. Dealing with the question of space in music, Langer states that musical space is not

> purely metaphorical. . . . There are definitely spatial illusions created in music, quite apart from the phenomena of volume, which is literally spatial, and the fact that movement logically involves space, which may be taking movement too literally. . . . But the space of music is never made wholly perceptible, as the fabric of virtual time is; *it is really an attribute of musical time, an appearance that serves to develop the temporal realm*

in more than one dimension. Space in music is a *secondary illusion.* But primary or secondary it is thoroughly "virtual," i.e., unrelated to the space of actual experience. (P. 117, emphasis added)

While I am in basic accord with Langer's views on the durational aspects of music, I find her altogether vague on the subject of musical space. True, she recognizes its existence in music unequivocally; but she does not make explicit enough how space functions in music other than to assign it a secondary role as an "attribute of musical time," never "wholly perceptible," "an appearance that strives to develop the temporal realm in more than one dimension"; therefore a "secondary illusion." In effect then, she maintains that the substance of musical space, i.e., the sound properties of music, exists less for its own sake than for the sake of enriching duration, the "primary illusion" of music, "to develop the temporal realm in more than one dimension." According to Langer, duration literally absorbs the functions of musical space, relegating them to a subordinate role.

The reader may have already observed how far these views are removed from those expressed in my opening paragraphs. The entire weight of Langer's statements is on musical time. For her, music is movement or passage of "sonorous forms in relation to each other" which create "an order of virtual time," i.e., duration. If these "sonorous forms in relation to each other" which comprise musical space are merely "an attribute of musical time," there is, then, no way to describe music other than as an embodiment of duration; no way to characterize subtle stylistic changes which have to do with the properties of musical space; no way to account for the historical evolution of musical styles, especially those developments which mark twentieth-century music off from the past.

Langer fails to see that musical space is literally coextensive with the sonorous bodies moving in time, creating duration. While she understands that the space of music is "unrelated to the space of actual experience," she fails to comprehend the extent to which musical space is created by the movement of sonorous bodies. Space does not lie outside a particular disposition of sounding pitches; it *is* that disposition of pitches, definable at any given moment by the particular articulation of that disposition. In other words, musical space is a created order of sound which, while not the temporal order per se, nevertheless is the only means by which temporal order can be made perceptible. It is the moving sound substance which constitutes the space of music; its movement which constitutes the duration of music. This is another way of saying that music is a conjunction of time and space. For each piece of music the conjunction of musical space and musical time will be different. There may be correspondences (and there very often are); but if musical time and space are "virtual," i.e., artistically created illusions—and here I certainly agree with Langer—then it follows that the space and time of one composition can never be repeated in another. Each work is a unique presentation of their conjunction, an organism with its own structure and metabolism. This will be true whether we are talking about two different compositions by the same composer or by two different composers (correspondences are more likely to be present in the works by the same composer than in those by different composers, but not always nor necessarily).

Langer is right to separate musical time from clock time and musical space from the "space of actual experience." It must be clear, however, that both the time and space of actual experience, i.e., of the phenomenal world, are present when a piece of music is performed, or imagined when composed. That is to say, the duration of a piece of music, while meaningless if measured by clock time alone, is so measurable and occurs within a certain number of clock time minutes or hours. Musical space on the other hand cannot be measured by increments of physical space (as we measure time) but it does take place in the area of physical space, a point to which we shall return later. The importance of this separation lies in making us aware that music is, as Langer says, "virtual" time and "virtual" space, i.e., created illusions for human perception. Music thus holds up to our aural apprehension artistically created symbols of our physical mode of existence, cleansing them of contingency, accident, and absurdity which invariably accompany human life.

My most serious objection to Langer's views is that, by placing too much emphasis on duration and subsuming space under duration as one of its attributes, she has oversimplified and therefore misread the evidence provided by music itself. Music is a perceptual unity like all gestalten; and it is only by conceptualizing perception that we begin to recognize the relationships of which music is comprised. These relationships of time and space are not, as Langer suggests, of only one order, i.e., a hierarchic arrangement in which duration as primary illusion absorbs space as secondary illusion. This is not true of all music, though it is of some. For example, it is true of Baroque and Classical music. And I suspect that it was by too much concentration on these types of music which form the great body of the heard repertoire that Langer stopped short of a larger vision of the potential relationships in which musical time and space may be conjoined. By disengaging space from time, by giving it greater structural independence, Langer might have penetrated more deeply than she has into the fundamental nature of music. I believe that she has been too quick to accept repertoire music as the only music (just as Schenker, whom she frequently quotes, did). Admittedly, Bach, Haydn, Mozart, and Beethoven are very great composers who wrote truly great music. But there have been, historically, other kinds of music, and there are today still newer (though perhaps not better) kinds of music. One cannot apply, therefore, to all possible types of musical expression philosophic-aesthetic concepts drawn only from one kind of music or stylistic expression (no matter how remarkable that music or style and its accomplishments may be) and achieve satisfactory results, either from an analytic or a critical point of view.

Space must be disengaged from time in order to be able to conceptualize the structural forces which make music. There are at least two excellent reasons for doing so: first, the internal organization of space qua space is structurally independent of duration, i.e., timbre, dynamics, intensity—all spatial properties—are not contingent on rhythm or meter any more than pitch-intervallic content is; second, in actual practice, composers have concerned themselves as much with the problems of spatial articulation as with time. That is why I believe that space must be seen as potentially equivalent to time in musical composition viewed outside of historical influences, that is, in the abstract. For this reason I hold that the use of the term *time-space conjunction* permits us to achieve a conceptual vantage point from which we can survey the historical evolution of music and recognize that music may vary in infinite ways in accordance with the articulations of the time-space conjunction. Time and space in music form a duality; but this duality is not fixed in a final state except in actual composition. Until then, it remains flexible, malleable—subject to every degree and shade of emphasis or tendency, now on time, now on space.

I turn now to a statement of Arnold Schoenberg which provides us with a further opportunity to explore potential meanings and functions of musical time and space. In an essay which appears in his *Style and Idea* (New York: St. Martin's Press, 1975), entitled "Composition with Twelve Tones (I) 1941," Schoenberg gives the basis of his compositional method. In the process of discussing composition with twelve tones he offers this definition of musical space.

> The two or more dimensional space in which musical ideas are presented is a unit. Though the elements of these ideas appear separate and independent to the eye and ear, they reveal their true meaning only through their cooperation, even as no single word alone can express a thought without relation to other words. All that happens at any point of this musical space has more than a local effect. It functions not only in its own plane, but also in all other directions and planes, and is not without influence even at remote points. . . .
>
> A musical idea, accordingly, though consisting of melody, rhythm and harmony, is neither the one nor the other alone, but all three together. The elements of a musical idea are partly incorporated in the horizontal plane as successive sounds and partly in the vertical plane as simultaneous sounds. The mutual relation of tones regulates the succession of intervals as well as their association with harmonies; the rhythm regulates the succession of tones as well as the succession of harmonies and organizes phrasing. (P. 220)

Two aspects of this statement draw our immediate attention: first, the character of musical space *as a unit* which contains within itself all musical events—melodic, harmonic, rhythmic; and second, the absence of any mention of duration per se. Aside from his reference to rhythm as either a cooperating element in the musical idea or as a regulator of the succession of tones, harmonies, and phrases, Schoenberg overlooks time in its durational aspect entirely. What he has given is a description of the association of melody, harmony, and rhythm in an integral ensemble—what he calls "the musical idea." What precisely does he mean by "the two or more dimensional space in which musical ideas are presented is a unit"? And what does he intend by the use of the term *plane?* We can only speculate as to what he means on the basis of inferences we can draw from his statement. The opening sentence contains three clearly discernible elements: (1) two or more dimensional space; (2) the presentation of musical ideas in that space; and (3) the space as a unit. We infer from "two or more dimensional space" a possible analogy with physical space which has length and breadth, height and depth; i.e., tones are organized horizontally as well as vertically. Schoenberg states that "all that happens at any point of this musical space has more than a local effect. It functions not only in its own plane, but also in all other directions and planes." The inference here is clearly a space whose volume is unrestricted, and which, therefore, may be considered analogous to the volume of physical space. Ideas exist on their own plane but have structural ramifications elsewhere in the space, "in all other directions and planes." Direction and movement anywhere in the space is thus potentially free, if our attempt to understand Schoenberg's ideas so far is reasonably correct. Furthermore, this space, "in which musical ideas are presented," appears to lie outside the musical idea and its components, to have its own existence, separate and apart from musical ideas per se. If this inference is correct, then we must add the corollary: that this is also an a priori space, not only existing separate and apart from whatever musical ideas may be presented in it but also existing *before* the presentation of any musical ideas in it. Finally, Schoenberg's idea that space is a unit would appear to be confirmed by the foregoing inferential analysis, namely that musical space is analogous to physical space (also a unit) and that, like physical space, it not only lies outside the elements which fill it, but exists before being filled by them— which is not to say, however, that physical space is a void, a nothingness.

If our speculations up to this point are on the right track, there is one basic conclusion to be drawn: the musical space Schoenberg apparently has in mind is a passive, static space. While it permits action within its field, it is not itself active. It merely provides an existing condition within which musical events may occur. Moreover, the space is always the same, regardless of the particular ideas and their articulations which occur in it—which is to say that potentially the same space exists for different works as well as kinds of music. In other words, space, according to this view, in no way determines either the nature of the musical ideas which happen in it or their articulation. While the musical ideas may be articulated according to their component functions (melody, harmony, rhythm) the space in which they are presented has no effect on these articulations. Perhaps we are justified in suggesting that what Schoenberg had in mind was "acoustical space," the realm of aural perception which is capable of sustaining manifold patterns of simultaneously occurring sound and noise phenomena. Acoustical space would appear to correspond far better with our speculative analysis of what Schoenberg intended by his definition than the term *musical space* does. Acoustical space is essentially passive, activated only by vibratory disturbance. Its primordial state is silence. It lies outside the realm of musical ideas but is capable of receiving them—or, we should say, transmitting them. It exists before and after their occurrence. Acoustical space relates to the physical realm through the hearing process which involves aural perception and discrimination (separation of sound elements from each other in relation to the sound source, determination of direction, etc.) of what is heard in the physical realm—music, noise, natural sounds, human talk.

One can go no further with this line of inferential speculation. We are still not absolutely certain of what Schoenberg meant and certainly do not intend that he meant what we have inferred from his statement. However, where musical space is concerned, we have at least established a fundamental distinction between his views (as far as we are able to understand them) and Langer's. Schoenberg's indifference to the role duration plays in music allows him to stress the unit he ascribes to what he calls "musical space." Here we are not forced to speculate, for it is perfectly clear that he does not accord musical time any special importance in the musical scheme of things. Even assuming that by "rhythm" he meant the whole temporal structure of music *as duration*, it still remains only one component in the structure of the "musical idea" along with melody and harmony: "neither the one nor the other alone, but all three together." There is, as he says, "cooperation" among these elements but this is not the same as saying they function as separately definable articulations in the conjunction of time-space; nor is the remotest relation to Langer's idea of time as primary illusion and space as secondary illusion implied. We are again thrown back on the concept of spatial unity; and, as I suggested previously, a unity which is acoustical, derived from aural perception. If, until now, there has been any uncertainty about this, we can dispel it by quoting another statement from the same essay which appears a few pages later.

> . . . the previously stated law of the unity of musical space, best formulated as follows: *The unity of musical space demands an absolute and unitary perception.* In this space . . . there is no absolute down, no right or left, forward or backward. Every musical configuration, every movement of tones has to be comprehended primarily as a mutual relation of sounds, of oscillatory vibrations, appearing at different places and times. (P. 223)

Thus Schoenberg unequivocally relates the unity of space to the unity of aural perceptions. One can only conclude (1) that this musical space exists only in aural perception, not in the articulations of spatial properties (pitch, timbre, dynamic, intensity) and is, therefore, acoustical space; and (2) that as a concept it is abstracted from the realm of aural experience of the physical world, separating musical events made up of elements of sound and rhythm from the aurally perceived "space" itself.

The fundamental contradiction which results from juxtaposing Langer's views with Schoenberg's is fairly obvious: Langer unifies musical events solely in terms of duration; Schoenberg, solely in terms of space. Even though Langer recognizes space as an element in the musical gestalt, it is secondary to duration and subsumed under it; consequently it loses its identity as space, becoming merely another dimension of time. Even though Schoenberg recognizes rhythm as an element in what he calls "the musical idea," it is only one of three elements, the other two being melody and harmony, which cooperate in mutual relations to form the musical idea; consequently it loses its identity, being one aspect only of a whole. For my purposes, therefore, neither of these views is satisfactory because they depend entirely on a conceptual unity which results in the loss of structural identity of one or the other of the two terms of the time-space conjunction. The assumption of either concept of unity would appear to be based on the premise that the musical situations defined by one or the other are true at all times and under all circumstances. But since neither the practice of composition nor the evolution of music bears this out, we are unable to accept the critical restrictions they impose upon us. We turn instead to the functional duality contained in my initial concept of the conjunction of time and space which permits us the latitude and scope we need in order to solve the problems which lie ahead. In positing a duality of the time-space relationship, this relationship or conjunction, as I prefer to call it, implies the existence of a level of mutual interaction between the elements out of which music arises without specifying whether this interaction, when it takes place, is between members of equal or unequal rank. Each retains its identity in the relationship or conjunction, regardless of the relative weight or importance accorded one or the other in a specific musical context. By maintaining this duality conceptually, time and space may be considered potentially free to combine and recombine in an infinite variety of ways. Nor does the term *conjunction* necessarily assume any degree of homogeneity in the articulations of time and space. Rather it provides for the possibility of heterogeneous relations, never determining in advance what the specific musical result will be. Thus it is conceivable that there are musical situations in which space is dominated by time and vice versa, but even then, never to the point where the domination of the one destroys the identity of the other, structurally or perceptually. The premise that the time-space conjunction retains a functional duality makes possible the investigation of the special characteristics of each aspect, separately and conjointly, from new angles and opens up to exploration a whole range of new problems.

It is time to explain what I mean by the "articulation of the time-space conjunction" and, in the process, sketch in the main outlines of my concept of musical time and musical space. One peculiarly unique musical circumstance provides us with the key to this discussion: the condition of silence, and the so-called musical rest. There is another kind of silence which, unlike the musical rest which may be characterized as "cessation of sound," I will call the "absence of sound." The distinction is worth making because it will lead to another point to be made later. In any performance situation, whether it be a concert or a play, there is usually a brief period of settling *into* silence, a preparatory silence as it were, before the performance starts. This silence has no structural function in the performance that follows. It is a condition of focusing attention and concentration on what is to follow. It is the threshold of action—musical, dramatic, or whatever. Though this silence may have no structural function within the context of the artistic action, it has another function related to that of preparing the action: it separates the artistic action from the mundane environment in which the action will take place. Not only does it separate the two realms of illusion and reality; it also transforms the real environment into one in which illusion can occur. This is why when the lights dim in the theater a hush falls on the audience and, suddenly, in the silence just before the curtain rises, the theater is transformed into a place of magical expectancy. Something of a very similar nature attends the appearance of the conductor, the ready attention of the orchestra, and the concentrated expectancy of the audience—the concert hall is transformed, ready for the great illusion that is live music.

Silence within a piece of music is not of this category; it is not mere "absence of sound." It is the purposeful "cessation of sound"; and therefore has a structural function in the context of the music. This silence is the negative of sound, but not the negation of sound. In its use composers have found a means of powerful effect, particularly in its direct juxtaposition with sounding bodies. If silence is the "cessation of sound," is it also the "cessation of movement"? The reader will recall Langer's view of duration as movement or passage of sonorous, audible forms. Logically, then, if the passage of sonorous, audible forms ceases, and is replaced by silence, movement or the sense of duration would also cease. But this is not what happens, as every musician will attest; for silence in music is part of the structure of the time-space conjunction and is itself an *audible* form, taking the place of sounding pitches. Duration or the sense of passage, therefore, is not abrogated; it continues unimpeded. The verbal syllogism "silence is the cessation of sound and therefore the cessation of movement because there can be no movement without sound" does not work here; it fails to reckon with the realities of the musical situation which is rooted in the conditions of the phenomenal world and therefore is not susceptible to this kind of verbal logic. We must seek an answer in the nature of silence itself and its relation to the musical space.

Musical space constitutes the concrete structural relations of pitch (and all its components) and silence. It is created by these relations and therefore is not a constant, either for a single work or for different works. Its integral structure is unique to each work—though admittedly there can be correspondences between the musical space, i.e., the articulation of internal pitch-silence relationships, of one work and another. This space is coextensive with the fluctuations of the order of pitch and silence and is realized in the articulation of these fluctuations. This is the space which the composer is making, shaping, articulating when he works. It is an aural conception, a mental projection in terms of structural relationships, which issues forth in performance as physically projected aural images. The question now is: how do we hear this musical space? The answer: in acoustical space, via auditory perception. Thus we are back to Schoenberg's idea of the acoustical space of "unitary perception" which he erroneously called "musical space." A distinction can now be drawn between the space of the composer's mental projections (which is coextensive with the articulated structure of the pitch-silence elements) and the space in which it is perceived. The concrete, physically rendered space of the composer is an active, characteristic force projected on or against the passive, neutral acoustical space of auditory perception (which is the same for all kinds of characteristic sound projections whether they are musical or nonmusical). The primordial condition of acoustical space is silence. Otherwise, it would not be possible to hear sounds of any kind—musical, human, or natural. As precondition it is the "absence of sound"; but when silence occurs in a piece of music we experience a unique phenomenon: we hear acoustical space, no-sound, the negative of sound. It is as though a hole were torn in the fabric of sound and there, as concrete as sound itself, acoustical space suddenly becomes perceptible, i.e., we hear it as part of the structure of the music itself. It now has meaning in the concrete musical space; it has become a technique of articulation, i.e., it separates for structural purposes audible pitch forms, itself audible as another type of form. Since it *is* audible and therefore structural, it does not cause the cessation of movement. On the contrary, movement contains silence as a temporal element. Silence may replace pitch; but movement continues, the silence now a structural element in the meter or in the rhythmic phrase, articulating in a special way the character of meter or phrase. When the meter in poetry or music is regular and a predictable pattern of beats is established, entire feet or individual units of the metric foot may be silent; nevertheless the meter continues its steady march as though every part of it were being physically sounded. Thus silence, though it may be characterized as "the cessation of sound" in a musical context, does not cause the cessation of durational flow. As heard acoustical space it becomes a structural element in the musical space. Like pitch itself, it is that point in the musical context where time and space conjoin, performing the simultaneous function of articulating the conjunction. The particular mode of articulation will determine the shape of both the metric-rhythmic and spatial aspects—and, therefore, of the music itself. Silence, as a structural element in the musical context, is drawn from the same acoustical space in which the "unitary perception" of what is physically projected takes place. Yet silence, as acoustical space, retains its essential character of passivity, thus permitting a constant oscillation of active-passive states in the heard flow of the music (sound-silence-sound-silence).

Let us consider some instances in which silence, as I have described it, plays a significant role as an articulating factor. In the opening measure of the last movement of Beethoven's String Quartet in A Minor, Op. 132, silence functions as an important element in the spatial-metric articulation.

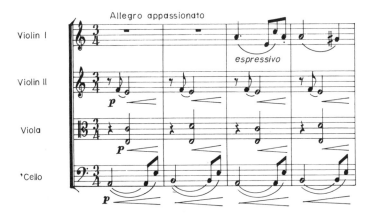

The two inner voices (violin II and viola) develop a simple metric as well as spatial design. The persistence of the eighth rest in the second violin and the quarter rest in the viola provide the "openings" through which acoustical space is heard as silence. Nevertheless regularity of motion is ensured by the constancy with which the cello and first violin sound the first beat left open in the design Beethoven has provided for the inner voices. What is accomplished is rhythmic oscillation within a fairly static spatial projection, an almost perfect symmetry of active-passive states over which the melody of the first violin traces its contour. This particular use of silence is common to all composers. Less common is the opening gesture of Beethoven's String Quartet in C-sharp Minor, Op. 131, No. 7.

The abrupt figures are forceful. But their force, their energy needs room in which to expend themselves. Hence the silences. It is not certain what will happen, not until the fifth measure when rhythmic regularity establishes clarity of metric order and the force inherent in the opening gesture is gathered up and directed. The impact of the opening figures comes from their very separation by silence which creates an expectancy which is not satisfied until the marchlike melodic-rhythmic design is reached in measure 5. The number of beats which are actually unsounded and the number which are sounded in the first four measures after the opening C-sharp (measure 1) balance each other exactly—eight and eight—creating, as it were, a perfect symmetry of active-passive states. However, the musical importance of silence weighs heavily here; for it is from the condition of silence that the two shapes which comprise measures 2–3 and 4–5 (first note) are literally wrenched. These concrete spatial tracings, therefore, have proportionately greater vigor and outline as a result. An examination of this movement of the quartet indicates the extent to which Beethoven is committed to this dramatic juxtaposition of sound-silence (see, for example, measures 117–25; also measures 268–78). The intensity of this structural use of silence exceeds in marked fashion its use previously pointed out in the passage from Op. 132. A still more intense use of structural silence which articulates the temporal and spatial aspects of Beethoven's music occurs at the outset of the Scherzo of the Ninth Symphony.

There is no passage like this in all Western music. Its assertive vigor and stark simplicity stem from essentially the same sources as the opening of Op. 131, No. 7; but where the latter provides a symmetry of sound-silence, the opening gesture of the Scherzo develops even greater force, not only because its instrumental resources and concrete spatial range are greater, but because the rhythmic alternation of sound-silence is asymmetrical. If the first four measures are taken as a unit and the second four similarly, it will be noted that the symmetry which underlies the first four is shattered by the second group of four: the actual sounds of measures 1–4 which take up one measure each are followed by one measure of silence after each, thus sound-silence-sound-silence; whereas measures 5–6 form one unit of concrete sound, followed by a unit of silence, measures 7–8, equal in durational value. Despite the internal symmetry of each four-measure group, the eight measures, taken as a larger group, comprise the entire musical phrase in which the juxtaposition of these two smaller symmetries creates one large asymmetry. The climax of the concrete space is reached in the sixth measure; but the durational flow extends beyond to encompass the seventh and eighth measures, heard as silence. The ultimate logic of this phrase reveals itself in the gathering-up into a single two-measure unit (5–6) the single-measure sound ejaculations (1 and 3), balancing this with the gathering-up of silence in a similar two measures (7 and 8), previously distributed in single measures (2 and 4). The power of silence, in this instance, is unmistakable. It sharpens the cutting edge of each pitch figure, lending special clarity to the timbre distinction, particularly in the sudden emergence from the silence of measure 4 of the timpani notes of measure 5.

It was inevitable that I drew these first examples from Beethoven's work, for a major facet of his dramatic power resides in his intuitive sense of the relation of concrete musical space to acoustical space, reinforced by his instinct for handling duration. Nor do I believe that in Beethoven's case it was purely intuition and instinct which led him to develop the articulations of the conjunction of time-space to such an intense degree. Even though these time-space conjunctions are purely musical, i.e., nonverbal awareness—it need not follow that they are merely intuitive or instinctive. While Beethoven may not have thought about these problems of space and time rationally (as, for example, I am trying to elucidate them verbally), surely he *knew* them as a composer and musical thinker, i.e., he was fully conscious of the properties of space and time to the extent his historical position permitted (and beyond).

I draw my next examples from the works of another composer also supremely aware of the art of articulating the time-space conjunction—Gustav Mahler. It is strange how little Mahler is yet understood as a composer; yet it is precisely in the internal structure of his music that he reveals he is in the great tradition of Beethoven. The opening statement of Mahler's Second Symphony will serve as corroboration.

The rhetorical grandeur of this passage rests not only on the guided upward direction of the pitch elements which comprise the total musical gesture, but also on the silences which separate the main pitch points which outline the rising C-minor triad. The expectancy of the next motion upward is further intensified by the silences which follow the arrivals at E-flat, G, and C. These silences are relative, not absolute, in duration. In a footnote to the conductor, Mahler writes:

> In den Ersten Takten des Thema's sind die Bassfiguren schnell in heftigen Ansturm ungefähr ♩ = 144, die Pausen jedoch in Hauptzeit- mass ♩ = 84–92 auszuführen. Der Halt im 4. Takte ist Kurz—gleichsam ein Ausholen zu neuer Kraft. [In the first measure of the theme, the bass figures are in quick and violent attack (around ♩ = 144), with the follow- ing pauses however in the main tempo of ♩ = 84–92. The fermata in the fourth measure is short—as if to marshal new power. (Trans. WB)]

With this footnote Mahler projected himself into our own time. The attempt to provide clear directions for producing rubato, i.e., elastic durational values, is a twentieth-century trait, typical of Webern and taken up by many others since. Mahler is thinking of silence primarily in terms of durational value (he assigns a metronomic range of 84–92 to the first and third measures where the celli and double basses do not play; note that he wants the fermata in the fourth measure short so that the final rise to the C in measure 5 can be taken up with "neuer Kraft"). The drama of this opening, like that inherent in the opening of Beethoven's Scherzo, is intensified by the searing emergence of the celli-basses from the silence which encompasses their own register. The middle register $(g–g^1)$ has been activated from the beginning; but, after the first mea- sure, recedes from aural attention to make room for the important action which emerges below it. The tremolo on the octave G becomes static, an oscillating disturbance in acoustical space. It is because of the differences in register between these two levels of static and active motion and the tendency of the static level to virtually lose itself in acoustical space that the bass figure can develop the sound-silence juxtaposition to a maximum degree of intensity. The

tremolo (g–g^1) which is spatially static, and therefore passive, is also dura-
tionally static; i.e., it is not articulated metrically and therefore does not define
itself rhythmically. These conditions, combined with the acoustical space left
open in the bass register, provide the basis for the projection of the concrete
spatial characteristics of the bass figure as well as the rubato rendering of the
durational flow called for by Mahler's footnote.

Finally I turn to an examination of a passage from the second movement
of Mahler's Fifth Symphony where silence again plays an important role, but
quite different in its structural implications from those we have discussed so
far.

Here we enter into consideration of a type of spatial articulation which
depends to a large extent on "timbre-modulation" (See Istvan Anhalt's review
of new recordings of Varèse, *Canadian Music Journal*, Winter, 1961, pp. 34–39),
a device which varies the color while retaining the essential shape of a concrete
spatial image. In this instance two elements fuse into a single spatial image: the

F-minor triad (*a*), a harmonic constant for fifteen measures (see p. 57, Edition Peters, No. 5), unites with the melodic motive (*b*) in varied woodwind timbres, creating the spatial environment in which the cello melody is projected with apparent ease because both its shape and timbre mark it off, aurally, from the woodwind figures reiterated above it. The distinction between the two spatial components which make up the whole passage is further enhanced by the rhythmic structure of each. The cello melody phrases according to the main beats of the alla breve (¢) signature of the movement; the woodwind repetitions of the fused triad (*a*) and motive (*b*) form variant lengths of duration, each separated by silence. For example the first five measures:

show clearly both the symmetry of the durational lengths of (*a*) and (*b*) and the articulation of active-passive states of sound-silence. Each timbre change of the spatially constant image composed of triad and motive is prepared by the silence which precedes it, separating its color distinctly from its previous presentation and from that which follows. The subtle oscillations of timbre-modulation become an aural fact in the perception of this passage, made structurally evident by the use of silence in its dual function of simultaneously articulating space and time in the musical context. In this case, as in many typically Mahlerian passages, the chief delight lies in perceiving how he handles the time-space conjunction as much as in following the contours of his melodic spans.

This discussion of the structural function of silence in the articulation of the time-space conjunction has brought into sharp focus the relationship between the concrete musical space and the acoustical space in which it is perceived, and has also shown to what an extent the articulation of the concrete musical space is bound up with that of duration in music. I have tried to indicate that there is no single condition that defines the time-space conjunction, but that there are infinite ways in which the conjunction can be articulated, each way characteristic of a certain kind of music. The organization of concrete musical space in terms of specific techniques or devices is directly related to the organization of the duration of the music, and vice versa. I hope to show later that the dominance of one over the other is the result of fundamental notions about what music is or can be, notions which are rooted in prevailing tendencies of the time.

Concrete musical space is as much an artistic creation as musical time. The aural images which comprise musical space are the physical projections, first conceived and imagined by the composer and heard in acoustical space, which employ acoustical space as silence in their structure. As sounding, audible bodies their movement creates the sense of duration or musical time, which is disposed and articulated in organized lengths of motion to create a structural time. The structure of movement also employs silence, or acoustical space, in a variety of ways in order to create one or another kind of sensation of motion. The musical gestures which result from this inflection of motion contain the aural image, sound-silence, or the active-passive musical space. The articulations of musical time and space not only constitute the organic process of composition itself; they also establish the form of the content (the aural images and musical gestures), which is to say the organic form of the created musical substance. Form is thus coextensive with content, i.e., with what is formed.

The shape of a tree, its height, thickness, and spread, are the outward manifestations of every movement and tendency of the internal growth process and interactions of the substances which go to make what we call "a tree," even to the texture and shape of the leaf by which it is identified. In much the same way the time-space conjunction issues forth as music according to the mode of its articulation, creating the illusions of musical time and space. In turn, the aural images and gestures—the substance of musical time-space—derive their expressivity, intensity, and quality not only from the mode or technique of articulation but also from the human stance toward reality, which is a powerfully determinative factor in the choice of the technique of articulation, whatever it may be. Because the stance toward reality is constantly undergoing modification and change according to the experience of the race, it is inevitable that music alter its structural forms and qualities from epoch to epoch; and that, whatever its present state, we have no reason to believe that it will not continue to alter under the impact of ever-new forms, conditions, and styles of human life. The evolution of musical style in Western civilization bears this out, whether we witness history or present developments.

II. Two Prototypes

I turn now to an examination of current musical terminology in order to discover, if possible, the existence of terms which might help us in our further analysis of the problems we have posed. What we are looking for are commonly understood terms which have a direct bearing on the conjunction of musical time and musical space and/or its modes of articulation. Do we have such a terminology at hand? Conventional musical terminology contains a host of terms of a surprisingly wide variety of meaning and connotation. Some of them offer interesting clues which are worth following up, and it is these I wish to investigate. If we are fortunate enough to find already known terms which will serve our purpose, our task may be lighter. Otherwise, we shall have to invent our own terminology in order to be in a better position to discuss these problems, for, while we may apprehend the phenomena already described in a general way, to go deeper into their structure requires a verbal technique which will permit definition and analysis of organic processes. Most important is the necessity to define and analyze these processes without violating their integral characteristics, i.e., without destroying the living substance of musical actions in the very act of verbalizing about them.

We possess three terms—*monody, homophony,* and *polyphony*—which contain a spatial implication; in each case we are informed by ordinary understanding of the terms that X number of parts make up the musical space. It is clear that by the term *monody* we understand one part (or voice); by *homophony,* three or more parts (or voices) sounding together; by *polyphony,* two or more in counterpoint. However, there are no further indications regarding the specific characteristics of the concrete organization of the musical space, i.e., no knowledge regarding the internal structure can be elicited, unless we accept a further refinement of the general structure: for example, that monody is a single-voiced melody (Gregorian chant or Varèse's "Density 21.5" for solo flute); or that homophony describes a melody accompanied by harmony (a Bach chorale or the opening measures of Schoenberg's Fourth String Quartet); or that polyphony arises through the association of independent melodies (a Machaut motet or a Hindemith fugue from *Ludus Tonalis*). Our efforts to derive more information from these terms will be fruitless, for each time we try we will be forced back to generalities. Two of the three terms suggest a general condition of articulating musical time—homophony and polyphony. When we say "monody," we do not know immediately whether we are referring to music which is measured or unmeasured: the term does not tell us whether the monody is pure melisma or metrically organized. But when we say "homophony" it is instantly evident that we mean a piece of music in which clearly established metric divisions of time regulate the simultaneous movement of both the melody and other parts; or when we say "polyphony," that we mean a piece of music whose temporal organization, whatever its structure, regulates the rhythmic movement of the parts, leaving them free to follow their own course regarding entry and exit. Beyond these general inferences, which I believe can be safely drawn from these terms, nothing more can be said about the specific techniques of articulating the time-space conjunction. What is of real interest, however, is that they contain as much information as they do, leading one to suspect that musicians have traditionally intuited the conjunction; otherwise how explain the long use and prevalence of these three basic terms?

There are other terms commonly used which have direct semantic ties with either musical time or musical space.

Time	Space
Arsis, thesis	Tone, note
Upbeat, downbeat	Pitch
Tempo	Chord
Meter	Triad
Rhythm	Harmony
Rubato	Sonority
Measure	Density
Phrase	Texture
Period	Register

Note that in some cases these terms offer more specific information than others. For example, *upbeat-downbeat* defines a relationship which is both metric and rhythmic; *measure* defines a metric division marked off from either a similar or dissimilar division; *triad* defines a three-note chord; *tone* defines a single pitch, and so forth. These are bits and scraps of information which, unfortunately, do not tell us what we want to know: how, specifically, do they function as articulating elements in the time-space conjunction? The two sets of terms are mutually exclusive; therefore, they offer no insight into the conjunction per se. While they may be factors in the articulation of either time or space, they are, with the few exceptions pointed out, too general to be meaningful. In association with more specific terms they may take on greater semantic weight. For example, if we combine pitch and rhythm we arrive at one of the most common terms of all, *melody*. Now, *melody* strongly implies the conjunction, no matter what definition is offered. Whether the definition states the two primary elements as pitch and rhythm, as we have just done, or tone and time, the results are essentially the same, at least in meaning and intent. Unfortunately, melodic concepts are as infinitely variable as the articulations of the time-space conjunction, and therefore the term *melody* is still too general for our purposes. Even a more specialized term like *harmonic rhythm* remains too vague although it suggests a relationship to the conjunction.

If we examine terms which designate formal organization, are we any closer to the mark? Consider set form types such as minuet, scherzo, rondo, sonata-allegro, gavotte, bourée, gigue, aria da capo, or strophic song; or what I shall call procedural types—forms which derive from a priori principles without specifying the macroshape, such as canon, fugue, chaconne, passacaglia, fantasia, or ricercar. None of these I have named are precise designations of the mode of articulating the time-space conjunction. To be sure, some are suggestive of either a general type of temporal or spatial articulation or of their conjunction. For example, *canon* clearly posits that two or more voices will follow each other at a prescribed metric and interval distance. This diagonal relationship necessarily involves the time-space conjunction. However, it cannot be said that *fugue* can be described this way because the parts are not bound to each other in as predetermined a fashion. Fugal entry is governed by interval relationships but, unless we know whether we are discussing a "real" or "tonal" fugue, we cannot know what we need to know about the interval content. (One might ask at this point, by way of interjection: is not the first movement of the Bartók *Music for Strings, Percussion and Celesta* a fugue despite the fact that it is neither "real" nor "tonal" in the traditional sense?) *Chaconne* and *passacaglia* suggest spatial properties, because we know that the harmonic structure of the one and the bass line of the other are generating forces of these procedural forms. With such forms as *minuet, scherzo,* or *aria da capo* we understand a tripartite temporal macroshape—but no more than that unless one takes the "trio" of the minuet and scherzo literally as meaning a three-part spatial structure. We could perform this semantic exercise endlessly but the results would be always the same: general clues, but not enough precise information to go on.

It ought to be clear by now that there are no terms in our present musical vocabulary, with the one exception of *canon,* which refer directly to the mode of articulating the time-space conjunction. This is not surprising, especially when one considers that there can be no answers until there are questions first. Since there has been no need in the past to define the problems this study raises there has obviously been no need for the terms in which to state the definition. But why does this need arise now? What conditions affecting the musical situation have brought this circumstance about?

At the very outset of this study I said that the articulations of the time-space conjunction were infinitely variable and that each kind of music which has evolved in the art music of the West is the result of its unique mode of articulating this conjunction. Further, I said that Western music had raised the conjunction of time-space to "ever-increasing degrees of intensity of integration." One need only examine a sample of Notre Dame *organum purum* and compare it with a page or two of Webern to realize to what extent this integration has been intensified. That there has been, between these two extreme types of music, an evolving series of unique modes of articulating the conjunction is historically self-evident, but it would be misleading to suggest that, simultaneously, these unique modes which issued forth in different styles were accompanied by the emergence of an analogous series of unique conjunctions. In a severely restricted fashion this is true only if we include the developments which have so radically altered the structure of twentieth-century music. For it must follow from the two terms which comprise the conjunction that only two orders are possible: time-space and space-time. This type of verbal logic is no idle exercise, for it is completely corroborated, as we shall see, by the evolution of music, particularly twentieth-century music. The two conjunctions, time-space and space-time, may be viewed as prototypes of fundamental significance. As prototypes, they will serve as the basis for penetrating structural relationships which resist traditional approaches. These prototypes will permit us to comprehend structural relationships which define totally different types of music and, at the same time, provide us with insights into the reasons for the crisis which has driven the audience of our own time from the music composed contemporaneously with it—a problem which cannot be taken lightly.

Until the twentieth century, Western music was rooted in one prototype: time-space. Regardless of changes in formal organization or combinations of temporal-spatial elements, i.e., different ways of realizing their simultaneous articulation, this prototype remained unaltered and intact, binding together in a chain of evolution centuries of constantly changing concepts of the aural image and the musical gesture. Its elemental strength ensured the continuation of tradition and common practice. At the same time it was able to extend tradition in an unbroken line, despite stylistic shifts in direction and the pull of new tendencies. Its power was such that it retained its essential structural characteristics throughout approximately one thousand years, from roughly 900 to about 1925. Small wonder that Beethoven could derive nourishment from Handel's scores, that Mozart felt duty-bound to study J. S. Bach, that Stravinsky in his early days could "return" to the music of (pseudo-)Pergolesi and adapt it to his purposes in *Pulcinella*, that Berg could incorporate the chorale harmonization of "Es ist Genug" by J. S. Bach into his Violin Concerto, that Wagner could consider himself Beethoven's spiritual heir, that Brahms could interest himself in the music of Samuel Scheidt, and so on. A fundamental tradition rooted in the prototype: time-space bound these men and their music together. It is because of this tradition that we are today able to accept without hesitation or distinction side-by-side performances of works from widely separated epochs, works expressing different tendencies and interests. Our aural faculties comprehend these stylistic differences without basic adjustments in our mode of perception. We do not require a uniquely different apparatus of perception for each style. Metaphorically speaking, the prototype created the conditions for a basic musical language, each style in that language a different dialect. While we may respond more directly, for one reason or another, to one dialect or another, we find we are nevertheless capable of apprehending to some degree all the dialects derivative of this language. The stylistic differences between Monteverdi and Mahler, for example, are considerable; yet we can understand both, as dialects of a common musical language, with comparatively little difficulty. I believe this to be as true of the musically educated layman as of the musician. The layman will accept with perfect equanimity a sonata of Domenico Scarlatti and a nocturne or scherzo of Chopin because their stylistic differences are external; they do not affect the basic prototype conjunction.

Does our aural apparatus function in the same way with twentieth-century music? The answer must be equivocal. It does when the act of perception focuses on music of Prokofiev, Shostakovitch, Bartók, Hindemith, Milhaud, Vaughan Williams, early Stravinsky, early Schoenberg, or Britten. With somewhat greater difficulty it will apprehend later Schoenberg, Webern, or Berg because the spatial properties have undergone a radical change particularly in regard to intervallic content and tonal direction. Nevertheless the basic prototype remains intact for the most part—I say for the most part, because there are mutations, artistic sports, in the music of Schoenberg and Webern which have caused fissures in the walls of the prototype, fissures deepened and widened by developments after 1945 yet already prefigured in the early part of the twentieth century in the work of Edgard Varèse. Our aural apparatus does not function in the same way when faced with the serial music and its various offshoots written "after Webern," i.e., since 1945. While our perceptive apparatus functions perfectly for Mozart and soon adjusts to Bartók, it simply breaks down when confronted with the new world created by serialism. This does not mean, however, that there is no value or validity in the music resulting from the new serial procedures. One of my purposes is to try to show what is positive in serial music and to demonstrate what may be meaningful for the continuing evolution of music. Before we can do this, however, we must deal with the question of why the perception of serial music is, in itself, a problem.

The music of the twentieth century which extends in various ways the principles of the harmonic functions of tonality is rooted in the same basic prototype as pre-twentieth-century music: time-space. Duration and space, though varied for stylistic reasons, remain in much the same structural relation to each other as before. By merely listening we soon acquire familiarity with these new aural images and musical gestures derived from new modes of articulating the particular time-space conjunction. However, by merely listening to serial music, our aural perceptions, no longer able to function in the "normal" way, become confused and bewildered and finally register non-comprehension. It is not, as some would have us believe, simply a question of acquiring familiarity with this music through repeated hearings. This will only create further exasperation and bewilderment because we will still be listening for images and gestures which are not there; it is rather a question of adjusting the perceptive apparatus itself to an entirely new set of conditions, to learn to listen for and to hear what *is* there. For serial music has utterly abandoned the traditional prototype, time-space, and established in its place a completely altered conjunction of musical time and musical space, a new prototype, space-time, which is the source of altogether new aural images and musical gestures. This new prototype, however, did not, like Aphrodite from the head of Zeus, suddenly spring forth full-grown from serialism. Serialism has merely confirmed a fundamental inversion in the structural relationship of time and space which has its roots earlier in the twentieth century. To identify the new prototype with serialism would be a great mistake, for it is only one potential mode of articulating the space-time prototype. Nor is this new prototype bound up with the fate of serialism any more than the traditional time-space prototype was bound up with the fate of any one of its many modes of articulation which evolved during the course of the centuries. By assigning serialism a role as a historical mode of articulating the new space-time prototype we shall find ourselves on surer ground, better able to deal with it and other articulations of this prototype which emerged almost simultaneously around 1925.

The reader will have seen by now that there is more than ordinary significance attached to the word order of each of the prototypes; and that in each instance the first term indicates the chief emphasis in the structural relationship of the prototype. When, a while ago, I referred to the dual nature of the archetypal conjunction of time and space and, indeed, insisted on this duality not only as the only means by which each could retain its identity, though in relationship with the other, but also as the only view sufficiently flexible to permit us to conceptualize their conjunction without predetermining structural emphasis or weight, it was precisely this end I had in mind. Time-space, as its word order implies, defines a basic structural relationship in which duration plays the dominant role, relegating space to a lesser role in the musical situation. Space-time, the second prototype, defines a structural relationship in which the roles are reversed. The reversal of the roles of time and space in the second prototype is so far-reaching in its effect as to alter the character of time and space and consequently the structure of music. This is not to say that the time or space of the second prototype is a different time or space from that of the first, i.e., a *new* time or space. Not at all; but the radical shift in emphasis does create sharp differences of degree.

To appreciate fully the essential difference between time-space and space-time it becomes necessary to discuss first "direction in music." Essentially, direction in music is the creation of an integral order which is perceived or sensed as structural goal or purpose. This is to say that when a composer creates an order in his music which defines its own form as it emerges in concrete sound, one can sense its direction, or, as we say: "we know where it is going." Direction in music derives from a clear perception of, and therefore corresponds to, the clear presentation of temporal and spatial points of departure and movement or passage en route to points of arrival or destination. The sense of direction coincides with, or runs parallel to, the actual growth process of the music and the order in which the growth process occurs. The classical music of Haydn, Mozart, and Beethoven offers us a prime example of the growth process of such an integral order in which structural direction is dependent on two essential conditions: periodicity of rhythmic motion and tonality. By their very nature, both are essentially directional, i.e., both are conditions which can fulfill their structural destinies only in future actions. Periodicity of rhythmic motion requires a regulated continuity of motion which in music is provided by meter and rhythm. In an unusual study of the forces inherent in meter and rhythm Victor Zuckerkandl points out that "the same force that forms the wave of the individual measure expresses itself, in reaching beyond the measure, as a demand for ever more embracing symmetries. The whole of a group is always at the same time the half (a half either demanding symmetrical completion or fulfilling that demand) of the next higher group." (*Sound and Symbol* [New York: Pantheon Books, 1956], p. 179.) In positing his wave theory of beat, meter, and rhythm, Zuckerkandl lays a sound basis for periodicity which is not only regulated continuity of motion but at the same time a cumulation of intensified energy produced by this motion.

> The succession of equal metrical beats produced the wave; the repetition of the same metrical wave now produces intensification. Every new wave, in comparison with the similar wave that preceded it, is experienced as an increase. . . . The two phenomena, the wave of the individual measure, the intensification of the successive waves are closely connected. . . . As the impulse that sets it in motion, the first wave lives on in the second, the first and second together in the third, the first three in the fourth, and so on and on. . . . As measure follows on measure, wave upon wave, something grows, accumulates; it is a dynamic process through and through, only to be understood as the result of a constantly active force. (Pp. 175–76)

Periodicity, then, is not mere succession in the extension of rhythmic motion but a process of intensification through accumulation of rhythmic forces which balance each other as they seek the next point of arrival, and the next, and so on. The order of this dynamic growth through accumulation is perceived through the melodic phrase which embodies this rhythmic wave force and consequently activates the next phrase. It is because of this process that classical music conveys such a powerful sense of direction, realized as periodicity in the cumulative drive of rhythmic motion. This is clearly demonstrated in the following passage from the scherzo of the Seventh Symphony of Beethoven.

The phrase structure coincides with the rhythmic groupings of measures into either twos or fours. The upbeat or arsis character of the first two measures drives to the third measure and releases its energy in the first four-measure group (measures 3–6) which, while thesis to the first two measures, is antecedent to the next four (measures 7–10). These two phrases drive into measures 11 through 16 to explode their total force at measure 17. The energy of this initial push from the first measure to the G-sharp of measure 17 expends itself through the first two beats of measure 24, which we sense as a rhythmic caesura. Thus the rhythmic point of departure, a two-measure arsis, sets off a drive through successive waves until the total motion arrives at measure 24. En route the rhythmic force reaches its maximum intensification at measure 17 and, from there, spreads its energies, like a breaking wave, over the next eight measures only to begin again a rising wave with the upbeat to measure 25.

As the second direction-producing force, tonality in classical music organizes the structural grouping of tones and chords around tonal points of orientation and ensures the pitch articulation of the rhythmic phrase-wave, at the same time confirming the directional structure of the rhythmic phrase-wave. In the movement away from one tone toward another tone (or from aggregate to aggregate) there exists the condition of fulfillment aroused by the expectancy which incomplete tonal motions produce. Take for example this melody from Mozart's Piano Concerto, K. 503.

The arrival at the first E-flat is a fulfillment of the individually incomplete motions from G to C, C to D, D to E-flat, each in turn fulfilling an expectancy created by the previous motion. The consequent phrase which falls in the opposite direction, after the outlining of the C minor triad, to D is the result of the balancing force which holds the first two phrases in symmetry. The second large period contains an intensification of tonal ascent to G and the final descent and cadence to C. All of these motions ultimately associate themselves with a single pitch locus, C, as the tonal center of gravity which controls pitch direction. Note also how the main points of tonal association coincide with the rhythmic periodicity of the melody—which, in this case, falls into units of two measures which combine into two units of four to make the total single unit of eight. This particular example is simple enough to grasp, but if one examines the opening of the scherzo from the Beethoven Seventh Symphony, one sees immediately how much more extended (and therefore more difficult to grasp)

is the distribution of the energies inherent in the direction-producing tonal forces in this case. The ascent through the horizontalized F major triad in the Beethoven example establishes the tonal locus. The fall from f² of measures 3 to g¹ of measure 6 is immediately counterbalanced by the sequential fall of the g² of measure 7 to the a¹ of measure 10. The reiterations of measures 11–14 which prepare measures 15 and 16 confirm F, the tonal point of departure. However, it is in measures 15 and 16 that the tonal intensification occurs and the directional force of the passage drives it to the major mediant (A major) which the subsequent phrases confirm beyond doubt. All these tonally directed pitch motions are coextensive with the rhythmically directed waves that drive the music forward; the one lives in the other as mutually interpenetrating structural forces.

Zuckerkandl's position is very close to my own on these matters. Even the coincidence of terms is remarkable, especially in his discussion of "points of departure" and "arrival" (pp. 97–98). In regard to individual pitch motions he says:

> no musical tone is sufficient unto itself; and each musical tone points beyond itself, reaches, as it were, a hand to the next, so we too, as those hands reach out, listen tensely and expectantly for each next tone. To be auditively *in* the tone now sounding means, then, always being ahead of it, too, on the way to the next tone. (P. 94)

According to Zuckerkandl the motion of tones is more than acoustical phenomenon, it is a "rise and fall in relation to tonal forces, a departure from —— and approach to ——; ——. All paths always lead back to their point of departure" (p. 103). Of course he is speaking here only of tonal music. In regard to the tonal cadence he remarks:

> The chordal step V–I is called the cadence in all languages. Does this not, after all, contain an explicit statement of its direction—specifically that it is a step directed downward? We understand to what this statement refers: to the dynamic meaning of the chordal succession, the "going to ——," the reaching the goal, the arrival at the center of gravity. (P. 114)

Zuckerkandl sums up his own position so well that I quote him here in full.

> Polarity and intensification—in these Goethe believed that he had discovered the two principles governing all the phenomena of animate nature. Now we find them in the two-fold activity of the forces that give all musical phenomena, in so far as they are temporal succession, their characteristic organization: in the tendency that closes, establishes symmetries, equalizes every weight by a counter-weight; and in the tendency

that drives on or, accumulates, is responsible for constant augmentation. How the two tendencies work with each other and with the tones, or rather let the tones work with them; how tonal forces and metric forces work together in general; how the tones bring out now the intensifying driving-on tendency, now the closing, symmetry-establishing tendency, let the one gain the mastery here, the other there; produce all possible syntheses between the two; bring asymmetrical structures into equilibrium; how, finally, in its ever increasing outreaching, *the twofold activity of the metrical forces in conjunction with the tonal forces bring into existence the forms of music, the ever astonishing, often overwhelming constructions of an architecture in time, serial structures and symmetrical structures of the smallest and largest dimensions, and structures in which the two principles interact in the most various ways* [Zuckerkandl is using *serial* in its sense as a series of pitches, rather than as a twelve-note series.]—all these are questions that we must leave to musical theory to discuss in detail. (P. 180, emphasis added)

While it would be foolish to claim that the greatness of the classical masters lies solely in the two direction-producing forces of rhythmic periodicity and tonality which were at their disposal, it is not farfetched to suggest that through their imaginative use of these they were able to infuse their music with an integral structural intensity and purpose which had not existed before them and which gradually altered its characteristics after them. The ability to establish an audible continuity which existed on two interpenetrating planes, rhythmic periodicity and tonality, made it possible for them to extend their forms to larger and larger proportions without fear of loss of direction, of structural goal or purpose.

Direction in music, as we have seen so far, requires audibility of structure based on an integral order of continuity and tonal orientation. The rhythmic periodicity and tonality of classical music provided structural direction in more than adequate measure, which explains, in part at least, why it continues to exert such a powerful influence on the musical life of our own time. By tracing the careers, as it were, of periodicity and tonality we shall see a pattern of evolution emerge which parallels the intense struggle of composers of the twentieth century to find a new form of musical expression. The pattern reveals the slow disintegration of the classical structural order which produced direction through periodicity and tonality, arriving by mid-twentieth century at new types of structural order which are essentially nondirectional.

The practice of rhythmic periodicity and tonality continued well into the late nineteenth century, and in varied, modified forms under the guise of

neoclassicism into the twentieth century, especially in the work of those composers who saw no need to break away from the past but took refuge instead in
history, wishing to perpetuate and/or to expand its basic principles of composition. However, it is well known that by the end of the nineteenth century
tonality was in a state of exhaustion, burdened by an overextended harmonic
vocabulary which was no longer or solely dependent on simple triads and their
functions or related melodic motions. There is no need here to describe once
again how *Tristan* affected the musical consciousness of the late nineteenth
century, signaling the overthrow of tonality. By the time Debussy had completed his work, atonality was already a living force in music (1908–15). The
struggle of Schoenberg to solve the problem posed by the abandonment of
tonality finally led to his discovery of the twelve-tone method, a rationale for
establishing once again a systematic order of pitch relationships on both the
horizontal and vertical planes, thus ensuring a new type of structural integrity
and the organized incorporation of the intuitive nonfunctional harmonic vocabulary of atonality (1923). During this time, however, periodicity continued
to exert its influence. Composers who, like Schoenberg, Berg, and Webern,
had abandoned functional tonality did not turn away from periodicity. The
musical phrase, based on the metric-rhythmic wave, became more supple,
plastic, and asymmetrical; but it remained, nevertheless, the structural means
for establishing an audible continuity. In Webern's intensely concentrated miniature world of sound, periodicity underwent subtle transformations which
prepared the way for the next steps which took place after 1945. With the
emergence of pointillism, the musical phrase which had previously embodied
motivic entities and their continuity (thus ensuring melodic shape) was abandoned, and with it rhythmic periodicity. An audible continuity, reflecting an
integral structural growth process based on beat, meter, and phrase, disappeared entirely; the meter and phrase lost their pulse. As a result a unique
phenomenon occurred for the first time in music: sound, as concrete musical
space, emerged as an independent structural force, no longer subject to periodicity; and duration, formerly embodied in the growth process of periodicity,
emerged in a totally new role.

This outline of the gradual abandonment of periodicity and tonality as
direction-producing forces in music will grow more meaningful as we retrace
its major steps in an examination of passages from works which exemplify the
tendencies described. The remarkable Five Pieces for Orchestra, Op. 16 of
Schoenberg, composed in 1909, exhibits the full attainment of atonality. The
abandonment of key and functional harmony in this work and its consequent
loss of audible tonal direction in the classical sense is characteristic of the pitch
content of atonality. However, by retaining the musical phrase and periodicity,
Schoenberg was still able to produce forms whose shapes were perceptible,
i.e., which made audible sense in terms of heard structural direction.

Copyright 1953 by C. F. Peters Corporation. Copyright renewed 1980 by Ronald Schoenberg. Used by permission of Belmont Music Publishers, Los Angeles, California 90049.

The passage shown here from "Premonitions," No. 1, follows twenty-five measures of clearly laid out phrases in 3/8 meter. From measure 26 on rhythmic intensification is produced by pitting a new meter against the original 3/8: four eighths in the time of three divided into asymmetrical groups. The piece grows in rhythmic force until it breaks into a savage ecstasy which reaches its peak at measure 79. From the point where the cellos begin the four meter (measure 26) to the entry of the oboes, clarinets, and horns (measure 36), we discern one rhythmic period whose subdivisions cannot be marked off, so integrated are the units of four, three, and two eighth figures. The total effect of these metric groupings is to destroy any sense of metric symmetry. At measure 36, a second period begins where the 3/8 is reestablished by the wind-horn motive whose shape, rhythmically speaking, is sharply defined so as to stand out from the rush of four around it. The pedal chord, D-A-C-sharp, tied over through many measures, acts as a gravitational force holding the volatile movements of the other material in its magnetic field, as it were. Its constant presence through the entire movement from measure 26 on confirms this. Direction is clear in this movement but it derives basically from rhythmic periodicity and phrase distinction rather than pitch content per se. If we turn to *Pierrot Lunaire*, we find the same forces active: direction is generated not so much by pitches as by periodicity and phrase shape.

As the example shows, meter is clearly established in "Mondestrunken," No. 1 of the first part. The shifts from 2/4 to 3/4 are in the tradition of the scherzo from Mahler's Sixth Symphony, no longer a "radical" technique by 1912, the year of *Pierrot Lunaire*. Not so clear is the directional structure of pitch which carried music still further into the atonal realm, although in the example given the piano and violin figures surely create a sense of tonal orientation (as pitch locus) by simple reiteration which, however, is soon dissipated. Pitch in *Pierrot Lunaire* became the means of producing a timbre environment which derived, as a structural tendency, essentially from Debussy. We shall have more to say about this later. In Alban Berg's Lyric Suite for String Quartet, written in 1925–26, a work divided in allegiance between atonal and twelve-tone pitch organization, rhythmic drive through phrase grouping and accumulation of dynamic thrust marks the fifth movement as a continuation of traditional practice.

The passage shown here is still "atonal." Direction is structurally audible as a result of the growth process of rhythmic motion through three phrase-waves, measures 1–3, 4–7, and 8–14. Its periodic structure is asymmetrical: a three-measure group followed by a four-measure group, followed by a seven. Measure 14, though silent, is a structural element in the last group of seven. In the first phrase-wave the overflow of energy into the next is structurally associated with the tied A of the second violin; similarly, the end of the second phrase-wave drives its force into the third by tieing over both violins and viola. At measure 15 a new phrase-wave begins, separated from the initial phrases by the silent measure. Thus the rhythmic directional force of the opening of this movement is, despite its asymmetry, clear. Less clear is the motion of the pitch. However, ascent, arrival at the upper register plateau, and descent, which coincide with the first three rhythmic phrases, make audible the shape of the pitch line even if individual or aggregate pitch motions lack tonal locus in the classical sense.

This attenuation of the aural meaning of pitch, i.e., its ability to offer the ear acoustical orientation, is part of the problem which affects the twentieth century. It also led, by a gradual process of stripping away from pitch meaningful structural relations and connections between specific notes and chords as notes and chords, to a generalization of the sound medium; that is to say, toward electronic music and the noise spectrum. Even though electronic music can still produce the twelve tempered chromatic pitches it is hardly relevant to the image of electronic music. The precise relationships of traditional music (including Schoenberg and Webern) have given way to a field of generalized relationships where individual pitches are replaced by a band of sound and

structural relationships depend on general sound complexes rather than specific ones.

When Schoenberg achieved the historically necessary rationalization of
pitch which no longer had tonal associations or meanings, he made possible an
integral order of twelve tones, capable of responding to his creative needs. The
solution of the pitch problem did not, however, carry with it any marked
change in the rhythmic or formal structure of his music. Schoenberg continued
to write, as he had before, "phrase-music," which was structurally rooted in
periodicity. The theme of his Variations for Orchestra, Op. 31, written in 1928,
is not organized exactly like a classical or romantic theme; but in its phrase
structure it exhibits strong ties with the traditional process of linking a series of
successive phrases which generate and establish a melodic line.

Copyright 1929 by Universal Edition. Copyright renewed 1956 by Gertrude Schoenberg. Used by permission
of Belmont Music Publishers, Los Angeles, California 90049.

It is essentially "vocal" in that the phrases are marked off by rests for
"breathing." The inflections of the distinct phrases, i.e., the rise and fall of the
pitch line, create pitch shape rather than directional tendency. In the classical
period, shape was the inevitable result of directional tonal forces which established connections between tones. While audibly present, shape did not exist
as an independent entity apart from the tonal field of pitch relations. When
shape replaced tonal pitch direction, as it did in Schoenberg's atonal and
twelve-tone music, it was in order to render the melodic content perceptible, to
retain as much as possible determinate contour. To this extent direction continued to play a role through the tendencies of shaped motion independent of
traditional conventions of note connections. So long as the idea of a tonal
center no longer existed, tone to tone relationships could only have meaning in
a shaped inflection of melodic movement but no longer as pitch elements in a
hierarchical order. It is the tension and release of ascending-descending motions, i.e., their inflection resulting in shape, which hold Schoenberg's melodies in a balanced perceptible frame, not their specific tone to tone relationship. It will be instructive to compare a theme of Mahler with one by
Schoenberg to see how tonally oriented direction anchors the contour of a line
while nontonal motion can produce contour but not direction.

By applying the simple test of singing through these two melodies, one becomes immediately aware that in the case of Mahler's melody, by singing the notes themselves, paying no particular attention to their tendency in one direction or another—either ascending or descending—the contour or shape of their motions is directly apprehended; but that in the case of the Schoenberg melody, first one must grasp the essential contour before one can achieve any degree of security where the precise pitches are concerned. This odd reversal is indicative of the inability of a nontonal melody to develop a predictable pattern of pitches, to be able to signal, as it were, what tone follows next along the melodic axis. As I have already pointed out, this is because there exists no hierarchic relation between tones in nontonal music and therefore, from a certain point of view, any tone can follow any other tone of the twelve chromatic pitches. Where a twelve-tone row is concerned, the situation is not quite so arbitrary; but without prior knowledge of the precise order of tones of the row, the perceptive result is virtually the same, i.e., it *seems* as though any tone follows any other tone of the twelve chromatic pitches. All that remains in the contour of a twelve-tone melody such as this one of Schoenberg's is the tendency to balance ascending and descending motions in order to develop a determinate shape. Contour alone, however, cannot produce direction. The next step in this inexorably evolving process of stripping music of its traditional order of integral structural direction was taken by Webern in his instrumental twelve-tone works—for with these works shape itself is attenuated. The tendency toward the "single note" and the dependence on motivic interval structure, both bound together in a mosaic of homogeneous textural design permeating all registers, brought about the so-called pointillist style. Although metric uniformity was still characteristic of Webern's style, the loss of an evident melodic shape took its toll of the directional force inherent in rhythmic periodicity. For the first time since the beginning of nontonal pitch orders (atonality and twelve-tone), periodicity and the phrase were brought to a state of near-equilibrium. One of the techniques which reinforced this condition of virtually suspending rhythmic motion was structural symmetry for which Webern had a strong penchant. This may be observed in the opening measures of his Variations for Piano, Op. 27. The phrase exists, to be sure; but the tendency of the growth process is frustrated. The beat and meter is now a frame, not a process—a frame on which to construct symmetries of pitch and rhythm.

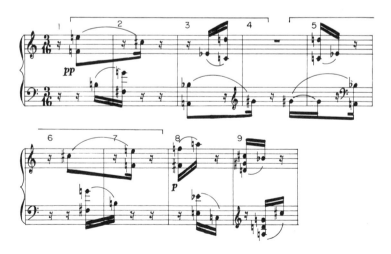

In this example the beats which comprise each measure are merely successive and, as such, constitute a frame or scaffolding which supports the structure: uniform, discrete, individual units of time which have no more relation to each other than the seconds which a clock ticks off. The structure in this example has a relation to the three sixteenths per measure only insofar as these beats provide the struts and joints of the supporting frame on which it rests. Unless the initial pulse of the meter is activated, propelling itself upon the next pulse and the next, the beat and the meter become static entities, succeeding each other but not progressing *to* each other. When the beat becomes merely a referential point in time, as it does in much of Webern and later in serial music, it is no longer dynamic; it has assumed a purely mechanical function by means of which a structure may be spread out in time but lacking the impetus of periodicity whose very life depends on the metric pulse. The introduction of the beat as a referential point marked the end of periodicity and the dynamism of the beat as pulse. This example is instructive from yet another point of view. The first three measures plus G-sharp of the fourth measure, first beat, enclose two small phrase units. This structure is symmetrically balanced by the G-sharp, third beat of measure 4, plus measures 5, 6, and 7. In this case (a bilateral symmetry or retrograde) the symmetry becomes the shape of the structure. There is no other shape or contour perceptible. However, perception is taxed to the limit in such a case because shape is attenuated, has become abstract, no longer embodied in a single line. Paradoxically, despite the determinate nature of this structure its perception is weakened by the spreading out of shape over its totality.

The metric order of Webern's music is not always a frame. Traditional periodicity continued to exert its influence especially on his vocal music; almost of necessity, since the human voice is the phrase-producing instrument because it must *breathe*. Even in some of his instrumental movements the process of metric growth asserted itself again—the third movement of his Concerto for Nine Instruments, Op. 24, for example.

This particular movement develops an intensity of rhythmic drive, and there-fore direction, which is almost classical in spirit. With Webern the great tradi-tion of directional, audible, structural order would appear to have ended.

Under the influence of Webern's most radical tendencies—those which tended to suspend shape and periodicity—the final steps were taken. In the music of the generation "after Webern," a rational serialization of pitch and rhythm, in other words space and time, completed the destruction of shape and periodicity, simultaneously altering the character of music itself. Serial music thus arrived at nondirection in terms of both an integral structural order and audibility. Whatever the inherent order of serial music, whatever its ra-tionale, it was now in a state of utter abstraction, existing apart from audibility of its intrinsic order and rationale. Any semblance of determinate structure, whether classical or nontonal, was now virtually abandoned, giving way to structural and, therefore, perceptual indeterminacy. This tendency is clearly illustrated in the following excerpt from No. 6, "Bourreaux de Solitude," from Boulez's *Le Marteau sans Maître.*

No individual line develops its own shape. If a shape emerges at all it is in the total pitch ensemble. Metric pulse does not emerge though a meter is indicated. This music moves in a realm of spatial-temporal equilibrium. However, not all of *Le Marteau sans Maître* exists in this state. There are sections, more obviously vocal ones, where tradition exerts its influence again in the form of shape and periodicity (Nos. 3 and 5) though attenuated; nevertheless, the prevailing structural tendency is nondirectional—the suspension of shape and periodicity have been accomplished. The same is basically true of Nono's *Il Canto Sospeso*, even though this is primarily a vocal work and one might have expected this tendency to be somewhat mitigated by the nature of the voice, the phrase-producing instrument. On the contrary the vocal phrase is virtually nonexistent; pitch inflection is distributed through the ensemble pointillistically, rarely appearing in individual parts as phrase shape. This is well illustrated in the opening measures of No. 9, the final chorus.

Thus a tendency which first emerged in serial instrumental music finally affected serial vocal music as well, establishing nondirection in all media of composition. It is worth noting that the time signatures in both the Boulez and Nono examples designate simple meters—but the beat is referential, a frame, not a pulse. The tendency we observed in Webern became a convention in the next generation.

So far I have associated the prototype space-time conjunction only with serial music mainly because this is its chief historical manifestation. (Later it will be necessary to backtrack historically in order to show that the spatialization of music has other sources as well; for the present, however, I will confine my remarks to the effects of serialism on the tendency toward spatializing music.) In tracing the steps which led to the emergence of nondirectional tendencies characteristic of serialism, we observed how space gradually freed itself from its traditional dependency on periodicity, emerging as an independent function more concrete than ever.

What do I mean by "more concrete than ever"? Since I have already described musical space as the concrete manifestation of pitch, coextensive with the sounding bodies of which it is composed, how much more "concrete" can space become, given the structural conditions of the space-time conjunction? So long as periodicity articulated the passage of duration, musical space as sonorous bodies served as a means to an end, conveying a process of musical rhetoric physically projected as melody and accompaniment, harmonic progression, counterpoint, or the like—in other words, structural relations which sought to express or convey a cohesive musical discourse through sound and the forms of sound. Whether the forms were based on melodic phrase succession or on procedural forms like the fugue or canon, spatial components projected a musical discourse in which timbre and dynamic level were expressive elements associated with pitch but lacking any objective value in themselves; nor could pitch per se be viewed *in abstracto* so long as it existed as the sonorous means for projecting, say, a melody and accompaniment. With the demise of periodicity and continuous passage based on the growth process of traditional musical discourse, pitch, timbre, dynamic—in short all spatial components—emerged as potentially objectivized elements which had no meaning beyond their own projection; they could be presented in a musical context for their own sakes. This abstraction of spatial components from a cohesive discourse created the possibility of the sound structure comprised of all the parameters associated with pitch and time. No longer a function of periodicity and the melodic phrase, the sound structure now existed as a concrete manifestation in its own right. Thus a tone, C-sharp, may be part of a composite sound structure which includes instrumental timbre, dynamic level, method of attack, registral position, density, and durational proportion. The new space created by means of sound structure is essentially homogeneous, i.e., musical events are free to occur in any register, no longer subject to the traditional stratification of registral levels which articulated a relationship of melody and accompaniment; it is a space without hierarchical order. Requiring no preparation or resolution as part of a continuously evolving discourse, each individual sound or aggregate of sounds is a concrete projection of itself. Thus sound structure has emerged as an independent abstraction, no longer a functional element serving another end. The sound structure is coextensive with itself; it is the music. This, then, is what I mean by "more concrete than ever."

What of the relation between the "new" space and time? The spatialization of music throughout the sound structure, following the demise of periodicity, radically altered the concept of time. Subject to the same principle of objective rationalization as space, time became durational proportion, having no relation to metric pulse or beat but signifying only what segment of time a given tone or aggregate of tones was to occupy. Thus time was abstracted from durational flow and cast in a frame of beats whose metronomic speed bore no necessary relation to the assigned proportion. The measure, as a frame of beats, and its speed were no longer functional; they existed only as a convenient scaffolding to support the objective measurement of time lengths. Abstracted from the beat, the meter, and rhythmic phrase, time became antidynamic. No longer a rhythmic force, time also became spatialized; since every tone or aggregate of tones comprising a sound structure occupied a segment of time or durational proportion, time became subject to the dominant influence of space. Under these conditions, continuity became unpredictable; there was no way of knowing or sensing what came next. Hence the structurally and perceptually random, indeterminate, discontinuous nature of serial music. On the positive side, however, we can say that by freeing space of its former dependence on metrical duration, serialism released the power of space to project itself in concrete, audible, sound structures which exist in their own right, creating new values in music as well as new problems.

In his recent book, *Since Debussy* (New York: Grove Press, 1961), André Hodeir has offered an account of this phase of musical development which, for all its glib journalese, possesses some valuable insights. Speaking of Pierre Boulez, he says:

> The reign of ambiguity had begun, giving the lie to those for whom "The repetition of an *audible* structure" as Michall Fano has put it, determines "whether or not a work is constructed." . . . The great classical works were the fruit of an architectural approach to music, and as such they made no secret of their structural patterns; the modern work conceals its structures in a network of countless subterranean channels. (P. 157)

The reader should have no difficulty understanding Hodeir's statement in the light of my previous discussion. Hodeir accepts 1945 as a turning point in Western music. In the work of Boulez composed up to about 1952, "the world of 'athematic' and discontinuous music really began" (p. 157). By 1957 Boulez himself had arrived at a position where he could say:

> This is why we have seen the row of 12 equal tones replaced by rows of block-sonorities, the densities of which are never the same; why we have seen metrics replaced by the row of durations and block-rhythms (either rhythmic cells or several superposed time-values); and why we have seen the parameters of intensity and tone-color outgrow their decorative and emotional virtues and, without losing these privileged attributes, go on to acquire a functional significance that has increased both their powers and dimensions. (Pierre Boulez, "Aléa," *La Nouvelle Revue Francaise*, November, 1957; quoted by Hodeir, p. 157)

The new consciousness of the still-open possibilities of music is clearly manifest in this statement. Taken together, Hodeir's and Boulez's ideas offer a capsulized version of what I have taken pains to elucidate so far. We see that the structural differences between the music based on the two prototypes— time-space and space-time—are differences of kind, not merely of degree. The prototype time-space generates dynamic architectural forms in which duration as passage shapes the course of the events in the musical discourse along a structurally continuous axis. The prototype space-time generates forms in which spatial projection, freed from the dynamism of rhythmic periodicity, occurs in unpredictable patterns, occupying a time structure which stands outside the propulsive influence of the beat and metric pulse. An essentially static structure is the end result, verified by aural perception. Thus the expressive values of each kind of music define totally different views of articulating the conjunction of time and space. One of the largest questions we face is that posed by the nondirectional tendency of the space-time prototype. Are directional tendencies and the spatialization of music incompatible? Can direction be established by means other than periodicity and tonality?

III. Speech-Form and Space-Form

To distinguish between the two prototype conjunctions without the necessity of calling attention constantly to the specific word order which identifies each, I have chosen to coin two terms which I hope will prove meaningful and yet simple enough to render them useful as general categories. The reader should understand that each of these new terms stands for the more technical term which embodies the "synthetical unity," as Kant calls it, of the manifold (*Critique of Pure Reason*, trans. J. M. D. Meiklejohn [London: G. Bell & Sons, 1887], pp. 80–81) which is the conjunction of musical time and musical space in either one or the other of the prototypes. These new terms will serve to emphasize even more strongly what I consider to be the essential characteristic of the music which issues from one or the other conjunction. The term which stands for the prototype time-space is *speech-form;* for the prototype space-time, *space-form.* The reader may wonder why, in coining a term to stand for the time-space conjunction, I have chosen *speech-form* instead of *time-form*—particularly as the latter makes a better verbal symmetry with *space-form.* Granted that the time-space conjunction generates *time-form* in the sense that the music is time-dominated; but the major shortcoming of *time-form* as a designative term is its inability to state directly the essential characteristic of the music which issues from the time-space conjunction. For while the present generation of composers is directly involved with the tendency to spatialize music (a fact which thoroughly supports the use of such a term as *space-form* to designate as a broad category the results of their efforts) for those earlier generations which produced the vast body of musical literature structurally rooted in durational continuity, it was not time per se which absorbed their conscious efforts but *expression.* Once the Middle Ages had passed and measure in music had been established, a specific concern with temporal problems and its theory receded from consciousness, replaced by the search for expressive qualities. It is the characteristic quality of expression in music and its human source which are summed up in the term *speech-form.*

In the long historical association which has existed between tones and words, musicians have exhibited a variety of attitudes, some of them contradictory, toward their expressive union in a musical context. To trace this history would require a separate study by itself; nor is it essential to my purpose. However, a brief examination of the views held by musicians of the early Baroque, the seedbed of the long tradition which came to an end between 1925–45 after more than three hundred years, will place the idea of speech-form in the frame of reference in which I intend its meaning to be understood. I am reminded of passages in *Dr. Faustus,* where, in describing a work of Leverkühn's, Thomas Mann writes:

> The *Lamentation* is expression itself; one may state boldly that all expressivism is lament; just as music, *so soon as it is conscious of itself as expression at the beginning of its modern history,* becomes lament and "lasciatemi morire," the lament of Ariadne. . . . A lament of such gigantic dimensions is, I say, of necessity an expressive work, a work of expression, and therefore it is a work of liberation; *just as the earlier music,* to which it links itself across the centuries, *sought to be a liberation of expression.* (Pp. 485–86)

Mann is speaking, of course, of the Baroque era when he refers to the "beginning of [music's] modern history," and of Monteverdi, the first great master of expressive music, when he refers to the lament of Ariadne.

During the transition from the late Renaissance to the dawn of the Baroque, certain musicians began to express extreme dissatisfaction with the Renaissance practice of stylized verbal imitation and a type of counterpoint which obscured the sense of words. Speaking of his contemporaries, in 1581 Vincenzo Galilei said:

> And that in truth the last thing the moderns [i.e., the contrapuntists—*Ed.*] think of is the expression of the words with the passion that these require, excepting in the ridiculous way that I shall shortly relate, let it be a manifest sign that their observances and rules amount to nothing more than a manner of modulating about among the musical intervals with the air of making the music a contest of varied harmonies according to the rules stated above and without further thought of the conception and sense of the words. (From "Dialogo della musica anticae della moderna," quoted in O. Strunk, *Source Readings in Music History* [New York: W. W. Norton & Co., 1950], pp. 312–13)

Galilei was inveighing against those who were intent on merely tickling the ears of their listeners, whose minds "being chiefly taken up and, so to speak, bound by the snares of the pleasure thus produced" had no "time to understand, let alone consider, the badly uttered words" (pp. 314–15). He goes on to describe the "treatment of the most important and principal part of music, the imitation of the conceptions that are derived from the words" (p. 315). He ridicules the practice of those contrapuntists who hold

> that they have expressed the conceptions of the mind in the proper manner and have imitated the words whenever, in setting to music a sonnet, canzone, romanzo, madrigal or other poem in which there occurs a line saying, for example, "Bitter heart and savage, and cruel will," which is the first line of one of the sonnets of Petrarch, they have caused many sevenths, fourths, seconds and major sixths to be sung between the parts and by means of those have made a rough, harsh and unpleasant sound in the ears of the listeners. . . . at another time they will say that they are imitating the words when among the conceptions of these there are any meaning "to flee" or "to fly"; those they will declaim with the greatest rapidity and the least grace imaginable. . . . with words meaning "alone," "two" or "together" they have caused one lone part, or two, or all the parts together to sing with unheard-of elegance. . . . finding words denoting diversity of color, such as "dark" or "light" hair

and similar expressions, they have put black or white notes beneath them to express this sort of conception craftily and gracefully, as they say, meanwhile making the sense of hearing subject to the accidents of color and shape, the particular objects of sight and, in solid bodies, of touch. (Pp. 315–17)

Galilei, having studied the ancient Grecian and Roman cultures intensively, had come to the conclusion that ancient music had the power to induce in the listener the "same passion that one feels oneself" (p. 317); that between the effects of oratory and speech and the effects of music there were strong bonds rooted in that which was to be said or expressed and the manner of its delivery and expression. (Such views directly contradicted those held by Zarlino, one of the great theorists of the Renaissance, who said, "What becomes the orator does not become the musician" [Strunk, p. 319].) The kernel of the idea which eventually became known as *stile rappresentativo* (from which issued Baroque monody and opera) is here stated by Galilei.

> When the ancient musician sang any poem whatever, he first considered very diligently the character of the person speaking: his age, his sex, with whom he was speaking, and the effect he sought to produce by this means; and those conceptions previously clothed by the poet in chosen words suited to such a need, the musician then expressed in the tone and with the accents and gestures, the quantity and quality of sound, and the rhythm appropriate to that action and such a person. (P. 319)

As a member of the Florentine Camerata centered around Giovanni Bardi, Galilei's ideas were taken up by others in the group—Caccini, Peri, and Rinuccini. Peri, who played an important role in these first efforts to realize *stile rappresentativo*, produced an opera, *Euridice*, on a text by Rinuccini. In his foreword to the opera, printed in 1601, Peri says:

> Seeing that dramatic poetry was concerned and that it was therefore necessary to imitate speech in song (and surely no one ever spoke in song) I judged that the ancient Greeks and Romans (who, in the opinion of many, sang their tragedies throughout in representing them upon the stage) had used a harmony surpassing that of ordinary speech but falling so far below the melody of song as to take an intermediate form. . . . I devoted myself wholly to seeking out the kind of imitation necessary for those forms. And I considered that the kind of speech that the ancients assigned to singing and that they called "diastematica" (that is, sustained or suspended) could in part be hastened and made to take an intermediate course, lying between the slow and suspended movements of song and the swift and rapid movements of speech, and that it could

be adapted to my purpose (as they adapted it in reading poems and heroic verses) and made to approach that other kind of speech which they called "continuata," a thing our moderns have already accomplished in their compositions, although perhaps for another purpose. (P. 374)

In his bitter fight against the reactionary critic Artusi, Monteverdi, the greatest composer of his time, proclaimed his *seconda prattica*, maintaining that words were the "mistress of the harmony" and determined the "perfection of the melody" (Strunk, p. 409). In extending the practice of *stile rappresentativo*, Monteverdi developed specific categories which correspond to the passions or affections of man as well as to the human voice. In presenting his *Madrigali Guerrieri ed Amorosi* of 1638, he wrote in the foreword:

I have reflected that the principal passions or affections of our mind are three, namely anger, moderation and humility or supplication; so the best philosophers declare, and the very nature of our voice indicates this in having high, low and middle registers. The art of music also points clearly to these three in its terms "agitated," "soft," and "moderate" (*concitato, molle,* and *temperato*). In all the works of former composers I have indeed found examples of the "soft" and the "moderate," but never of the "agitated." (Strunk, p. 413)

Monteverdi goes on to describe how he rediscovered the genus of agitated music, referring to Plato and Boethius as sources for his new approach to music.

After reflecting that according to all the best philosophers the fast pyrrhic measure was used for lively and warlike dances, and the slow spondaic measure for their opposites, I considered the semibreve, and proposed that a single semibreve should correspond to one spondaic beat; when this was reduced to sixteen semiquavers, struck one after the other, and combined with words expressing anger and disdain, I recognized in this brief sample a resemblance to the passion which I sought, although the words did not follow metrically the rapidity of the instrument. (Strunk, pp. 413–14)

The idea that the range of human emotions, the passions and affections as they were called in the Baroque era, could be expressed in, represented by, conveyed through music—an idea which seventeenth-century musicians believed they had reclaimed from the long-forgotten art of the ancients—had a profound effect on the future of music. Employing every contemporary means at their disposal and inventing new ones as the creative situation demanded it, composers in succeeding generations sought increasingly to develop and intensify the expressive power of music. (See Gluck's letter of October 1777 to M. de la Harpe, specifically the third paragraph, in *Pleasures of Music*, ed. Jacques Barzun [New York: Viking Press, 1960], p. 529.) The unrelenting search for increased power of expression had its inevitable effect on the development and standardization of instruments and, not least, on the form of instrumental music. This intensification of musical expression reached its peak especially during the nineteenth century; composers demanded greater scope, brilliance, flexibility, color, and range of nuance of their instrumental resources. The expansion of structural forms as reflected in the purely instrumental works of Beethoven, Berlioz, Bruckner, and Mahler, for example, resulted in truly imposing sound edifices matching the great vocal forms—opera, passion, mass, oratorio—which had emerged earlier. Though lacking the direct emotional stimulus that a text or dramatic situation provides, instrumental music became a powerful medium for the expression of human feeling and states of mind. The common bond between vocal and instrumental music was melody. Through continuously evolving melodic thought, both vocal and instrumental music produced an expressive musical discourse through representations of feelings and states of mind. The melodic phrase, the central creative act during this long period of development, formed the basis of musical thought which, regardless of stylistic differences, lived through time, *became* time, as it were, embodied in the passions and inflections which comprised the movement of melodic passage. As Langer says:

> The phenomena that fill time are tensions—physical, emotional or intellectual. Time exists for us because we undergo tensions and their resolution, their peculiar building-up, and their ways of breaking or diminishing or merging into longer and greater tensions, make for a vast variety of temporal forms. (*Feeling and Form* [New York: Charles Scribner's Sons, 1953], pp. 112–13)

Langer is speaking of the way in which the content of human experience fills our lifetime, becomes the durational structure, as it were, of living. The durational structure of speech-form can be described as analogous. While its logic is strictly its own, the content of speech-form—the passage of a sonorous melodic-harmonic content—also builds in a cumulative way, preparing, culminating, dissolving; the resultant expressive discourse representing in its order states of mind or feeling, "tensions and their resolutions," as Langer calls them. Music as speech-form abstracts from human experience the feeling tone, the tension structure of feeling, and conveys this as expression. It cannot convey experience directly but rather *represents* the content of experience as tension structure through its ability to order "tensions and their resolutions," nor can it be said of music that the order in which it presents this representation of the content of experience is the same as the order in which human experience takes place. The unpredictable nature of existence for human beings prevents life experience from developing a purposeful order in the sequence of life's events. Contingency, accident, and randomness prevent such an order from emerging from the pattern of life. The great achievement of speech-form lies in the fact that through its ordered musical discourse an expressive structure was created which transcended phenomenal existence, lifting music above the level of contingency, accident, and randomness.

I spoke earlier of the musical phrase calling it "the central creative act in music." Roger Sessions puts it in his own way when he asks: "What, for instance, is a so-called 'musical phrase' if not the portion of music that must be performed, so to speak, without letting go, or, figuratively, in a single breath?" (*The Musical Experience* [Princeton, N.J.: Princeton University Press, 1950], p. 13). Regarding the musical phrase "as the most important musical fact" because "it bears on the nature of . . . 'musical movement' . . . ," Sessions states that

> a melodic motif or phrase is in essence and origin a vocal gesture; it is a vocal movement with a clearly defined and therefore clearly expressed profile. And . . . it too is sensitive to infinitely delicate nuances of tension and relaxation, as these are embodied in the breathing which animates the vocal gesture and shapes its contours. (P. 19)

Thus Sessions makes a direct connection between the qualities of states expressed in music as "tension and relaxation" and their inflection as "delicate nuances" derived from the nature of the vocal gesture. Sessions also speaks of what he calls the "musical train of thought" pointing out that it "differs from any other train of thought only in the fact that its medium is tones, not words or images or symbols" (p. 56). He qualifies this by saying that "in music it is the logic of sensation and impulse that determines the ultimate validity of the train of thought and gives the musical work not only its expressive power but whatever really organic unity it may possess" (p. 58). The idea of continuity of melodic passage, the "musical train of thought," in which the musical phrase as vocal gesture "in essence and origin" is the central "musical fact," as Sessions puts it, is at the core of the meaning of the term *speech-form;* for in speech-form, musical expressivity attains a state of eloquence of discourse or rhetoric, "musical speech" in other words, which is made manifest in continuous melodic movement. This eloquence of discourse is speechlike in character, an embodiment of what Langer calls "impassioned utterance." In vocal music we can relate the character and quality of utterance to the emotional stimulus of the text and the states suggested by either its general atmosphere or specific images. But in instrumental music we cannot trace the utterance to anything as specific as a text; we cannot say *what* is being uttered, i.e., what the music is "saying." However, it is undeniable that speech-form music in its instrumental form is a discourse with the quality of "impassioned utterance." The theorist Heinrich Schenker corroborates this view of the expressive content of instrumental music when he remarks in his book *Harmony* (ed. Oswald Jonas [Chicago: University of Chicago Press, 1954], p. 14): "It is easy to understand . . . why music . . . assumes a rhetorical, declamatory character, with verbal associations lurking ghost-like behind the tones—words, denied by an inscrutable fate their realization and complete expression; words, however, speaking to us the more penetratingly and the more mysteriously." In an enlightening discussion of the relation of music to the speech elements of vocal music and their transference to instrumental music, Langer states that

> instrumental music strives for the expressiveness of song, the sound of direct utterance, "voice." . . . This, I believe, is the basis of the qualitative difference, which has often been noted, between singing and all other kinds of music. It is not . . . the power of our emotional association with the voice that makes it pre-eminently "human," but the fact that utterance, which is an intellectual function of the human organism, has always a fundamentally vital form. When it is abstracted from any actual context, as in music-conscious song, it becomes art, but keeps its *Lebensnähe.* The fact that song grows in musical power by constant formalization, approaching the sound of instruments, whereas all other sources of tone are somewhat schematic and lifeless until they attain "voice," the semblance of singing, marks a peculiar dialectic in the total phenomenon of music. (*Feeling and Form,* p. 144)

Langer's use of the German *Lebensnähe* refers to an earlier statement in her discussion where she says: "Throughout its career as a bearer of musical ideas, the voice keeps its readiness for pathos, its association with actual feeling— what a German would call *Lebensnähe*" (p. 141). Thus when instrumental music, through the musical phrase as vocal gesture, attains "voice," it becomes utterance even though its tendency toward inflection may derive solely from the nature of the phrase itself. This tendency toward inflection in melodic thought, though abstract in nature, has its roots in the vocal gesture which is the source of utterance. The very abstractness of melodic inflection in instrumental music renders it freer, more flexible—open to greater flights of fantasy and greater degrees of intensity—than purely vocal music which is bound by the limitations of a text. This enlargement of the possibilities of imagination inherent in instrumental music is attested to by Berlioz who wrote somewhere in connection with his dramatic symphony, *Romeo and Juliet:*

> If in the famous balcony scene and in the funeral vault the dialogue between the lovers, Juliet's asides and the passionate pleading of Romeo,

are not sung; if, in a word, the duets are entrusted to the orchestra, the reasons are several and easily grasped. The first—and this would suffice by itself—is that the work is not an opera but a symphony. Secondly, duets of this character have been composed for voices a thousand times before and by the greatest masters. It was, therefore, the part of prudence, as well as a challenge, to attempt a new mode of expression. Lastly, since the very sublimity of the love story made it a perilous task for the composer to depict it, *he chose to give his imagination a wider latitude than the positive meaning of words would have allowed; he resorted, instead, to the instrumental idiom, a richer, more varied, less fixed language, which by reason of its very indefiniteness is incomparably more powerful for the present purpose.* (Emphasis added.)

Speech-form then, sums up in one general category music in which the phrase as vocal gesture establishes a melodic continuity or melodic discourse which is an expressive "train of thought" as "impassioned utterance"; its semblance of speech deriving from utterance, its quality as expressive form from its continuous flow of states of tension alternating with relaxation, experienced as melodic inflection.

What, if any, are the expressive tendencies of space-form? To answer this question we must first attempt to understand how space-form manifests itself in music. The great pioneer of space-form is Edgard Varèse, whose first major works in this direction are "Octandre," "Hyperprism," and "Intégrales," composed between 1922 and 1924. What makes these works significant is their embodiment of tendencies reaching back to the earlier part of the twentieth century in a new concept of music in which space becomes the focal point of musical structure. The dominant tendency toward atonality, the increasing interest in timbre for its own sake, and the new possibilities of rhythmic structure were molded into a unique formulation by Varèse which is remarkable for its anticipation of the sound structure of serialism, but with a difference—the difference consisting essentially in the fact that the structure of Varèse's music is audible in its unfolding movement, i.e., its macroform grows clearly and organically out of the relations of musical events to each other. This is in sharp contrast to the inaudibility of macroform in serial music and the ambiguity (or indeterminacy) which is intrinsic to serialism. The fact that serialism arrived at spatial formulations (sound structures) analogous to Varèse's, produced twenty-five or more years before, only serves to confirm the fundamental significance of his work and the insights which led him to his concepts of music. In a lecture first given in 1936, and more recently quoted in an article he published in his *Poème Electronique le Corbusier* (Paris: Les Cahiers Forces Vives aux Editions de Minuit, 1958), Varèse described his idea of *spatial projection*, which formed the conceptual core of "Intégrales." I will not repeat it here, since I have quoted it in full in an earlier essay in this book (p. 22).

It is not a mere transposition of words to say that Varèse's "spatial projection" is actually a type of space-form, *in fact the first conscious effort by a twentieth-century composer to realize through music spatial images in sound*. By using the analogy with the visual field, Varèse has made clear what his intentions are: to create new musical images whose structure and function are spatial and whose movement contributes to this essential characteristic. Varèse formed a new kind of musical space through concrete, aggregate structures of sound substance which are defined by what Istvan Anhalt calls their "inseparable pitch-timbre-intensity entity." The indissoluble unity of these properties creates new functions for the constituent elements in the unity and therefore new possibilities for variety and shape in spatial imagery. This, combined with a new concept of time and motion, which by their controlled relationship to the aggregate sound structures present maximum freedom of projection, extends the entire range and scope of Varèse's space-form. Unlike the serialists who mistakenly equate duration with all other parameters of music, Varèse employs duration as the means by which his spatial images are disposed in a planned sequence of nonperiodic movement. His idea of the "seemingly unpredictable" projection of his spatial images necessarily subordinates the function of duration to space, for a time-dominated music cannot function in a "seemingly unpredictable" fashion without its durational flow being disrupted and ultimately destroyed. Motion in Varèse's music is free of periodicity, providing the temporal field within which the spatial images are able to move as he chooses to make them move. As Anhalt points out, "only sparingly does he allow the emergence of a pulse in music." It is this purposeful suspension of metrical pulsation which makes possible nonperiodicity in Varèse's music and the "seemingly unpredictable" projection of his spatial images. (Indeed, it is only *seeming*; for his images unfold with a sense of rightness and inevitability which can only occur in the work of a master.) If we call Varèse's "vertical sonorities," as Anhalt puts it, densities, we can evoke not only the sensation their audition produces but also their meaning as function which is quantitative. The concept of density, which Varèse realizes in his music, is basic to space-form, for it is the means by which a spatial image is created in its sound constituents. Language is too limited to permit us to ascribe to density specific degrees of mass and concreteness. All we can do is to speak in general terms, to say, for example, that a density is more or less opaque, or more or less translucent. Even though this language is metaphoric, it is inescapable.

The pitch constituents of a density may be "chords" or "harmonies" in the traditional sense. However, space-form is concerned with chords or harmonies only as pitch aggregates or complexes, i.e., only as they contribute to the indissoluble "pitch-timbre-intensity entity" which becomes the form of the density. From the harmony of *basso continuo* to functional tonal harmony to nonfunctional nontonal harmony to density: this has been the general course of the historical evolution of the pitch complex since about 1600. For the first time in modern history the sounding together of different pitches is freed of melodic domination and the "laws" of voice leading and harmonic progression. Density emerges in Varèse's music as the richly varied, constantly fluctuating movement of sound substance within the spatial images themselves, the object of musical process without reference to anything beyond itself. Liberated from the traditional stratification imposed upon it by figured bass and harmonic progression, register, too, is free to take on a new function; with the consequence that registral distribution of the musical elements and forces which constitute the density plays a significant role in determining the character of the spatial image, even to some extent the actual *weight* and *mass* of the density. Whatever the individual macroforms of his works, they are essentially space-form in the sense we have been discussing. While there are hints of the space-form to come prior to Varèse, it remains essentially his creation. Just as speech-form as an expressive utterance found its beginnings in the music of Monteverdi, so space-form as projection may be said to begin with the works of Varèse.

In his Ars novae musicae, a treatise dealing with the new concepts of mensuration which were being developed at the beginning of the fourteenth century, Jean de Muris, philosopher-mathematician, wrote, "Prolonged sound measured by definite time is formed in the air not so much in the likeness of a point, line, or surface, as rather *conically and spherically* (in the likeness of a sphere, as light is found in free space)" (Strunk, p. 174, emphasis added). This statement is arresting, indeed, and to my knowledge unique in its attempt to define metaphorically the form or shape of a musical sound which, given sufficient duration, becomes subject to aural contemplation. That de Muris's statement is metaphoric indicates a constant inability from the beginnings of Western theory to develop a precise enough language for certain musical phenomena. One can only speculate as to the ultimate value and correctness of his metaphor; nevertheless I quote it because it suggests rather strongly the nature of space-form sound structures—the way they form themselves "in the air," so to speak—and links itself directly as a metaphor of prolonged sound shape to Varèse's metaphoric remarks dealing with the geometric figure:ground relations which define his spatial projections. It is as though sound structures, formed as densities of varying degrees of opacity, were moving in relation to each other in acoustical space in much the same way a constantly changing series of conical or spherical objects were to move in relation to each other, singly or compositely, in physical space. In point of fact, space-form music, lacking as it does a bass line which, in harmonically structured music, acts as a field of gravitational force, functions in a state of gravitation-free movement, forming itself in acoustical space in a series of single or composite "spherical" densities which can combine and recombine in an endlessly varied succession of aural images. Nothing exists in space-form to restrict the free movement of these images, since the total register of acoustical space is a completely homogeneous unit within which the sound substance can move according to the various forms (whether they are metaphorically conical or spherical in the sense of de Muris's description or not) it takes on as density; nor does the temporal aspect of the density, which is an integral part of it, prevent it from functioning in this way. The movement of a spatial image is determined solely by the form it takes in relation to the context it establishes with other images; hence the nonperiodic temporal structure of space-form music and its seeming unpredictability. Varèse's metaphor of the geometry of the spatial projection evokes for us directly the abstract nature of space-form and the concreteness of the densities themselves. The integral self-sufficiency of the spatial image, a self-sufficiency which requires nothing beyond itself to make its function clear, derives from its abstract quality and its concrete sound structure. Thus the geometric figure-ground metaphor of Varèse is not at all fanciful. It is, in fact, a profound insight into the illusion of musical space which is produced when sound substance, organized as density, is projected for its own sake and is no longer subject to the tyranny of periodic time. The process which generates space-form music is abstract, but not necessarily inexpressive. On the contrary, the projection of density structures opens up entirely new possibilities for expression in music similar to nonfigurative painting, which treats the canvas not as a means for representing extrinsic visual images but for projecting or stating only those intrinsic relationships which are integral to paint itself—color and line. Space-form music projects new types of sound relationships as tensions in themselves, not as representing subjective tensions which we have associated with speech-form music. The inflection of speech-form melody which derives, as I have tried to show, from utterance, does not exist for itself, so to speak, but in order to give "voice" to musical utterance. This is absolutely clear in vocal music and imperceptibly less so in instrumental music. Nevertheless, the latter, historically, derives from the former and is only one step further removed, as an expressive medium, from the subjective sources which determine the character of vocal melody. Speech-form music is essentially "singing" (even in dance music) and retains its *Lebensnähe* in instrumental forms. As "song" it can never be separated from those states which determine the subjective structure of human feeling and the tensions which characterize that structure. Whether vocal or instrumental, speech-form music remains one or two steps removed from its emotional source; i.e., it cannot express the subjective states which characterize the source directly—it can only parallel them, so to say, as musical representations. Space-form music, however, is a direct, concrete projection of energy tensions in the form of highly charged aural images which exist in their own right. Nor can we speak of the possibility of two categories of space-form music—vocal and instrumental—for if the sound of the voice is used other than as a component in the pitch-timbre-intensity unity—even though in conjunction with a text—immediately the structure of melodic inflection will be invoked and space-form will become speech-form. Of course, it is to be expected that, if the human voice *is* treated as a component in a density structure even though singing a text, verbal imagery will no longer influence the inflection of vocal line because "line" per se will be nonexistent and the words of the text will be reduced, as for example in the choral music of Luigi Nono, to a series of successive syllabic sounds. Space-form music, therefore, though it may use the human voice, is essentially instrumental and achieves its greatest effect through the use of instruments projecting sound substance as concrete, self-sufficient densities.

As abstract expression, space-form not only finds its analogy in mid-twentieth-century painting but also in what the poet Charles Olson calls "projective verse." Olson juxtaposes "projective verse" with "nonprojective" verse, the former "OPEN, or what can also be called COMPOSITION BY FIELD as opposed to inherited line, stanza, overall form, what is the 'old' base of the nonprojective." In his essay on the new state of poetry, written in 1950, Olson suggests "a few ideas about what stance toward reality brings such (open) verse into being, what that stance does, both to the poet and to his reader. (The stance involves, for example, a change beyond, and larger than, the technical, and may, the way things look, lead to new poetics and to new concepts from which some sort of drama, say, or of epic, perhaps, may emerge.)" He goes on to describe projective verse kinetically as "a high energy construct and, at all points, an energy discharge." The source of this energy involves the fundamental principle of projective or open verse: "Form is never more than an extension of content" and the process by which "the principle can be made so to shape the energies that the form is accomplished." (This, as Olson states it, is very close indeed to Varèse's "the form is the result of a process.") Olson makes clear what he means by *process:* "*ONE PERCEPTION MUST IMMEDIATELY AND DIRECTLY LEAD TO A FURTHER PERCEPTION.* It means exactly what it says, is a matter of, at *all* points . . . get on with it, keep moving, keep in, speed, nerves, their speed, the perceptions, theirs, the acts, the split-second acts, the whole business, keep it moving as fast as you can, citizen!" After describing the relation of syllables as sound to the word they compose as sense—syllable as belonging to the head and the ear of the poet and the line to the heart and breath, Olson says:

> It comes to this, this whole aspect of the newer problems. (We now enter, actually, the large area of the whole poem, into the *FIELD,* if you like, where all the syllables and all the lines must be managed in their relations to each other.) It is a matter, finally, of *OBJECTS,* what they are, what they are inside a poem, how they got there, and once there, how

they are to be used. . . . every element in an open poem (the syllable, the line, as well as the image, the sound, the sense) must be taken up as participants in the kinetic of the poem just as solidly as we are accustomed to take what we call the objects of reality; and that these elements are to be seen as creating the tensions of a poem just as totally as do those other objects create what we know as the world. The objects which occur at every moment of composition (of recognition, we can call it) are, can be, must be treated exactly as they do occur therein and not by any ideas or preconditions from outside the poem, must be handled as a series of objects in field in such a way that a series of tensions (which they also are) are made to *hold*, and to hold exactly inside the content and the context of the poem which has forced itself, through the poet and them, into being.

The objects which compose the content and context of the poem and therefore its form leads Olson to posit what he calls *objectism*,

a word to be taken for the kind of relation of man to experience which a poet might state as the necessity of a line or a word to be as wood is, to be clean as wood is as it issues from the hand of nature, to be shaped as wood can be when a man has had his hand to it. Objectism is the getting rid of the lyrical interference of the individual as ego, of the "subject" and his soul, that peculiar presumption by which Western man has interposed himself between what he is as a creature of nature (with certain instructions to carry out) and those other creations of nature which we may, with no derogation, call objects. For a man is himself an object, whatever he may take to be his advantages, the more likely to recognize himself as such the greater his advantages, particularly at that moment that he achieves an humilitas sufficient to make him of use. ("Projective Verse," in *The New American Poetry 1945–60*, ed. Donald M. Allen [New York: Grove Press, 1960], pp. 386–97)

The analogy between space-form as projective music and Olson's poetics of projective verse is so close that, in many instances, his statements would seem to apply as well to space-form music as to projective verse. For example, his reference to the kinetic structure of the open poem as a "high energy construct and, at all points, an energy discharge" describes very well, I feel, space-form densities as tension structures. His remarks to the effect that form is the process by which the energy of the poem is shaped, and that process consists of one perception leading directly to another perception, apply directly to space-form. Particularly meaningful is the second which suggests strongly the "seemingly unpredictable" spatial images of Varèse leading from one to the other without preparation or transition—in other words, doing away with all irrelevancies so that the main business of projecting the spatial image ("get on with it, keep moving, keep in, speed, nerves, their speed, the perceptions, theirs, the acts, the split-second acts, the whole business, keep it moving as fast as you can, citizen!") moves freely, unimpeded, without waste motion or energy. The kinship is most relevant and striking in Olson's reference to the "objects" of the poem—"the syllables, the line, as well as the image, the sound, the sense." Substitute for the objects of the poem the objects of space-form—the sound substance shaped into densities consisting of pitch, timbre, intensity functioning in the open, homogeneous acoustical space as spatial images in relation to each other. Both the objects of the poem and the objects of space-form music are concrete, to be "taken up as participants in the kinetic of the poem [read "space-form"] just as solidly as we are accustomed to take up what we call the objects of reality." The objects of the poem and of space-form music create the tensions of their respective media "as totally as do those other objects (of reality) create what we know as the world." The crux of the analogy lies in Olson's next statement.

> The objects which occur at every moment of composition [of poetry and of music alike] . . . *are, can be, must be treated exactly as they occur therein and not by any ideas or preconditions from outside the poem* [read "space-form"], *must be handled as a series of objects in field in such a way that a series of tensions (which they also are) are made to hold, and to hold exactly inside the content and the context of the poem* [read "space-form"] *which has forced itself through the poet* [read "composer"] *and them, into being.* (Emphasis added.)

From his statement of objects as constituting the content and context of the open work, Olson derives his idea of objectism, which is "the getting rid of the lyrical interference of the individual as ego, of the 'subject' and his soul." The "lyrical interference of the individual," expressed in poetry as nonprojective verse or closed verse, is expressed in music as speech-form utterance—which is also a kind of closed form, preconditioned from outside music itself by ideas about the form music is to take and what music is capable of expressing in that form. In space-form the sound "objects" cannot be predetermined by such prior notions but can only occur as a process by which the energy tensions dictate the forms the spatial projections will take on as well as their succession, thereby establishing both their content and context. In other words, the densities, the concrete sound objects, of space-form function in an open field of musical composition, having no source outside themselves to make manifest—no subjective states of mind or heart or soul belonging uniquely to the individual composer to be uttered—yet expressive as tension structures which vary and fluctuate only in relation to each other as spatial images. The sound substance of space-form is "as wood is, to be as clean as wood is as it issues from the hand of nature, to be shaped as wood can be when a man has had his hand to it." Taking his stance toward sound substance as he would toward any other object of reality, the composer puts "his hand to it," shapes and projects it in a new form invested with his human energy, his vital being.

There is still another view from which the problem of space-form music can be seen, yet closely related to the objectism of Olson's concept of projective versus nonprojective verse. The tendency toward the spatialization of music ultimately derives from profound changes affecting contemporary consciousness and the twentieth-century stance toward reality and experience. Space-form music reflects these changes and may be said to stand as a musical representation of the new consciousness. By subordinating duration to space, music no longer exists in its former state of anticipation of the future. It projects itself as a series of present moments, holding up to aural perception each spatial image as the self-sufficient object of perception as it occurs, not as it will realize itself in some future event. The state of music in which "it will realize itself in some future event" destroys the present qua present. In such a case the present can function only as a link between past and future events. This is the underlying assumption of Zuckerkandl's idea of the wave motion of periodic music which is a striving beyond the present event, thrusting the immediately preceding past event across the bridge of the present into the future. That is why speech-form, as a music dominated by periodic duration, can be described as articulating actions of time. Because these actions of time are in a constant state of incompletion and therefore require the future tense, so to speak, in which to complete themselves, the highest manifestations of speech-form occurred during the classical period of tonality. Speech-form, viewed as actions of time, to be aurally perceived with utmost clarity, requires some such means of pitch orientation as tonality in order to provide a constantly defined locus (or place) at every point of the flow of duration. Without a clearly established locus, speech-form runs the risk of losing itself in structural and perceptual meandering. In the spatialization of music we discern the increasing importance of locus and the slowing down or arrest of durational flow. Space-form, dominated by locus and articulating actions of place, readily dispenses with tonality per se because it is already a music in which place is *presence*—defined by the spatial image which uses nonmetric durational proportion to establish this presence as the immediate, directly perceived event. Speech-form is always *becoming*, never completed action in the present; space-form *is*, all events occurring as completed present action, and though successive, requiring no future for their realization.

Completely opposite attitudes or stances toward reality are reflected in these forms of music. Subjective man views existence as change, as becoming, himself and his culture at the center of the process of change and becoming. For subjective man, life is an experience of duration in which the present is a link with the past and to the future. The present is charged not only with memory images of the past but also with the restless, often anxious anticipation of the future. In this sense life cannot be lived in the present because only the past is real, only the past is solid and has meaning. However, when man seizes on the present as the real moment of existence, he overcomes duration and spatializes his existence; i.e., he objectifies his perceptions of himself and external reality, charging the present perception with maximal meaning and energy. I believe this is what Olson had in mind in positing his notion of "objectism" in relation to projective verse: man fills his present moments with objects of perception which take on solidity, his world becomes a world of space and place, permanence is established. It is this consciousness of the world as place rather than time which seeks to overcome the impermanence of existence, the process of becoming, to establish the present as the only real time, and to grasp therefore the present as eternal. In an eternal present, past and future tense are absorbed and lose their reality and time becomes spatialized. It is only by returning to subjectivism that man reinstates past and future, depriving the present of its reality. The West would seem to be shaking off this subjectivism, having been dominated by it for at least two centuries; and is gradually turning toward objectism. Since the early part of the twentieth century the movement to overcome duration as the reality of existence has increased in intensity and, since mid-century, the spatialization of consciousness has begun to assert itself with increasing force and energy. (The world as place, as an eternal presence, would seem to be more in keeping with the space age into which we have entered, and its concomitant consciousness of the cosmos, than the old pre–space age world of time and change.)

Many of these ideas constitute the core of a difficult and voluminous essay by Wyndham Lewis, *Time and Western Man*, written in 1927 (Boston: Beacon Press, 1957). (The coincidence of the composition of Varèse's first space-form works at approximately the same time as the appearance of this critical study of time and space is striking.) Lewis sought to stem the tide of temporal consciousness which had, since Bergson, reached its climax in Western culture, sweeping our modern literature, philosophy, and art. Because his was a "spatial" mind, Lewis was drawn to "classical man," *objective* or *plastic man,* as he put it, rather than "Faustian Man," modern Western man, *subjective* man. "We have seen," he said,

> the subjectivism of the Faustian or modern Western man, associated fanatically with a deep sense for the reality of *Time*—as against Space. And the classical man who was so shallow and "popular," as we have been told by Spengler, not only because he based his conception of things upon the immediate and sensuous—the "spatial"—but because he entirely neglected, and seemed to have no sense, indeed, of *Time*. His

love of immediate "things" found its counterpart in his love of the "immediate" in "time." He was that creature of the Pure Present so admired
by Goethe. The "timelessness" of Classical Man, then, his *objectivity*, his
sensuousness, his *popular* and *common-sense* view of things, were what pre-
eminently distinguished him. . . . Classical Man—that inveterate "spa-
tializer"—was in love with *plastic*. Modern, Western, "Faustian" man,
on the other hand, is pre-eminently interested in *music*: he spurns and
abandons *Plastic*, and all its ways. It is in music that he supremely expresses himself. (Pp. 392–93)

Lewis, developing the Spenglerian view of Western culture, was anything but
sympathetic to Spengler.

There is no person more persuaded of the political, or historical, nature
of *everything* than is Spengler: and that is, of course, the "Time"-na-
ture. . . . If music is the art most appropriate to the world-view of the
time-philosopher, then history is certainly the form in literature that
must be above all others congenial to him. For the "time" view *is* the
historical view *par excellence*. And the great prevalence of archeological
and scholarly subject-matter in contemporary art is, aside from the effect
of the rapid elaboration of the technique of research, the result of the
hypnotism of the time-cult. Spengler is the most characteristic bloom that
has so far made its appearance out of this entire school. The mere title of
his book (*Decline of the West*) is an invitation to extinction for the White
European, or Western man. It says to the West: "I am an *historian;* I have
all the secrets of *TIME;* and I am able to tell you with a wealth of detail
that will take your breath away (if you have any left after your War) that
you White Peoples are about to be extinguished. It's all up with
you. . . ." (P. 254)

Lewis's resentment of Spengler stems, among other things, from his basic
antipathy to the whole notion of the time doctrine.

It is the transformation of a space-reality into a time-reality that is involved—that is the trick of the time-doctrine that is important to grasp.
Dispersal and transformation of a space-phenomenon into a time-phe-
nomenon throughout everything—that is the trick of this doctrine. Pattern, with its temporal multiplicity, and its *chronologic* depth, is to be
substituted for the *thing*, with its one time, and its *spatial* depth. A crowd
of hurrying shapes, a temporal collectivity, is to be put in the place of the
single object of what it hostilely indicates as the "spatializing" mind. The
new dimension introduced is the variable mental dimension of time. . . .
In place of the characteristic static "form" of Greek Philosophy, you have

a series, a group or, as Professor Whitehead says, a *reiteration*. In place of a "form" you have a "formation"—as it is characteristically called—a repetition of a particular shape; you have a battalion of forms in place of one form. In your turn, "you" become the series of your temporal repetitions; you are no longer a centralized self, but a spun-out, strung-along series, a pattern-of-a-self, depending like the musical composition upon time; an *object*, too, always in the making, who *are* your states. So you are a *history*: there is no Present for you. (P. 176)

The reader cannot have helped but observe the frequent references Lewis makes to music as the art form most representative of the time-doctrine. His understanding of music as a durational form is penetrating.

Movement, or things apprehended in movement, are very much more abstract than are static things. The object of contemplation is less abstract, evidently, than the objects of experience of the objective of action. To put this in another way, *time is more abstract than space.* But the process of *de-spatialization*, undertaken by Bergson and carried on by the philosophers we are considering (Alexander and Whitehead) denies any "concreteness," except such as can be obtained from a time-pattern, like the structure of a piece of music. But it can only be apprehended as music can be apprehended, in *time*—not in space. It requires movement, as well as duration, to unfold itself. There is no one instant at which it can be apprehended in its totality; you have to take it bit by bit, you have to *live* it, and its pattern will unfold as a melody unfolds itself. . . . In the case of the music there is no concrete shape existing altogether, once and for all, or spatially. There is a shape, an organic completion, but it is a pure creature of *time*. It cannot spatialize itself. (Pp. 174–75)

The perceptive reader will immediately recognize in Lewis's description of the way music happens—what it can do and what it cannot do—the limitations of view forced on him by his historical position. Paradoxically, at the very moment he was writing, music had already begun to spatialize itself, consciously in the work of Varèse, unconsciously in the work of Webern; speech-form music which Lewis is describing because, apparently, it was the only music of which he was aware, was in its decline. As to Lewis's remark that music "cannot spatialize itself": while it is true that music can never attain the totality of the one-time, all-at-once state of concrete objects, natural or man-made, it can, and does in space-form, create the illusion of concreteness of the spatial by reinstating the present, therefore the illusion of timelessness. Perception of each single or composite projection of sound substance in the form of densities (or spatial images) is "immediate and sensuous," to use Lewis's phrase. Undeniably music cannot escape time entirely—but to the extent to which it converts metric time flow to nonmetric time proportion, it arrests duration and overcomes it in space-form. We experience space-form music as the *spatial sensation of time*. Thus, while movement still prevails, it is not the "crowd of hurrying shapes" or "temporal collectivity," "spun-out, strung-along series," to use Lewis's language, which would seem to characterize speech-form music, that we perceive. The sense of motion, on the contrary, is of an entirely different order, tending toward either an arrested or a static state, what we might term the illusion of *motionless motion*, which allows us to contemplate aurally each spatial image, to "take our time," as it were, in the actual hearing of the musical events. If speech-form music as a general category is a reflection of the time doctrine which reached its climax in the early twentieth century, space-form music is a reflection of a new, contemporary tendency to assert the primacy of the world as object, of the immediate and sensuous perception of the object and ultimately, therefore, of space and place. Nowhere today is there more active concern and awareness of this tendency than in the world of painting, in which the problem of creating the illusion of space—whether deep or shallow—is unquestionably primary. In a 1954 essay, "Abstract, Representational, and So Forth," Clement Greenberg writes:

> Shall we continue to regret the 3-dimensional illusion of painting? Perhaps not. Connoisseurs of the future may prefer the more literal kind of pictorial space. They may even find the Old Masters wanting in physical presence, in corporeality. There have been such reversals of taste before. The connoisseurs of the future may be more sensitive than we to the imaginative dimensions and overtones of the literal, and find in the concreteness of color and shape relations more "human interest" than in the extra-pictorial references of old-time illusionist art. They may also interpret the latter in ways quite different from ours. They may consider the illusion of depth and volume to have been aesthetically valuable *primarily* because it enabled and encouraged the artist to organize such infinite subtleties of light and dark, of translucence and transparence, into effectively pictorial entities. (In *Art and Culture* [Boston: Beacon Press, 1961], pp. 137–38)

As a representation in music of this developing spatialization of consciousness, space-form is as authentic for us as speech-form was for previous centuries. The parallel with abstract art in this connection is hardly coincidental—and, indeed, revelatory of the manner in which basic problems cut across different contemporaneous cultural phenomena. Space-form defines musically our position vis-à-vis ourselves and the external world, our changing stance toward reality. It is, therefore, a profoundly human musical form, a potentially intense artistic expression, through which the structure of reality, as we experience it *now*, may be perceived.

The Structure of Time in Music

If we say that "time is an essential feature of the universe,"[1] presumably we mean not only that time is built into the very fabric of the physical reality of the universe but that it also exists apart from man. But, since man is himself part of the fabric of that same physical reality, there is ultimately no way to separate his consciousness from it. He is inextricably bound up in it; his perception and consciousness of the universe are mental reflections and refractions of it. Because temporal order in music is an ordering or *rhythmatization* of something other than itself—sound vibrations which have their own interacting laws of autonomous physical structure and artistic musical combination—music provides us with a cosmic metaphor in which we may examine more closely and directly the properties of duration, continuity, and the direction of events, as well as their relation to repetition and recurrence of event patterns and their connections with the functions of perception and memory.

Music, of all the arts of man, enjoys that peculiar position of intermediary link or interface between the physical universe and ourselves because music endows physical vibrations, i.e., objective, measurable properties of sound, with human form. The special feature of that human form is the creation of temporal order without which sound qua sound cannot be raised to the level of music. Seen in this way, music becomes that unique aesthetic form which arises spontaneously in every culture from the action of an autonomous, deeply intuitive sense of time implanted in man's mental makeup, on a fundamental reality of the physical universe. Man creates in music a palpable metaphor of the universe in a passionately colored succession of expressive events, which become a transformation of the raw data of physical reality in and of themselves. Man's rhythmic energies, rooted in his physiological and neural constitution, are inextricably bound up with his ability to create time in music.

Even the most cursory examination of the history and theory of Western art music must reveal the curious fact that the study of the structure of time in music—or to use the usual terminology of the musician, the study of rhythm, tempo, and motion—has received scant attention compared with the conscious care and concern lavished on problems of sound in the form of pitch and its possible combinations in the construction of melody, harmony, and polyphony. One would have thought that musicians—who literally became artificers of time, practicing the temporal art par excellence—would have concerned themselves consciously and systematically with the devices and practices by

137

means of which they created and regulated the flow of time through sounding forms. Yet this has not been the case, as the history of Western music of the past three centuries shows. Over this same period of three hundred years, composers developed articulation of temporal structure to remarkable degrees of subtlety and imaginative skill in matters affecting phrase lengths, rhythmic combinations, musical form, and structural proportions. The nineteenth-century composers who came after Beethoven especially accomplished brilliant feats of temporal ordering, became master artificers of time, but their achievements were neither matched nor accompanied by rational/theoretical considerations of the problems they faced or their solutions.

One must assume, therefore, that with two notable exceptions, the approach to the handling of time in music has been and remains largely intuitive rather than rational. However, these special cases exhibit all the characteristics of a rationally ordered approach to time in music but from radically different directions and for totally different reasons. They are the periods in the history of music when the intuitive necessarily had to give way to the systematization of rhythmic modes in order for music (1) to develop into an art form; and (2) to extricate itself from what appeared to be a dead end by arbitrary, rationally determined systems or principles of order. I am referring in the first case to the medieval period, extending from about the middle of the thirteenth century—when the establishment of fixed rhythmic modes, based on what musicologists now claim to be garbled versions of Greek poetic foot lengths, resolved problems of notating two or more simultaneous parts—to the more subtle and flexible mensural notation of the fourteenth century and beyond; and in the second case to the twentieth century when, after the crucial break with tonal practices, developed from the end of the Renaissance through the nineteenth century, composers once again took up a more self-conscious, rational-minded approach to their problems in order to find new ways of creating and controlling time in music.

It is of fundamental significance to the ideas I wish to advance that—except for these two not insignificant periods, the first of which gave birth to the basic formulations of the very language of Western music, the second of which ushered in a radical break with that same language at the point of its maximum development and maturation—composers have essentially behaved intuitively toward the handling of time, accepting as either convention or tradition or both the stylistic practices and devices of rhythmic motion of their particular day. Admittedly, these practices and devices changed as the styles of music themselves changed, but by no means radically or abruptly. It would appear then that especially between 1600 and 1900—the three centuries which saw music evolve toward an increasing command, subtlety, and flexibility of melodic, harmonic, and polyphonic expression, and the concomitant expansion of temporal structures, climaxing in the seventy-to-eighty-minute symphonies of Bruckner and Mahler and the two-to-three-hour and sometimes longer operas of Wagner and Verdi, composers struggled with and overcame problems of giving adequate size and shape to their increasingly intense and expressive intentions. Theory, however, lagged behind in the academic doldrums of the same old harmonic/polyphonic considerations. The development of harmony itself cannot be divorced from the development of temporal structure; and, not surprisingly, in a symbiotic relationship such as exists between pitch and rhythm, what happens to the one must necessarily affect the other. As it turns out, the theory of music of the Classical and Romantic eras remains woefully deficient in dealing with the result of this symbiotic relationship, and the failure to deal with this very problem arises from the fact that music theory is obsessed with the specificities of pitch relations. The vast majority of theorists treat pitch relations as static ones unrelated to temporal motion. A further difficulty arises from the fact that temporal motion, though entirely specific as to notation, becomes meaningful only as aggregate time structures which become increasingly resistant to analysis by the means traditionally at theorists' disposal.

It seems logical to infer, then, that when a musical language is being consciously formulated or a new one consciously invented, rational involvement with all aspects of the craft and syntax of that potential language becomes mandatory. From the fact that an intuitive grasp of that craft and syntax is slow to develop and mature it also follows that composition itself is slowed down. Donald Tovey has remarked, "It is very seldom that a composer or writer can simultaneously concentrate his energies on the working out of a new language and on the construction of big designs."[2] In the case of early medieval music, composers had first to find a clear means by which to fix and establish the relationship between two or more parts; otherwise, it would not have been possible to regulate the flow of harmony of two or more layers of pitch motion. When such regulation was suspended (or became nonexistent centuries later as in certain varieties of twentieth-century music), disorder and chaos resulted. But medieval composers were trying to create order by combating potential disorder, not by making disorder part of their aesthetic arsenal. The suspension or nonexistence of regulated flow, resulting in either chaos or a newly won freedom (depending on who is perceiving the phenomenon and from what point of view), became only one aspect of twentieth-century music as composers, releasing themselves from traditional melodic/harmonic flow, sought out new means of pitch organization and motion and were thus led into the necessity of investigating new possibilities of creating time in music. To what extent they have succeeded or failed is a major concern of this essay.

While it is undeniable that the medieval and contemporary periods share a rational approach to musical time, it needs to be pointed out that there is a vast difference between the two. On the one hand, we see the first application of rhythmic modes to pitch in the medieval period, and on the other, the application of rationally based rhythmic and nonrhythmic schemata to new pitch possibilities in recent contemporary developments. It is not known for certain how pitch and rhythm finally came together in the dawning of polyphonic music. Donald Grout points out:

> It was obviously necessary to find some way of showing rhythm and duration by the shapes of notes themselves. Strange to say, a complete solution to this difficulty was not achieved until after the middle of the 13th century, when a simple set of signs was evolved for the notation of rhythm. In the meantime, 11th and 12th century composers and singers of polyphonic music devised a system in which the prevailing rhythmic pattern of a melody called the "rhythmic mode," was specified by certain conventional combinations of notes and note-groups.[3]

It can be reasonably conjectured, therefore, that the use of rhythmic modes helped to establish a musical practice and style of composition and performance which arose, if not spontaneously, certainly intuitively. Grout makes clear that the rational organization of rhythmic pattern followed after at least two hundred years or more of slow emergence and development. This separates the rationalist character of the medieval period definitively and distinctly from that of the twentieth century; the medieval being distinguished by slow, intuitive root growth, the contemporary by an arbitrary rationalism born in a cataclysmic upheaval wherein the effects are still present.

Having established the notion of a basic intuitive approach to the creation and regulation of time in music, I am now faced with the necessity of trying to locate or discover the source of this intuitive capacity, and to demonstrate the link between the rhythmic forces and energies bound up in this fundamental capacity and the flow of sound events as it emerges from the depths of the mental/perceptual structure of consciousness. As an absolutely unavoidable corollary, I am also faced with the necessity of trying to make clear how it happens that an intuitive temporal sense, minimally guided by the rational (via a practical, working system of conventional notation for marking off beats and groups of beats, controlling the flow of events articulated in phrases and their accumulation into larger and larger groups eventuating in precise and clearly ordered macrostructures), produces immediately graspable, clearly perceptible body rhythms or pulsations; while, in the case of rationally based contemporary systems and schemata which suppress or circumvent the physiologically-neurologically based intuition of time, we observe the introduction of a spectrum of perceptual difficulty and lack of graspability ranging from the merely vague or uncertain to the disordered and chaotic, not only affecting the perception of beats and groups of beats—if indeed they are present at all—but also stamping the macrostructural flow of events with the same characteristics.

It must be noted that we are dealing with different languages of pitch combination and construction. Directly associated with the intuitive temporal sense is the diatonically based language of key-centered tonality and its melodic/ harmonic constituents which emerged from a long process of development and maturation. Directly associated with the contemporary rational temporal sense, the product of a cultural break that occurred in the first decade of this century, is the chromatically and/or microtonally based language of non-key-centered atonality and its range from arbitrarily systematized pitch formulations (commonly known as twelve-tone music or serialism) to unsystematized pitch happenings resulting from what can only be called "game plans" based on chance or choice, otherwise known as aleatoric music—happenings which may or may not include noise elements or noise resultants. (The application of electronics to either side of this atonal or nontonal spectrum of composition alters in no way the nature of the perceptual results I have outlined.)

I wish to introduce here the criteria by which the conditions I have described in a general way may be recognized. Since I have made clear that, in my view, the repertoire of traditional music derives primarily from the exercise of the intuitive sense of time and that, in the case of the so-called advanced or experimental music of the twentieth century, the intuitive is usurped by efforts to establish a more rationally determined system of time controls, these criteria will necessarily reveal positive and negative faces with respect to the conditions of aural perception depending on which way they are turned.

These criteria flow from the kinds of relationships which connect music with *identity*[4] and, in turn, identity with memory. I am defining identity here as perceptual impression or gestalt, an organic totality, which can be remembered in all its constituent details as well as in overall design—that is, committed to memory, or recognized on repetition as essentially the same gestalt previously experienced, whether with large or small variations in the mode of projection (a common experience in the performance of music where the same work is subject to variant interpretations affecting, say, tempo and/or dynamics).

The properties of identity[5] are profile or shape of motivic or melodic ideas, direction of harmonic progression, and repetition or recurrence of melodic and/or harmonic ideas, either in the identical form as first stated or in variant structures retaining essential features of the initial statement or statements. These properties refer primarily to the shape and form given to pitch, through the action of time articulated as rhythmic periodicities. Such periodicities constitute the particular ways in which pulsation of beats and their organization into ever-larger groups affect phrase lengths and, ultimately, the extension and accumulation of phrasal, sectional, and movemental structure. In every case memory is potentially activated by the properties of identity. The degree to which these properties are well defined and artistically well wrought will affect their relationship to memory; conceivably, one can move from a condition of absolute identity to vague or uncertain identity to absolute nonidentity with their corresponding degrees of absolute memorability to difficult memorability to nonmemorability. Thus, we can see that music as a creation of temporally ordered events must achieve clarity, precision, and definition on all levels of articulation of its structural flow, if it is to possess identity and arrive at memorability.

At the root of musical time—its creation and regulation—are two unmistakable conditions which determine its essentially goal-oriented nature: *directionality*, which is produced by the relationships between pulsations and periodicities which move in only one way—toward the goal of structurally organic completion of the rhythmic forces and energies released in the music; and *causality*, which may be seen not only in the ways in which pitch elements affect each other through the response of melodic consequents to melodic antecedents, the striving of harmonic progressions toward points of cadence, but also in the tendency of metric/rhythmic forces to accumulate and drive to climactic points in phrases, sections, and movements, thereby releasing new momentum, or to fall away to make approaches to cadential points of temporary rest from which new beginnings may arise. The goal-oriented structure of time in traditional music starts from the smallest units of pulsation and, gradually through a multiplication of the effects of accretion and cause and effect relationships, builds a temporal organism which not only affects us physiologically but engages us emotionally and mentally as well. Comparing traditional music—which he calls "teleological"—to avant-garde music, Leonard B. Meyer reminds us that, despite obvious differences in structure and pattern as exists in the music of, say, Bach or Haydn, Wagner or Bartók,

> such music is perceived as having a purposeful direction and goal. . . . But the music of the avant-garde directs us toward no points of culmination—establishes no goals toward which to move. . . . It is simply *there*. And this is the way it is supposed to be. Such directionless, unkinetic art, whether carefully contrived or created by chance, I shall call *anti-teleological*.[6]

There are numberless statements by avant-garde composers which corroborate Meyer's view of the situation, if not his critical attitude. One such statement will suffice.

> The music has a static character. It goes in no particular direction. There is no necessary concern with time as a measure of distance from a point in the past to a point in the future. . . . It is not a question of getting anywhere, or making progress, or having come from anywhere in particular.[7]

Meyer sums up his position toward antiteleological music in these terms: "underlying this new aesthetic is a conception of man and the universe which is almost the opposite of the view that has dominated Western thought since its beginnings."[8] The juxtaposition of the two views could not be more clear. On the one hand, teleology, exercising the role of purposeful, directed tendencies moving along an axis of continuity and internally meaningful relations between cause and effect which serve to corroborate the unidimensional flow of events, becomes the tacit premise on which traditional music built up its power and effectiveness; on the other hand, antiteleology, exercising the role of aborting, frustrating, or circumventing direction and continuity, purpose, and internal causal relationships is established as the avowed premise on which aleatoric music rests. Once again the presence of the intuitive or the rational may be clearly traced out in these opposite aesthetics and implied conceptions of man and his relation to the universe. It is interesting to note that avant-garde composers are much drawn to philosophies which prefer stasis[9] to kinesis, and call on the implications of quantum mechanics, which revealed the potentially indeterminate nature of the microworld, for support of their aesthetic of macrocosmic indeterminacy.

If it were simply a matter of having to choose between the teleological and the antiteleological view, personal preference could decide the case. However, it is not that simple, for the very reason that the antiteleological approach to composition has brought out and emphasized an aspect which broadens the whole inquiry into the nature of the structure of time in music, and music itself as an artistic representation of the modes by which man knows the universe. I refer to the curious phenomenon of *music as space.*

If the temporal nature of music has received scant attention from composers and theorists, the spatial nature of music has received even less— probably because the idea that music could represent aspects of spatiality did not occur to anyone until after the premises of traditional music came into serious question and were replaced by a different set largely adhering to antiteleological views. While the case for time in music, difficult as it seems, is susceptible to various approaches including the one I have been making, the case for a spatial dimension in music is refractory in the extreme. Nevertheless, in view of the conscious efforts to suspend teleology in contemporary composition, it is imperative to understand the nature of the results which have emerged from this negative attitude toward the structure of time in music.

We must ask what happens to music if continuity and directionality, pulsation and periodicity are suppressed, subverted, or circumvented in favor of discontinuity, nondirectionality, and the suspension of pulsation and periodicity. The answer is twofold: first, the regulated flow of time is replaced by mere duration, which now assumes a passive, nondynamic, nonkinetic character; and second, musical sound loses its connection with melodic/harmonic motion and is therefore transformed into potential mass or density of vibratory forms which exist in and for themselves. Since pitch is that aspect of music whose source is the physical universe and cannot move by itself, but depends entirely on being moved by the action of the intuitive time sense, i.e., on being rhythmatized, pitch assumes new properties and, presumably, a new independence. When structured time acts on tone, motion or the illusion of motion is created. When structured time is divorced from tone, the illusion of space is created.

The most significant effect of these radical departures from tradition is discerned in the nature of the musical discourse itself. Traditional processes of thought had assumed tonality as the basis of melodic/harmonic organization and periodicity as the regulator of metric organization and rhythmic flow. When these fundamental direction-producing forces were replaced by freely chromatic atonality and an essentially nonperiodic rhythmic structure, a musical discourse based on readily predictable continuity was no longer possible. With the advent of atonality, melodic motion, lacking the organizing factor of a tonal center, became almost completely disjunct. As a result, melodic shape or contour tended to become less predictable, its direction less certain, its topological formation showing the strain of distortion and stretching. Because of this attenuation of shape, musical discourse, though it might be precisely ordered through the new procedures and mechanics of the twelve-tone method of serialism, stood in danger of perceptual disorder. With the advent of total serialization, this tendency was reinforced. While the stream of events in totally serialized works may be continuous in the sense that sound is always in motion, the discourse seems to have lost its sense of direction, resulting in a kind of unplanned indeterminacy in which the position and motion of any given pitch element become matters of considerable perceptual uncertainty. Planned indeterminacy in the guise of aleatoricism, on the other hand, seeks to be utterly discontinuous and perceptually unpredictable in order (according to the pseudophilosophy of its adherents) to preserve the spontaneity of the pure moment divorced from any past or any future, the absolute freedom and freshness of the living situation. In this kind of music, sounds emerge from silence only to sink back again. This view is considered to approximate the real conditions of "life" as human beings experience it. It is unequivocally described as something which "is always starting and stopping, rising and falling . . . so listening to this music one takes as a springboard the first sound that comes along: the first something springs up into nothing and out of that nothing arises the next something, etc. . . . like an alternating current."[10]

Thus we see that the new autonomy granted the sound material is largely due to its liberation from the process of establishing traditionally causal connections between melodic phrase shapes and the harmonic progressions which support them, all of which, in turn, derive their energy and movement from structured time. This liberation permits sound to create its own context apart from the forces of periodic time, a reversal of the traditional procedure.

The widely held view of sounds as objective, concrete, quantitative entities in themselves is revealed in the terminology which has grown up around it: densities, vertical pitch aggregates, sound objects, sound structures, etc. The nonperiodic motion of these new sound constructs requires that it not interfere with their projection but rather enhance it; the duration assigned them must give them full and ample opportunity to reveal their purely vibratory characteristics. Inevitably, the suppression of pulsation and periodicity radically affects the perception of time in music. One of its more obvious results is to slow down the passage of events, sometimes to the point of near immobility; and even when volleys of rapid projections of sound tend to increase the speed of the passage of events, the perceptual sense of the motion remains essentially nondynamic. It follows, then, that musical discourse in the traditional sense is out of the question and is replaced by a new phenomenon characterized by discontinuity and unpredictability.

The release of sound from tonal functions accomplished by atonality, the gradual suppression of beat and pulsation which parallels the evolution of atonality and its total systematization, and the resultant emergence of the unpredictable and the discontinuous are all paths which led to the overthrow of a long-dominant temporal structure, replaced by the spatialization of music where the sound substance is formed as the primary object of projection and perception, its motion entirely secondary and contingent on the emerging structure of the sounding forms themselves. The motion of this music—it must be emphasized that we are dealing with "musics" which cover a wide range of points of departure and compositional procedures—tends either toward a state of equilibrium or toward erratic gestures and rapidly changing shapes and speeds. The temporal aspect, long dominant, must give way to the exigencies of producing these new sound forms.

When Whitrow says, "mind, as manifested in consciousness, exists only in time: it is purely a 'process' and not a 'thing,' "[11] one immediately recognizes music as a manifestation of that mental process—an objectified manifestation through which one can more readily read back into the contents and structure of the process than by confronting consciousness itself or its effects head on.

It strikes me as a reasonable certainty that the conception and realization of a musical work is, in its special way, a complete manifestation of mental process, a projection of fundamental aspects of consciousness including time and memory; and that the physical projection and performance of such a work activates, to the highest degree possible, both the contents and structure of that process as well as the structure, shapes, and gestures of the sound material of that work through which the process is revealed and may be perceived.

Like spoken languages and mathematics, music is a deep expression of the central nervous system, perhaps even deeper than the others—although I see no way to prove this.[12] Just as language and logic are rooted in the central nervous system, music's roots can be traced to the same source. But between music on the one hand and language and logic on the other is a vast difference in the mode of manifestation: music is not simply a patterned structure of notated symbols or self-generated sounds and vocables possessing potential meaning and communicability; it arises from the action of the mental process on the entire range of audible vibrations (from the interaction of human biological reality and external physical reality) and is made manifest by the specific ways in which that process makes use of the physical substance of vibratory phenomena. By the interplay and interpenetration of mind and sound—and it must be remembered the mind not only perceives sounds coming from outside itself but can also imagine them apart from physical stimuli—music achieves a special form of unification which offers us an immediate and concrete way to study the phenomenon of time and its relation to memory and provides us with one of the major symbols of human culture in which we recognize man as the microcosm in whose nature we may trace out the lineaments of the macrocosm. Time is as truly perceived through the ear as space is truly perceived through the eye; both major organs of perception are the openings onto the living universe of which we, in turn, are physical/psychic manifestations and by which we may learn to know it and ourselves.

NOTES

1. G. J. Whitrow, *The Natural Philosophy of Time* (London: Thomas Nelson & Sons, 1961), p. 313.
2. *Beethoven* (London: Oxford University Press, 1944), p. 51.
3. *A History of Western Music* (New York: W. W. Norton, 1960), p. 74.
4. I am indebted to John Michon for the suggestion that, in the sense I intend, "identity" may be considered a *perceptual invariant*.
5. It must be remembered that aural identity must, in every case, corroborate visual identity, i.e., the notated representation of the music. Not surprisingly, this is not necessarily the case with aleatoric music; no necessary relationship exists between the sound and the appearance of the "score" which, often enough, may be a graphic design or a set of verbal instructions, etc.
6. "The End of the Renaissance," in *Music, The Arts and Ideas* (Chicago: University of Chicago Press, 1967), p. 72.
7. Christian Wolff quoted in John Cage, *Silence* (Middletown, Conn.: Wesleyan University Press, 1961), p. 54.
8. "The End of the Renaissance," p. 72.
9. It could be argued that this condition of stasis approaches the state of "nontemporality" and, therefore, reinforces the illusion of spatiality. The

difficulty here is that the literature of traditional music is replete with instances of music (e.g., Beethoven's Ninth Symphony Adagio) which approach stasis not through suppression of pulsation and periodicity but through *slowness of tempo or motion.* In the latter instance, direction and causality still operate, leaving unaltered the essential bases for temporality.

10. John Cage, *Silence,* p. 135.

11. *The Natural Philosophy of Time,* p. 113.

12. For a provocative and whimsical corroboration of this view, I refer the reader to the chapter, "The Music of *this* Sphere," in Lewis Thomas's *The Lives of a Cell* (New York: Viking Press, 1974).

On Music, Humanism, and Culture

- *In Search of Music (1964)*

- *No Center (1969)*

- *The Composer in Academia: Reflections on a Theme of Stravinsky (1970)*

- *Humanism versus Science (1970)*

In Search of Music

Something strange has happened to music—so strange, in fact, that I hardly know how to describe it. Up until the time of World War II, composers wrote music out of the conviction that somehow, in some mysterious fashion, music could and did express profound human states and emotions. Music was a record in sound of the most intense kinds of human experience; and in those early decades of this century the best music reflected this—it was what I like to call "depth music," an intensely moving counterpart to the psychological and literary introspection of those years, perhaps even a documentation, in a profoundly creative sense, of the dark and ominous shadows of human existence which characterized the mood of the early twentieth century. Whatever the changes in external style and technique, there was about the depth music of this period—the music of Schoenberg, Stravinsky, Bartók, Ives, Webern, or Berg—the sense of the supremely conscious effort to link up with the great traditions established by the masters of the eighteenth and nineteenth centuries. It seems perfectly clear now, though it was much less clear fifty years ago, that these composers were not radicals and revolutionaries but rather great conservatives, each with his own vision and voice, each stamping his music with the signature of his creative personality, each expanding the possibilities and dimensions of musical expression out of personal necessity rather than willful, arbitrary motivation. We value their discoveries today because they speak to us in expressive terms, and because it is the record of human experience which they have captured in these terms that validates their technical discoveries and innovations and not the other way around. But in the twenty years since the end of World War II, it seems that the growing impact of science and technology on all our modes of thought and existence has finally penetrated the art of music. And this is the strange thing that has happened: by applying the scientific attitude and ideology to the art of music, the composer has transformed music into a unique, if curious, form of applied science.

This is perhaps the strangest thing of all: that, despite the legacy of artistic tradition, composers should have succumbed at all to the enchantments of science or what they understand as science. In this case it really does not matter whether their ideas about science or those drawn from science are correct or not according to the view of science itself. What matters, what is of absolutely prime importance, is that they have adopted and adapted to the purposes of musical composition their understanding (or misunderstanding) of concepts, methods, and procedures which stem from the theory and practice of contemporary science. The end result of this application to musical composition of a predominately scientific orientation and cast of mind has been the *externalization* of music. By that I mean that the basic elements of music have become entirely objectified and materialized into temporal and sound phenomena. The properties of sound and the characteristics of duration (having been externalized as self-sufficient physical phenomena) have in turn been subjected to every conceivable kind of controlled analysis and experimentation in order to discover not only what they are made of, so to speak, but also how they function in and of themselves under varying conditions—quite apart from the subjective feelings of the composer.

The parallel with science is striking indeed. The scientist deals largely with the world of external phenomena. His primary task is to understand these phenomena and to learn to control them by discovering the laws through which they function. All of nature is the scientist's laboratory. It is a truism that science proceeds by means of the experimental method and necessarily under controlled conditions and with the aid of increasingly sophisticated techniques and instrumentation. In falling under the magic spell of science, the composer has necessarily had to emulate the scientist by adopting his essentially objective ideology and attitude. More important, however, in order to do this the composer has had to provide himself with a world of external phenomena, and so has turned music into such a world, one upon which he can perform operations of an analytic and experimental nature.

Some composers today believe firmly that musical composition is a form of research into the properties of sound and time and their possible combinations. In this sense it is said that a composition may be based on a theory or hypothesis of which the composition itself becomes a form of proof subject to validation by aural perception. This is indeed a new idea in music, at least in theory, and contradicts outright the traditional view that a musical work is the creation of an artistic statement which proves nothing but simply *is*. On the other hand, there are other composers of experimental music who are not at all concerned with music as forms of proof but simply as efforts to see what happens, what comes out, given certain situations—good, bad, or indifferent, as the case may be.

At the root of these notions of experimental music is the depersonalization of the act of composition itself, the withdrawal of the subjective self of the composer—the inevitable concomitant of externalizing music. The idea of composing music as a creative act is necessarily antithetical to such composers, because such an act implies the overriding presence of the personality of the composer and the exercise of that composer's faculties of intuition and imagination, in themselves mysterious aspects of mind which obey their own laws.

The irony in all this is that today many scientists are behaving like artists while too many composers are trying to behave like their poorly conceived image of the scientist. There is striking evidence that the best scientists of our time prize their faculties of intuition and imagination very highly indeed; they are not averse to "inspiration." This odd reversal in the roles of scientist and composer suggests that the composer's appreciation of the scientist's motivations and the way he works is superficial in the extreme and for this reason seriously endangers the composer's relation to his own field of endeavor.

Composers may have drawn on many of the fundamental concepts or principles which have animated twentieth-century science, but they have failed to appreciate the difference between hypothesizing in verbal or mathematical terms or symbols an already existing state in nature (the movement of atomic particles, for example) and applying such a hypothesis to a musical situation which has no prior external existence but must be arbitrarily manufactured or fabricated. Among the scientific concepts and principles which seem to have fascinated composers the most are (1) the principle of indeterminacy which applies to the microworld of the atom and seems to contradict the straight-line cause and effect which appears to operate on the level of the macroworld; (2) the concept of aleatoricism (or chance) which contradicts the logic of a purposeful direction, end, or goal; and (3) the concept of discontinuity which contends with the idea of a continuously moving, unbroken line of evolution and development. In addition to these, composers are also fascinated by (4) problems of aural perception which more properly are the province of the sciences of psychoacoustics and psychology; (5) problems of random and nonrandom groupings which are the province of statistical analysis; and (6) problems of information theory which are basic to computer technology and inevitably neurology, the workings of the human central nervous system (as Von Neumann has demonstrated so convincingly). It is obvious enough, simply by enumerating these areas of basic interest, that composers are too busy with the externals of music and the handling of time and sound as objectified phenomena to be much concerned, if at all, with the expressive aspects of music which are necessarily internal and subjective.

The truth is that the dominant temper of our times *is* scientific and there is no use being an ostrich about it and burying one's head in the sand. We must be alive to whatever values science can lend to the conditions of human existence and the pursuit of human ends. To this extent, I am firmly convinced that every serious-minded composer who goes in search of music today must know his time and be sensitive and responsive to its best ideas, warm himself with the vital energies that animate his world—but without capitulating to science and its methods. For better or worse, we live in a scientific age; that does not mean the artist must surrender his art to science. The artist's task is to make everything that feeds him from the world into art, and if he finds the concepts of science grist for his mill, why should he not use them? But the composer must understand the difference between himself and the scientist—that the two are engaged with the world in entirely different ways: the composer as artist has the power to create a new, immaterial world through the medium of art, while the scientist tries to understand an already created world and does not possess the power to create a new physical world.

The composer in search of music as an act of creation not only can discover himself in the process, but also man. For what warms and energizes music, what makes it vital and passionate, is not the movement of time by itself or sound in itself, but the human spirit through which movement and sound must pass before they can emerge as music. The composer in search of music must inevitably confront himself; in that act, he discovers the world to which he belongs, the world in which man is the self-aware, self-conscious, active, and creative element in the hierarchy of biological strata. The composer in search of music discovers that everything in nature (himself included) is in motion, that movement and rhythm are built into nature. In the composer, this awareness is translated into the shape of musical gestures. The composer in search of music discovers that everything in nature (himself included) *sounds;* everything has its sonic identity. In the composer, this awareness is transformed into the sounding substance he shapes into musical form and idea. There is that point at the far perimeter of experimental music where the composer must inevitably meet himself again as a human being, and it is this ultimate meeting with his essential humanity which I believe will eventually bring about the return to primary, root things, where it is man who counts far more than sound by itself, or movement by itself, and where it is the experience of the composer as a human being which makes the interpenetration of sound and movement into the music he seeks.

No Center

The winds of change are blowing. Harder. Stronger. Gusts up to twenty, thirty, forty miles per hour. Gale warnings all up and down the coast. Tornados and hurricanes; maybe. Tidal waves, too. It's getting so you can hardly stand on your own two feet without holding onto something or somebody.

Borman, Lovell, and Anders are in orbit around the moon.

They just brought the men from the *Pueblo* back to the States.

The Paris talks are getting nowhere. Fast.

Columbia. Berkeley. Martin Luther King. Robert Kennedy. Black. White. Yellow. Brown. Red.

There's a revolution going on. All over. Students and workers. There's a New Left. There's a New Right. There's also a new President.

Borman, Lovell, and Anders are orbiting the moon. They'll be home on Friday. With luck. After that the winds will blow even harder.

Art and Life. Life and Art. They've gotten all mixed up. And no one can really tell the difference anymore. It's causing terrific confusion.

Look at the theater. You can't tell the difference anymore between the actors and the audience. Participatory Theater: like Participatory Politics (Clean for 'Gene) and Participatory Democracy. Group grope. Love thy neighbor, all your neighbors. "Talk to me naked."

They want to erase all the old differences, all the old distinctions. Tabula Rasa. The "Now." Feel; don't think. Burn; don't create. Take over the university. No more classes.

The winds of change are blowing. Harder. Stronger. Gale warnings up and down the coast. If I were Black, I'd join the Black Militants, not because they're right but because I couldn't help myself.

Burn, Baby, Burn. Open wide the Doors of Perception. Acid, Pot. The Electric Circus is short-circuiting the Central Nervous System. The neurobiologists and biogeneticists are about to invade the CNS. RNA. DNA. Everybody look alike, sound alike, act alike. Don't know why there's no sun up in the sky, Stormy Weather. Let's make special people for special tasks. Let's change the world. Cybernetics, computers, servo-mechanics, loops, input/output, feedback, Brave New World. Soma holiday. Reentry. Dangers of.

> I must create a system of my own
> or else be enslav'd by another man's.
> My business is not to reason and compare
> My business is to Create.
>
> (Blake)

Malcolm Lowry said: "Never trust a writer who doesn't burn." Our business is to create, not to reason and compare. We are in the business of Poetry. "Intelligence," said Jorge Luís Borges when he was interviewed by Ronald Christ, "has little to do with poetry. Poetry springs from something deeper; it's beyond intelligence."

What's our problem? Syntax? Semantics? The trouble with Varèse's music is Varèse. Every man has his own deserts. What are you doing to fill your existential vacuum?

I'm trying to correlate everything I ever learned with everything I ever experienced. Metaphors. Correspondences. Analogies. Hallucinations of artistic vision. Plurality of sensibilities. Multiplicity. Simultaneity. Eternal Recurrence. Cyclical Return. The Eternal Present Eternally.

Blake's "contraries" appeal more to me than Aristotle's "unities." Unity of Varieties vs. Variety in Unity.

In the same interview Borges said something about style which reminded me of Ives's remark about Substance and Manner. He remembered that Bernard Shaw had said that "as to style, a writer has as much style as his conviction will give him and not more." Then Borges went on to say, "If a writer disbelieves what he is writing, then he can hardly expect his readers to believe it."

Our business is not to reason and compare—but to create—and burn—and make poetry, each in his own way—whatever way that is.

Rilke—war letter, June 28, 1915: "The whole sad man-made complication of this provoked Fate, that exactly this incurably bad condition of things was necessary to force out evidences of wholehearted courage, devotion and bigness. While we, the arts, the theater, called nothing forth in these very same people, brought nothing to rise and flower, were unable to change anyone."

Norman Mailer. *Why Are We in Vietnam*. Four-letter words of the whole sad man-made complication of this provoked Fate. The Language of Despair. The Obscenities of human suffering and Pain.

The saddest confession of all: "We . . . were unable to change anyone." Man only learns, if indeed he learns at all, from living, not from the example of Art. Then why Art?

I'm trying to correlate everything I know with everything I feel. Sense and Sensibility. So is everyone else. Are we making it? Can we make it?

The Art of Combination, "Ars Combinatoria." Borges. Rauschenberg. Robert Lowell, MacLuhan. Ives first and foremost. Günter Grass/Brecht/Shakespeare and Coriolanus/The Plebean Revolt/The Workers Strike in East Berlin. Velikovsky's "Oedipus and Ihknaton." Myth and History. Fact and Fiction. *The Theatre and Its Double*. Antonin Artaud. Borman, Lovell, and Anders. The Moon of the Mind in orbit around the Sun of the Heart.

The art of combination is an attitude, an exploration of deep inner space, mental space.

Are we making it? Can we make it? Beckett talks because he can't stand to hear the silence that surrounds him.

Where do you draw the line? Is there somewhere to draw it?

Right You Are If You Think You Are. Pirandello.

The Iconography of Imagination. Northrop Frye.

Poetic Vision. Blake.

Some people think if you put Noise and Revolution together you've got Art. Herbert Marcuse says: "So it (art) wants to become an essential part of reality, to change reality."

The saddest confession of all: "We . . . were unable to change anyone." Graffiti. The Obscenities of human suffering. Pain and Frustration.

That's how Dada got started. After the Great War, the War to End All Wars and Make the World Safe for Democracy, oh Woodrow Wilson. Intellectuals and coffee-house aesthetes proclaiming a new Revolution and a new Reality. A new Style of Life. Art vs. Power and Money. All they changed was art and made it "Modern."

Reality. Where is it? Outside or inside your head?

The New Left. SDS. Underground movies. Superstars. Pornography. Hippies. Futz. Hair. Acid. Pot. The Cop-out. Rock: Folk and acid. Strobe Lights: a fury of electricity. Mixed media. Multimedia. The New Confusion: where does Life End and Art Begin? Outside or inside your head?

The art of combination is not a theory. It is an attitude.

Art wants to "become an essential part of reality. It wants to change reality." The world outside your head is the world of politics and control, tanks and troops, science and technology. The world of power and money. War and Death. You can't change that with art. Then why Art?

In the end art gets pushed back into art, into the studio, into the gallery, museum, concert hall, theater. In the end art gets pushed back into your head. Poetic vision. Taste. Fire and Algebra. The Iconography of human imagination.

Art is the effort to keep man in the state of permanent Revolution. Until he becomes fully Human.

We are Faust, the Arch-Romantic.

Art is the Creation of a mental realm to which there are no known limits. Keep man in a state of permanent, perpetual Revolution. Until he becomes fully human.

We are Faust, the Arch-Romantic. We want Eternal Youth. And we want it Now.

We keep murdering Innocence over and over again to prove something to ourselves, but no one knows what that is.

New choices open up: Perception rather than Logic. Taste rather than Method. Imagination rather than Ideation. Existence rather than Predetermination.

The very multiplicity of human languages, dialects within languages, regional inflections of dialects proves the impossibility of predetermining any-thing. Which is the same as predicting anything. After you've thought that one through, think of the plurality of human cultures, past and present, and the infinite varieties of ways man has developed to live, to eat, to sleep, to make love, to bring up his children, to immortalize his spirit. Life transformed into Art.

We are Life. We are Faust. In love with Eternal Recurrence. With the Eternal Present Eternally.

Where are you? You have to decide. Because you can't have it both ways. Life or Art. Politics or Poetry. What do you want? You can't be outside and inside your head both at the same time. Where are you?

Only the first time is a surprise. After that it's either a bore or a pleasure. If it's a bore, who needs it? If it's a pleasure, it might be worth repeating. And who knows: You might become famous. What Price Glory?

Repetition. Children love to repeat things that give them pleasure. The Joys of Innocence.

Only Love makes Repetition possible. After the first time there's no surprise. The Repertoire is a form of Love. How does a new piece get into the Repertoire? Any Repertoire?

Why do you want to write music nobody can love? Do you hate yourself? Or do you hate them? But let's get one thing clear: record companies don't create the Repertoire.

Obsolescence. Cultural exhaustion. Perceptual weariness. The winds of change blow everything before them from view. Sometimes nothing is left in its path. Where are the Snows of Yesteryear. What is History? And Where?

I used a tune in my *Alchemist Music* which I thought was by Tylman Susato, a Renaissance composer-printer. A musicologist I know told me re-cently that Susato got it from someone else, they don't know whom. Does it make any difference? It's a good tune.

Borges tells the story of Pierre Menard who wanted to write Cervantes's *Don Quixote*. Not *rewrite* it. Write it. It was very hard work but he did manage a couple of chapters which, not surprisingly, came out word for word like Cervantes.

I stand in a circle of time, not on a line. 360 degrees of past, present, future. All around me. I can look in any direction I want to. Bella vista.

Time. History. Series of stepwise stages of evolution. Linear view. Cause and effect. The logic of events. Systematization with blinders.

The center piece of my *Music for the Magic Theatre* is a transcription, that is, a completely new version, of a Mozart adagio. I decided to repeat it in my own way because I loved it. People who don't understand think it's by Mozart.

Assemblage. Collage. A Complex of attitudes and ideas. *Dissimilar* atti-tudes and ideas. Surrounded by a vague aura of association.

Why does a collage or an assemblage need to be created from junk? Why not the opposite?

Tabula Rasa. Wipe the slate clean. Start all over again. Erase memory. Eradicate the Past. Can we?

The Emperor of China who built the Great Wall ordered all the books burned except those that dealt with agriculture and astronomy. The ancient Chinese were among the world's greatest historiographers. They kept complete records of everything that happened. He, the Emperor who ordered the book burning, wanted to be called the "First Emperor."

Ray Bradbury wrote a book called *Farenheit 451* in which the principal job of the firemen was to burn old books that would keep alive the memory of past ways and ideas the leaders wanted dead.

In Cromwell's England it was proposed that all the archives then residing in the Tower of London be burned. The idea was to start all over again.

Borges, commenting on Hawthorne's parable "Earth's Holocaust" says: "In other words, the plan to abolish the past had already occurred to men and—paradoxically is therefore one of the proofs that the past cannot be abolished. The past is indestructible; sooner or later all things will return, including the plan to abolish the past."

Why do you want to write music that no one can remember? Do you hate music?

Art is the alchemical process of transformation which takes place in the furnace of the heart and mind. We transform ourselves into Art. Transcendent use of Life. Use yourself.

Our perspective of history and time has deepened, lengthened, widened. On the way to the moon Borman, Lovell, and Anders saw the Earth. It is a small globe that hangs in Black Space.

Do you reject Evolution? Do you reject History? What are you trying to forget? The Past is indestructible. Sooner or later all things will return. We repeat Beethoven because he's worth repeating. Not to sell more tickets or more records. You've got to keep things straight.

Simultaneous streams of sounding bodies. A vibrating galaxy of suns, moons, and planets. Each different, each unique. Coming together, colliding, penetrating, attracting, and repelling.

Everything we love belongs to us. That includes the past and the future. We are the present.

Simultaneous cries of Pain, shouts of Joy, songs and dances of Love and War, Life and Death. All coming together, colliding, penetrating, repelling. Enlarging the inner space, the deep black space of the mind. Tracery of electric circuits in the Central Nervous System. Memory: a microsystem of orbits in the mental realm. Orbits, Ellipses, Penetrations of the Moon of the Mind, the Sun of the Heart.

We are in the grip of Evolution. Trials and Errors. Dry runs. Wet runs. Selection. Refinement. Maturation of human consciousness and its powers of perception and conception. Of its ability to master opposites, to hold in fine balance the ferocity of tension of opposites. Simultaneous streams of events, gestures, perceptions. To conceive and develop a sense of the whole pattern. You can't change anyone but yourself.

Linearity: series. One thing at a time. Exploration in depth of single impulse. Single vision. Exclusivity.

Nonlinearity: in the round. Time is a ring of fire, a circle, not a line. Movement in any direction. In all directions at once if you can keep your balance. Inclusivity.

The art of combination is not a theory. It is an attitude. New problems for the composer because he needs to depend entirely on his own taste, his own range of musical experience. Sensory order takes precedence over external logic and methodology. He stands unprotected before the winds of change. He stands only on what he has come to love. He is what he loves.

Anonymity. *Anonymous/Twentieth Century*. Leonardo Ricci, architect, city planner, dreamer. Earth is man's Home. What I mean is: how can composers presume to give the performer "freedom" in his name. Are *you* free? Can you give anybody anything but love? If you want to write music no one can remember, why ask the performer to share your nonact of love? Don't put your name on it. Do it anonymously.

Collective behavior. Indian music. Jazz. The Beatles. Free collectivity of performers/composers. Mutual sharing, give and take. Let's keep things straight. You've got to decide what you want.

A collage or assemblage is a composed collectivity of objects or gestures. What has that to do with being "original"? The copyright law was designed for the nineteenth century. To protect the inalienable right of each individual to the property he created. Publishers talk of "properties." Writers are in "stables." How do you pay royalties to the collective unconscious?

Ars Combinatoria. Inclusive vs. Exclusive. "Unity of Varieties" vs. "Variety in Unity." Combination of opposites. Blake's "contraries." Search for new inner balances and outer surfaces. The created illusion of new images. A new collective consciousness.

History is not our master. We can choose. Our real limits are defined by biology and the Central Nervous System. The liberation of the imagination from dogma implies the freedom to move where the ear takes us and to bring together everything which seems good to it. We are not Slaves of History. We can choose and create our own time.

Borman, Lovell, and Anders came home. Magnificent Men.

The winds of change are blowing. Harder. Stronger. Every minute.

I'm trying to stay on my own two feet.

The Composer in Academia:
Reflections on a Theme of Stravinsky

I would warn young composers too, Americans especially, against univer-
sity teaching. However pleasant and profitable to teach counterpoint at a
rich American Gymnasium like Smith or Vassar, I am not sure that that is
the right background for a composer. The numerous young people on
university faculties who write music and who fail to develop into composers
cannot blame their university careers, of course, and there is no pattern for
the real composer, anyway. The point is, however, that teaching is
academic . . . , which means that it may not be the right contrast for a
composer's noncomposing time. The real composer thinks about his work the
whole time; he is not always conscious of this but he is aware of it later,
when he suddenly knows what he will do.

—From *Conversations with Igor Stravinsky*
by Igor Stravinsky and Robert Craft
(Garden City, N.Y.: Doubleday and Co., 1959),
pp. 153–54.

The question before us is so frighteningly complex I can only suggest in the sketchiest terms my view of the issues involved. Also, I feel duty-bound to underline the thoroughly subjective nature of my way of looking at these issues.

Let me start off by saying that I believe we all fantasize our existence, and within the frame of our individual fantasies we seek our own "reality"—that which gives shape, meaning, and substance to the whole of our existence. Anything which falls short of that fantasy or inhibits its realization, we suffer as failure or frustration. Anything which continues it or helps it along the path of realization, we enjoy as success and justification. The two conditions are not unrelated, for it often happens that we define ourselves by negatives and develop our capacity to survive out of the abrasives which life puts in our way.

That is why I say that Stravinsky is right when he remarks that "there is no pattern for the real composer, anyway." If we measure Stravinsky's ca-reer—a phenomenal one to be sure—against, say, the career of Ives, we can see how right he is. On the other hand, precisely because "there is no pattern," his caveat against university teaching addressed to the young American composer is gratuitous. It is conceivable that university teaching may turn out to be no worse or better than conducting six to nine months of every year. How it turns out depends very much on the individual and not on how he makes a living.

But this part of the question is particularly complicated because it is not simply a question of what a composer decides to do with his noncomposing time but what options he has to choose from. For most of us the option of living independently as a composer—writing our music and involving ourselves in its performance directly or indirectly—did not or does not exist, simply by virtue of the accidents of family background and of individual fortune. So, leaving this option aside only because it is not widely available, let us examine the question of the *right contrast for a composer's noncomposing time.* Presumably Stravinsky means that we should be doing something which, while providing us with a necessary income, will not blunt the edge of our work nor eat us up alive physically and spiritually. We get back directly to his: "there is no right pattern." But more than that, we see that any activity other than composing, for which society is willing to pay a musician a reasonably decent salary or income, makes basic demands on his time and energy. And conscience and self-image require that the job be done well no matter what it is.

If the American landscape were dotted with tiny principalities and courts no doubt we would all be *Kapellmeistern* of a sort, like our seventeenth- and eighteenth-century European counterparts. Instead America has colleges and universities, in sufficient quantity and of a degree of enlightenment sufficient to have opened their doors (if not yet their hearts) to the hundreds and possibly thousands of composers alive today. The point I am trying to make is that conducting careers are virtually closed to composers (exceptions notwithstanding) because of the nature of our performance culture and its penchant for star conductors; it is also useless to talk seriously about pursuing a career in commercial music or journalism or publishing or the mass media in general. [It should be noted that Rochberg speaks here not from the usual, presumably snobbish, academic point of view, having been (among other nonacademic employments) a music editor himself for many years before teaching full time.—Ed.] The single decent option left the American composer, where he can pursue his work according to his own inner pressures and needs, is the academic life. Difficulties arise, however, because of the false sense of security and insularity induced by that life. For a composer purports to produce art, and art issues from plunging oneself into what Loren Eiseley calls the "roiling universe" and making (or trying to make) an artistic order out of its chaos. In a sense, then, a composer's work must not be limited by his economically engendered associations with a university consciousness vaguely dedicated to the traditions of rationality and the logics of reason. However much theorists have tried to reduce music to the neat frames of observable logics and orders, an artistic order is not ultimately rational.

Here is where Stravinsky's caveat develops strength and, I feel, must be taken seriously. For in the process of adapting themselves to the life of the university, composers have taken to identifying their goals with those of their colleagues in other disciplines. For reasons I do not fully comprehend, they feel they must justify their existence, not as artists, but as masters of logical procedures, demonstrable, observable, *and* (last but not least) teachable. From this has flowed all sorts of institutionalized nonsense and aberrations which (however short-lived I believe they will eventually prove to be) nevertheless have already done and are still doing plenty of damage. Almost all of this nonsense has to do with the teaching of theory and composition by means of precepts, systems, and methodologies—notions which are interposed between the student and music and which are defended to their academic deaths by self-protective, self-defensive individuals who have learned the academic game too well for their own good, and certainly for that of music.

What safeguards are there then for the university-trained and supported young composer to prevent the subversion of the unconscious impulses which led to music in the first place? How can he avoid being eaten alive by teaching duties and committee meetings, by the academic environment and its special demands and subtle pressures? Paradoxically, by resistance to it. Among other things he must resist identifying himself as an "academic" and maintain himself as an artist. He will have to find the strength to build an intensely private world while maintaining a fluid and open contact with the external world in which he must function. Certainly he will have to resist falling into the various traps of the short-lived fads in composing (and teaching) which are consistently appearing and disappearing. In short, once he has accepted an academic position he has waived the right, in my opinion, to blame his personal weaknesses or inadequacies on the university environment. For personal survival he has to practice the rebel's code stated so succinctly by Camus: No means yes. If he makes it, it will still be a miracle; but then all of life partakes of the miraculous and it is the artistic consciousness which helps to keep this knowledge alive. Occasionally a clear, beautiful signal *does* manage to come through the constant static and noise of existence.

Humanism versus Science

I suppose the usual or conventional thing for me to do would be to define, as succinctly and cogently as possible, the essential characteristics of the humanist mentality and the scientific mentality and then to go on to show in what way, as a musician and composer, I believe the former to be superior to the latter. But this would be a gross oversimplification of the issues involved and would make almost impossible the more difficult task I have imposed on myself, of showing how the alienation of art from human goals has resulted from the uncritical and unquestioning acceptance on virtually all sides of the validity of science and science's own uncritical and unqualified "pursuit of truth"—without regard to the consequences for the values of human existence. If science has been taken at its own word and scientists raised to the status of secular saints in governmental, industrial, intellectual, and popular mass media circles, it is largely, I believe, because the world that science and its technology have made has caught the same virus of rational madness which characterizes scientific mentality today. So long as the appearance of a lofty and impersonal objective rationality is maintained, the madman, like Claggart in Melville's *Billy Budd*, remains above suspicion and reproach until some accident occurs—and then, according to the ironies that Fate deals out to man, it is simple, honest Billy Budd who must die because he strikes out in a blind rage and kills Claggart.

On this issue of accident and Fate let me quote from the epilogue to Friedrich Dürrenmatt's play, *The Physicists*, wherein the author states his credo of the responsibility of the human spirit to life.

> The more premeditated man acts the more effectively he can be overtaken by an accident. Premeditating people wish to reach a certain goal. The accident strikes them most effectively, when as a result of it they arrive at the opposite of their goal. The very thing they fear and wish to evade. Oedipus for instance. Such a story is, to be sure, grotesque but not absurd. It is paradoxical. Dramatists are as little able to avoid the paradoxical as logicians. A drama about physicists has to be paradoxical. It cannot have physics as its goal, only the effect thereof. The content of physics concerns the physicists, its effect concerns all people. What concerns all, only all can solve. Every attempt of an individual to solve what concerns all must of necessity fail. Reality appears in the paradox. Whoever faces the paradox exposes himself to reality. The dramatic art

can trick the audience to expose itself to reality but it cannot force it to withstand it or to conquer it.

Like the dramatist, I hope to trick you into exposing yourself to reality— at least the reality I have in mind—but I cannot force you "to withstand it or to conquer it." There you are on your own, and not without the danger of becoming Billy Budds—whether out of heretical passion or moral fervor on behalf of man. Claggart cloaked himself, as does science, in a subtle form of self-righteousness. Billy Budd's fist was the unwilling instrument of a more open, naive species of morality. Whether or not the "accident" which overcame them was preventable is one of the great hidden fascinations of Melville's classic confrontation of good and evil. Whether the ultimate accidents inherent in the unchecked hubris of modern science are preventable at this late date poses to my mind an even more fascinating (because the frame of reference is actual existence, not a story) study of the moral catastrophes which have gradually overtaken man and have alienated him from his own basic needs and values.

Originally I wanted to tell you a story, a piece of science fiction of my own devising. It was not modesty which prevented me in the end, but the sheer difficulty of producing a piece of writing which, as writing, would have a certain value in itself. (This sense of the limits of one's own powers is part of the humanistic tradition and cast of mind, based as it is on the respect for the material to be worked with and the idea or vision to be projected through it. The production of art and the craft of art imply—or have implied, at least until our own day—that a wedding, not a rape, is the desire of the artist, a mating of inside and outside, of mind and matter, a marriage of human values with cosmic ones.) Although I decided that I lacked the skill to write the story, nevertheless I want to tell you what I had in mind and you may judge the applicability of the ideas to the present subject.

Imagine a time quite remote, say three to four thousand years from now. The people of this time live in wilderness, barely subsisting. Periodically they are driven underground by windstorms which still carry lethal radioactive particles. They speak of the "days of terror" in mythic form—stories, poems, ballads. They are as remote from a knowledge of what caused the terror as we are from knowing the real story of Noah's flood. Though their civilization is crude and daily survival their basic preoccupation, they have advanced to letters and music again and are especially consumed by a passion for the past; they are obsessed by the need to find out what brought on the universal catastrophe which their collective memory has formed and symbolized in myth. They practice a primitive kind of archaeology, digging wherever they can to uncover evidence of the "days before the terror." When the story opens, a vast collection of documents, books, records, tapes, newspapers, magazines has been discovered, presumably in the ruins of a once great library. The dilemma this presents the leaders of the community and the people themselves with is the crux of my idea. For while on the one hand they want to know in order to fill in the gaps of their tragic history, on the other hand they may not be able, once exposed to reality, in Dürrenmatt's words, "to withstand it or to conquer it"; for they live by the thinnest of threads, holding on to virtually bare rock, offering themselves and their children only the minimum of hope for continued survival, of joy in the sense of being alive, of pleasure in the simple and basic acts of living.

What is all-pervasive in their consciousness is the dark intuition that their remote ancestors grew mad with unlimited and unrestrained power and let loose on themselves and the world dread and terrible forces; that this did not happen suddenly but over a space of time; that the earth was desolate for an untold number of years; that, miraculously, life still clung to the earth and survived in conditions of utter despair and utmost terror. Hence the myths of the "days of terror" which centered on descriptions of fearful man-made catastrophes and destruction from aroused natural forces, on stories of heroes who survived, on vaguely generalized notions of the state of the world before the "days of terror." In the process of developing their culture, empty as it was of what we call science and technology, they went inward; from out of their passion for life and the necessity for sheer survival there grew a kind of religion—certainly an ethical and moral code—which taught that all forms of life were sacred, that the only knowledge worth having was in relation to the maintenance and replenishment of life wherever possible, that human consciousness was one of the mysterious glories of existence but had its limits and in no way, under no circumstances, was to be abused or misused. Everything in their dark past warned them of pride of spirit, of arrogance of mind, or the crime of separating the inner unmeasurable world from the outer measurable one.

The mechanical tasks of deciphering all the materials found must of necessity take time; and in the process, as each new aspect of the ancient mentality is revealed, the leaders grow more and more apprehensive about the impact on the people. It falls to the lot of one of them to study the music discovered. He comes to think of this music as the "music of terror"—not unlike the way an ancient Chinese philosopher, when describing the condition of a political state on the verge of disorder and chaos, refers to its music as the "music of decline." In the survivors' culture, music is synonymous with singing; for there are virtually no instruments and there is no interest in virtuosity. Singing is for them the sound of man; and through their voices they express the entire range of dark feelings and emotions which is their lot to bear. Associated with the myths of the "days of terror" are ritually ordained "songs of terror" and "songs of sorrow" plus a vast repertoire of more popular, simpler songs about daily life, about love, about the earth, about death, about survival, about man and the cosmos. The "music of terror" reveals the sound of man as he was before the "days of terror"; for the scores, records, and tapes date from the second half of this century and the music they document is, with all too rare exception, totally devoid of the warming touch of the human spirit or the magic of artistic expression. Either it is precisely logical and cold—mere patterns of sound relationships and configuration whose tiny, hard granules travel through musical space like myriads of lonely planets in the eternally frigid zones of cosmic space—or it is unrestrained in a hysterical, chaotic way: random bursts or flashes or driblets or points of sound crashing, clashing, milling around each other turbulently, driven from one excess and extreme to another until the nerves and the ears recoil in self-defense. This raw, ugly truth of man before the "days of terror" began was all there, a repugnant record of mental aberration and sickness of spirit, a frightening, terrifyingly clear insight into the conditions which ultimately came to be directly responsible for the cruel sufferings of the survivors. The musician-leader is repulsed by what he discovers and dismayed by the realization that sound can be so perverted, so tortured, so lacking in the sweetness and grandeur of human feeling in contrast to the music of his own people which is suffused with a sense of the tragic and beautiful. After long deliberation, it is finally decided by the leaders that the knowledge they have gained must be revealed to the people in order that they may be reinforced in their awareness that the myths of the "days of terror" are essentially true; that there was once a time when man knew no limits to his lust for power and knowledge and in the pursuit of both grew mad, all the while proclaiming the sacredness and inviolability of his search for the secrets of the universe and life and the desire to control them; that they, the survivors, must continue to hold existence holy and to govern themselves in the light of this first and last condition of human existence. Here the story ends.

I had intended to end it with the sentence: And now man knows that he is alone in the universe and the only sounds he hears are the sounds of nature and his own voice.

It would be presumptuous to attempt, or claim to attempt, a depth analysis of the abberations of the contemporary mind—but it seems to me there is a kind of rational madness let loose in the world which delights in manipulation for its own sake, usually, if not always, buttressed by self-justifying, objective principles, a kind of rational madness which understands no theoretical limits to its pursuit of these goals and which, worst of all, recognizes none of, or is blind to all of the possible consequences of its procedure when acted out in real life and among real people. The energy which feeds and drives the engines of this variety of consciousness is certainly not itself rational, but the faith—couched in rational, ideological terms to which it attaches itself—becomes the sole justification for its exercise. In turn, this rational, ideological faith gives rise to its own specially devised morality and assumes, therefore, the condition of a quasi-religious status among its followers and practitioners. In the process the faith becomes externalized, is abstracted away from the realities of human existence, and gives birth to an inviolate dogma or doctrine in its own right—somehow sacred, beyond the pale of examination, doubt, criticism, revision. The purer the stated motives, the more selfless the declarations of persons involved, the nobler the pursuit, the greater the chance for idealizing the whole process and giving it an aura of striving for the highest human goals.

The purest example I know, which my description fits in every regard, is science, for in science today we see the remarkable phenomenon of an unquestioned, worldwide agreement to pursue knowledge to its absolute limits, regardless of the ultimate consequences for human existence. We note the pride and loftiness of its objective impersonal pursuit of truth, we are impressed by its selfless ardor in carrying out this search for the ultimate secrets of the universe, and we have raised to the rank of culture heroes those men who have contributed the most toward unlocking the bonds which, according to their scientific faith, have kept mankind imprisoned in the darkness of ignorance. The horrible paradox in this almost four-century-old play of man's constitutional inability to foresee consequences while in hot pursuit of what he calls "truth" is that, as each discovery of this truth has brought man closer and closer to his own extinction, either through the prospects of physical destruction or through psychological maltransformation or biogenetic tampering, science itself remains supremely and arrogantly confident of its limitless purposes and indeed has the full support and encouragement of governments, industrial entrepreneurs, and people generally, all of whom continue to believe uncritically in its benefits. It may seem unduly harsh to refer to scientists as rational madmen who act out their blind Claggart-like roles under the guise of the purest of motives; but what other conclusion can one come to when, with all too few exceptions, scientists still remain impervious to the moral consequences of their research and findings, disclaiming any part of the actual consequences stemming from the technological application of their work to real situations?

It is not surprising that the world picture of the scientist from Galileo to today still remains as Schrödinger has observed, "without blue, yellow, bitter, sweet, beauty, delight, and sorrow." However regrettable it might be, the dehumanized objectivity of scientific methodology and procedural logic gradually entered into and became central to large areas of artistic thought and production.

The emergence of forms of art totally devoid of human content, and therefore meaning, owes everything to a naively accepting and uncritical belief in the values of machine technology and the scientific premises on which this technology has been firmly based. While it is true that humanistic traditions still prevail in some artistic quarters, it is nevertheless true that they have been abandoned largely in favor of varieties of production which concentrate on consciously devised technical manipulation of the optic nerve; on the application of pure geometric design to the plan of the pictorial or the sculptural space; on the development of factory-produced sculpture for which the artist provides a blueprint; on the emergence of the "happening" as a misapplication of the principles of indeterminacy which permits the artist to indulge himself without restraint or taste; on the establishment of "open theater" and "participatory theater" which, as far as I can see, derive from the principles of behavioral psychology in which stimulus and response play the greatest roles. In short, this kind of contemporary art either manipulates the central nervous system (sometimes in bizarre and grotesque, however systematic, ways) or ignores its needs completely by removing itself to realms of abstraction which, though patterned, refuse sense and meaning to the viewer. From either point of view it would appear that the artist treats his audience as though it were either automaton or comatose—certainly incapable of self-generated thought or feeling. It is therefore not surprising that we can see the likeness of the dehumanized, morally devoid specter of science in much of contemporary art. The same pretense toward lofty and impersonal objectivity is present in both; the same removal from the consequences of one's actions is present in both; the same preference for reducing the ineffable subject (man) to an eminently manipulable object (automaton) is present in both.

The success of this kind of contemporary art—in painting and sculpture primarily—is itself a commentary on the dominion of science in our present world. The psychology of the scientific mentality pervades our culture today and virtually guarantees the success of any kind of human effort which bears its imprimatur. The alienation of science from life is exactly parallel, in my view, to the alienation of the artist from art. In this regard, although we continue to use the words *artist* and *art*, it would perhaps be more accurate to speak of "technician" or "artisan" and of the work they produce as "product."

The separation of the immeasurable inside from the measurable outside, i.e., the propensity for converting the world around us into so much machinery to be mastered and controlled—leaving out the dark, subjective nature of the controller, himself an intrinsic part of what he attempts to control—is the hallmark of the scientific outlook starting with Galileo and Kepler. For three centuries painters, sculptors, musicians, poets, and writers went their way producing the body of our inherited culture, but in the twentieth century—the century in which science itself has finally overtaken and conquered the world—art has succumbed to the ethos which seems all-pervasive and inescapable, deadly though it may ultimately prove to be to man and his best interests.

Until the twentieth century it was clear that the worlds of science and art were separate from each other, sharing no basic premises in common. Though Kepler could say:

> As the ear is made to perceive sound and the eye to perceive color, so the mind has been formed to understand not all sorts of things but quan-

tities. It perceives any given thing more clearly in proportion as that thing is close to bare quantities as to its origin, but the further a thing recedes from quantities the more darkness and error inhere in it.

It was precisely in those areas where the mind recedes from quantities and moves freely and intuitively in the realms of qualities that the artist lived and worked his human miracles. It was there that "blue, yellow, bitter, sweet, beauty, delight, and sorrow" held sway and produced their magical images for the eye, the ear, the mind—images which attained a human reality and gave the brutish, hard life of men a possible sense of glory in existence, a sense of the miraculous. But science not only does not believe in miracles; it positively despises them. The choice of illusion open to man goes deeper than simply the choice between reason and miracle. Physics—whether of the microcosm of the atom or the macrocosm of deep space—is no substitute for cosmology; for it was cosmology, with its myths and magic, ritual and religion, which sustained and protected man over eons of time up to the very threshold of the age of science, largely because it allowed his image-making nature free rein to people his inner world with the fantastic, with the sense of awe in the face of forces whose power he sensed but could not know. And most of all it constrained his hubris. Modern man may view with disdain his primitive forebears for propitiating the gods as a means of defense and protection against the unseen and unknown—but it is doubtful he would even be here to practice this disdain had his ancestors practiced the modern variety of science. Rationally it is probably not demonstrable that man has survived through fantasy, but intuitively one knows we are still here today only because of that faculty for the fantastic, only because of our innate passion for images, symbols, myths, metaphors.

That science has removed much of the physical harshness of existence is certainly to its credit—but by the paradox of Dürrenmatt's premeditating man, science has simultaneously removed from us precisely that sense of our worth which art once embodied and without which human existence attains a new low of helpless misery. It has transplanted the once-eternal difficulties of human existence to the inside, the very core of man, leaving him frightened, bewildered, and uncertain of direction while at the same time propelling him in an increasing spiral of motion. If one compares the results of the "divine madness" which Plato ascribed to poets with those of the "rational madness" I am ascribing to scientists, it is not difficult to see which is to be preferred in terms of the present and future of man. But the "divine madness" has been almost totally replaced by "rational madness" in the arts of our times; and it is in certain and specific varieties of contemporary music one can see this best.

Music is the most discrete, the most potentially abstract, the most specific of all the arts. To Leibnitz it was "unconscious counting," a species of mathematics; to John Ruskin "frozen architecture"; but to musicians it was, until only very recently, "singing." Sound was simply the physical medium, the carrier of the increasingly expanding structures which based themselves primarily on the model of the vocal phrase and its psychology, and projected its human aspirations in clearly shaped, arching melodic lines with or without direct verbal association. As late as Schoenberg and Stravinsky, and even in Webern, the propensity for "singing" worked its magic even on purely instrumental works. And where "singing," in the sense of vocal or instrumental lyric expression, was modified to "dancing" in the sense of periodicities with directly felt rhythmic pulsation, music retained its uncanny balance between inner and outer, remained a wholly human creation of human realities—memorable, repeatable, meaningful, if not always beautiful according to individual taste. By another of the great ironies that pursues premeditating man, as soon as composers began to think of music as sound and sound as quantity, singing and dancing in the traditional musical sense were replaced by conscious counting (going Leibnitz one better) and by *literally* attaining the condition of "frozen architecture"—sound events designed in time but not rhythm. Since present-day composers are extremely, if not excessively, verbal and given to different varieties of intellection and abstraction, they have fully documented their peregrinations in endless articles and books, few of which ultimately reveal the slightest awareness of the erosion of their own art at their own hands. Because they are fascinated by mathematics, logic, and science and have taken on the rational madness of their scientific confreres, we read much these days about information theory and its relation to the psychology and composition of music; about statistical probabilities, stochastics, and the Markoff Chain and their compositional possibilities; about group and set theory as applied to serial music; about aleatoricism and indeterminacy and entropy. Every possible scientific metaphor and analogy is invoked. Every possible scientific discipline is ransacked for potential connections with and corroborations of theoretical postulates of how to expand the possibilities of sound itself and its theoretically limitless arrangements, compositionally speaking. Musicians study computer programming, probe the latest linguistic findings, revel in the communication sciences. They read widely in logic; they take courses in advanced mathematics. All this would be admirable if it were for the personal cultural enrichment of those who feel so inclined—but it is in the name of music and exploring its possibilities in every conceivable direction, regardless of where it leads or what outlandish conclusions result, that this incredible display of misguided diligence is carried on. It used to be that a musician who wanted to compose schooled himself in the disciplines of counterpoint and harmony, learned his craft and went about the uncertain business of producing art; history tells us few succeeded. Today it is enough merely to want to become a composer (without benefit of evidences of a musical "ear") to generate a spate of studies which have nothing whatever to do with music as a craft or an art; observation shows us few are failing. As incredible as it may seem, musicians today have actually come to believe that music is susceptible to analysis and logic, that what it is as acoustical phenomena, as patterns of simultaneous and successive order, as embodiments of structure and design is ultimately knowable by the calculating, measuring, premeditating mind. The presumption of such notions has converted music into a new form of applied science, a kind of acoustical technology. The private cosmology of a Beethoven has virtually disappeared from the scene; and the pathos of this spectacle of misguided presumption is rendered even more pathetic by a contemplation of this memo of Charles Ives, written in 1924 in a London hotel room.

> Music is one of the many ways God has of beating in on man—his life, his ideals, his hope in everything—an inner something, a spiritual storm, a something else that stirs the man in one of his parts (consciousness) and "all at once"—we roughly call these parts (as a kind of entity) "soul." It acts through, or vibrates, or couples up to human situations in ways (or measures) man may hear and know: that is, he knows he hears them and says (or thinks or feels) he knows them. Further than this, what this inner something is which begets all this, is something no one knows—especially those who define it and use it primarily to make a living. All this means almost nothing to those who think about it. Music—that no one knows what it is—and the less he knows he knows what it is the nearer it is to music—probably.

It is not germane whether the musicians who are deeply involved with scientific ideas and notions understand or apply them correctly to their own production. Here again the scientist can sit on his lofty perch and disclaim any responsibility for what musicians do with his ideas, but the fact remains that his impact on the musician is deep and profound and has had no less deleterious effects on music than on other areas of existence. As in the Chinese box-within-the-box, we proceed in depth to ever-increasing disregard of consequences. For there are among us composers who renounce any responsibility for what they produce, claiming instead that the very nonrepeatability of their indeterminate works based on chance or choice lies in the very nature of physical phenomena and is therefore of a higher reality than any which pertains to man's limited possibilities, tied down as they are by cultural associations, memory, history. Even more interesting—if not revealing of the present state of psychic erosion—is the tendency on the part of certain very "advanced" composers to advocate anonymity for their productions, i.e., to remove the onus of a specific personality or stigma of a particular ego from the work itself so that the work can at least exist freely without any human ties whatsoever. (Usually such ideas are advanced to the accompaniment of vague murmurs about the virtues of collaboration, collectivity, the submergence of self in a larger societal whole, etc., etc.) But it is in the area of electronics, magnetic tape, and the computer that music today has received its greatest impress from the technology of science, and it is here where composers have entered into pure quantification and measurement of wave lengths, wave combinations, partials, and time segments and sequences. That music should thus be subjected to forms of automation is inevitable; that it should remove itself more and more from singing and dancing and embrace a world of sound devoid of human content is surely the end result of believing that music, like everything else today, is reducible to formulas, to equations, to statistical probabilities, to predictable and controllable functions and behavior—in short, to technology.

We are, I fear, in the days before the terror I described. While it would be gentler, though not kinder, to call much of the music being produced now a "music of decline," I'm afraid it is already the music of the "days before the terror." Any sense of the human limits of music has been lost. In my view, it is not likely it can be regained, at least not until we have passed through the terrors which science and technology have prepared for us and have been driven back by the sheer need to survive to a reevaluation of priorities in life and a renewed sense of the essential tragedy of man. The Greeks already understood the nature of this tragedy as the hubris of man, his vaulting pride, his lust for dominion over the very universe which made him. And as the Greeks had a word for everything, they invented the Eumenides, the Fates which, when provoked, cut premeditating men down. Must we wait until we are standing desolate and despairing in a man-made wilderness to understand the words of Dürrenmatt's physicist, Moebius?

> I am poor King Solomon. Once I was immeasurably rich and wise and god-fearing. I was a prince of peace and justice. But my wisdom destroyed my fear of God, and when I no longer feared God, my wisdom destroyed my riches. Now all cities are dead over which I ruled; the empire which was entrusted to me is empty, a desert shimmering in a blue light, and somewhere, around a nameless star, senselessly, eternally circles the radioactive earth. I am Solomon, I am poor King Solomon.

On the Fantastic and the Logical

- *Aural Fact or Fiction: Or, Composing at the Seashore (1965)*

- *The Fantastic and the Logical: Reflections on Science, Politics, and Art (1973)*

- *The Marvelous in Art (1982)*

Aural Fact or Fiction:
Or, Composing at the Seashore

The crisis which has overtaken the contemporary composer involves, at its deepest level, his relation to his art and the very process of composing—the making of the artwork. He is suffering from the triumph of abstractionism.

He is like a bird who first wants to examine the size of the sky or a fish who first wants to examine the extent of the water—and then try to fly or to swim. But the bird and the fish will never find their own ways in the sky or water because they have dissociated themselves—the fish from the water which makes his life, the bird from the sky which makes his. The fish and the bird have unlearned spontaneity, grace, naturalness. They have become self-conscious.

The triumph of abstractionism has led us to the cliff edge of dehumanization and depersonalization, nihilism and negativism. The more we have penetrated into the abstract—a process which has involved stripping away the surface and depleting or emptying out content—the more we have given ourselves up to an overriding faith in materials and procedures, in the factual levels of artistic production. What were formerly means have become ends, vitiating the fiction-creating power of the imagination. The impulse toward abstraction begins with the desire to rid ourselves of human encumbrances, to burn out excrescences, to unload superfluities. But as abstraction proceeds it devitalizes, constricts, and in the end defeats itself by producing a sawdust world whose longitude and latitude are narrowness and dullness, whose atmosphere is thin, dry, and cold. Art is reduced from its power to create mental fictions, works of imagination, to the mere production of trivial presentations of raw data—sounds, colors, lines, words.

The triumph of abstractionism has produced a unique form of paralysis. By analysis and analytic dissection we arrive at mechanics and inorganic structure. The Cartesian addiction, the rationalist's narcotic, to divide the world into body and spirit, machine and mind destroys the view of the totality of the living organism. What William Blake called the Spectre, man's reason, produces that frame of mind which tends to frustrate and paralyze the creative impulse. It kills or casts a pall on the artist's energy which is passion and his imagination which is intuition. I am reminded of Blake's couplet:

> If the Sun and Moon should doubt,
> They'd immediately go out.

When the center of creative activity is displaced from the region of the psyche to the region of the reason, fiction is reduced to fact, myth to reporting, and imagination is destroyed or crippled. All that remains, all that "art" is made of, is collections of facts, perceptual data. Abstractionism paralyzes "speech," i.e., the power to say, the capacity to utter and express—and when carried to its ultimate it ends in forms of inarticulateness. Music, of all the arts, has the power of directly communicated eloquence. But as abstractionism has taken greater and greater hold, musical eloquence has proportionately atrophied and died. And where it has not been reduced to being utterly inarticulate, it remains at the level of cold precision where nothing flows, moves, or lives. The musical discourse has become inhibited, blocked, frozen in its tracks, immobilized.

A composer does not need to have anything to say of an expressive nature in order to manipulate, order, and structure precise aural patterns and designs. The relationships he establishes in such a case are purely formal and syntactical. He is a kind of grammarian who interests himself only in the structure of his language, not its meaning. In this, however, he can keep his distance, remain personally detached, while he deals with aural facts in much the same way that an engineer deals with physical facts. On the other hand, a composer who does have something to say needs a vocabulary and needs to know how to use it. But his interest is not merely in the structure of his language; it is in its capacity to point beyond itself, its power to create meaning—musical meaning. The aural facts with which his language provides him are, by themselves, not sufficient to create the aural fiction which only his imagination can. Perhaps this is what Charles Ives is getting at when he bursts out in the epilogue of his *Essays before a Sonata:* "My God! What do sounds have to do with music!" Sounds, aural facts, acoustical phenomena cannot attain the level of eloquence; only aural fiction, the music which is in the composer, can.

But all that I have said so far is only one side of the picture. The abstract adventure has produced some very positive results, not the least of which has been its capacity to generate a whole range of new possibilities and to open up to the composer a totally new perspective. It has made it necessary for him to rethink his problems, to take nothing for granted. It has engendered a heightened sense of awareness, of the relationship between himself and the process of making the art work. Perhaps most important of all, it has taught him to recognize that this relationship is not static—that there is always something else, something still to be realized and made manifest, just beyond the tips of his fingers, as he pushes out his horizons further and further.

The abstract adventure in music, which began with atonality, has taught the composer the value of sound as sound, every conceivable kind of sound—its perceptual dimensions as well as its perceptual limits. To his surprise, he has in the process rediscovered that the sound of the human voice is the richest, the most fluid, the most flexible of all musical instruments. In his search for a new vocabulary the composer has expanded his color palette to include noise and electronically generated sound. His experience with noise produced by conventional percussion instruments, or natural phenomena, or man-made engines and machines, has influenced his attitude toward electronic music. Conversely, his experience with electronic music, and its new category of synthetically produced aural phenomena, has influenced his attitude toward live music composed for conventional instruments. The interaction has been fruitful, and beyond anyone's expectations. Precisely because of this the composer has come to place a higher value than ever before on those traditional instruments which are naturally rich and complex in their sound characteristics.

Unfortunately the discovery of the new dimensions and possibilities of sound has not been automatically or necessarily accompanied by a direct knowledge or sense of how to use them to their best advantage. So far two directions seem to have been indicated and pursued: first, environmental sounds, usually in the noise spectrum, and composed sounds of an analogous kind generally found in aleatoric music; and second, analytic sound research and analytic composition both in and out of the electronic music studio. Presently efforts are being made to combine both types. So far, however, it appears that they may turn out to be dead ends—mainly because they are unable to get beyond the level of aural facts and the mechanics of acoustical phenomena. The composer must eventually come to the realization that the new sound vocabulary is neutral (as are all sound vocabularies), "sexless," and cannot bear fruit by itself. It will have to be put to the composer's uses, not its own. Hermann Broch, the novelist, says in his trilogy, *The Sleepwalkers*, that "in our day technique has simply outrun creative effort, that we have not yet wrested from our new material its adequate forms of expression and that all the disquieting lack of proportion arises from imperfectly mastered purpose."

Granting that the mastery of purpose remains to be demonstrated and accomplished, still further significant changes have occurred in contemporary music as a result of the abstract adventure—namely the discovery of a new sense of gesture and a new attitude toward motion and time. The new sense of gesture can be best characterized as *juxtaposition of contrary tendencies*, i.e., unprepared and sudden shifts from slow to fast, high to low, loud to soft, and the like; the new attitude toward motion and time as *discontinuity*, i.e., stopping and starting, the use of silences, unexpected interruptions of flow, and so on. Sometimes, however, it appears that constant juxtaposition and discontinuity produce a narrow, constricted music because they pare down the possibility of a variety of levels of action. Their obsessive use tends to result in disruption of the flow of successive events and tends also to produce a flattened-out effect in the perception of how things happen. Nineteenth-century romanticism gave us the great climax which grows out of extension of ideas which, in turn, are part of a continuously expanding, unravelling melodic flow. In today's music, climax has been leveled out and is virtually nonexistent. It becomes increasingly important to see these new gestures and motions incorporated and integrated into a larger context of continuity where climax is possible again. I see nothing to prevent the composer from learning how to operate on both levels, increasing the gestural dimensions of his music and therefore its psychological, emotional impact. There is no logical reason to forbid the use of juxtaposition and discontinuity in a larger context which also embraces extension, growth toward climax, and climax itself. The new aural facts—sounds and procedures, the structural mechanics of today's music which have been made possible by the adventure with abstractionism—do not necessarily preclude new aural fictions, the creation of new and imaginative contexts. The importance of the whole crisis of contemporary art lies in the urgent demands it places upon us to renew our efforts to find a new focus without destroying the values of what we have learned from the abstract adventure.

With the preceding discussion as background I wish now to pursue the idea of "fact" versus "fiction" still further, drawing my examples not from music for the moment but from the novel, theater, film, and painting. When the medium of art is verbal or visual rather than aural, it becomes easier to discern distinctions between the factual and the fictional levels, between the material and the mental, and to observe the creative process which welds them into artistic entities—or fails to do so, as the case may be. At the same time certain difficulties do arise because these distinctions themselves are caught in the web of human experience, which is empirical and therefore may not hold in every instance. A critical evaluation of art from any point of view inevitably leads back to the world in which we live and our place in it—or what we think our place in it is.

When we say (as we often do), "Let the facts speak for themselves," we are oversimplifying. Facts do not speak for themselves; they need to be interpreted. Interpretation is a purely subjective process, and whether we claim it is our reason or our intuition or an interesting combination of both that does the interpreting, we can never be certain—unless we are confirmed fanatics, rabid rationalists—that the way we know, the way we experience the world and the way we have come to believe whatever we do believe about existence may not be so after all. The "facts of life," the whole range of cosmic, biological, and man-made phenomena, undergo constant alteration in relationship as cultural emphases shift from one epoch to another and the style of life changes. In this century we have virtually had to accept a position of relativism; and it is notoriously difficult to retain one's balance in such a precarious posture, especially if the work to which one is intensely committed—the practice of art—is rooted in and derives its motivations and energies from the intricate relation between one's subjective self and the world around it. (It may turn out that truth is not stranger than fiction, but rather that fiction is, after all, a form of truth—man's subjective truth.)

H. L. Mencken in his preface to the 1946 edition of Theodore Dreiser's *An American Tragedy* points out that the prototype of Clyde Griffiths was "a young man named Chester E. Gillette who drowned a girl named Grace Brown in a lake in Herkimer County on July 4, 1906, and was electrocuted for it on March 20, 1908." Dreiser, according to Mencken, "was probably the most matter-of-fact novelist ever known on earth. It was seldom that he departed from what he understood to be the record, and he never did so willingly." What then accounts for the great hold Dreiser's book has had on his readers, if all Dreiser did was to base his novel on the "facts in the case"? Mencken makes the point that "it is Dreiser who is telling the story, not some commonplace reporter. It offers a picture of profound tragedy seen through a suitably melancholy temperament. The author's brooding . . . is all over it. It is not only a minutely detailed picture of one unhappy man's life; it is a commentary upon human life in general." Dreiser has performed the essential creative act of the novelist by transforming a factual report into a living fiction, pure human invention, a subjective fantasy which undeniably conveys truth.

In the play *Rashomon* and the Japanese film (which the play follows very closely) a uniquely human situation enmeshes three participants in a brutal rape and death—the samurai husband, his wife, the bandit who cannot contain his animal appetites—and one observer, the frightened woodcutter. The fascination of the film and the play lies precisely in our interest in the four different stories told, each contradicting the other. The bandit emerges from his version as part poet, part hero, the irresistible seducer and brave man of action, who kills the husband in a duel, fair and square. The wife, though the bandit claims she submitted willingly, swears she was taken by brute force and kills her husband herself in a state of shocked amnesia. The husband, contemptuous of his wife because she has dishonored him by acquiescing in her rape, kills himself with his own sword after being released by the bandit. Finally, the woodcutter (who comes on the scene accidentally) reveals that neither the bandit nor the husband are as brave and honorable as they present themselves but rather cowards, egged on to fight each other by the wife. As the woodcutter reports it, the husband falls into a clump of bushes and accidentally kills himself. How can the audience tell what is true? It is clear that each of the participants in these tragic events interprets them as flattering to himself, as revealing himself in the noblest, most virtuous light possible. Within the structure of the story each subjective interpretation is clearly a fiction. Paradoxically, however, if we take the play (or the film) as an artistic entity, a created vision of human tragedy and folly, it seems quite clear that the conflicting versions are themselves the dramatic facts of which the dramatic fiction is fashioned and shaped. In *Rashomon* we have an instance of fiction, based not on a body of reported facts (as in the case of *An American Tragedy*) but on a body of invented facts whose model is drawn from an intuitive knowledge of the nature of human beings. In both cases a model of the world and of human experience serves the writers.

When we view a film like *Last Year at Marienbad*, we find ourselves in a realm of fantasy where the familiar model of the world, either explicit or implicit, has disappeared and we are completely removed from any semblance of external reality. The events in the film are pure fiction and could only happen in the film, never outside. Alain Robbe-Grillet, who produced the scenario, says in writing about *Marienbad* that he and its director Alain Resnais "decided to trust the spectator, to allow him, from start to finish, to come to terms with pure subjectivities." They wanted to make a film "addressed exclusively" to the spectator's "sensibility, to his faculties of sight, hearing, feeling." The film they eventually produced is a "composed" film, composed very much the way a piece of music is composed—or in the light of my previous remarks and others to come later ought to be composed—i.e., of "pure subjectivities." *Marienbad*'s compositional characteristics place it directly in the realm of created fiction. There is no external model of reality to which it refers except vaguely and ambiguously; hence it is a completely subjective and internalized expression appealing directly to our visual, aural, and emotional responses. For this very reason there is one scene in which one experiences a peculiar shock: the "other man" in the love triangle and the woman are standing before a statue of a man and a woman in classical robes. They are talking about the figures, less concerned with their identity than the attitudes and expressions they convey. Several different interpretations are offered by the "other man." Suddenly, the man who is presumably the husband—we are never sure—appears and says, "Excuse me, sir. I think I can supply you with some more precise information. This statue represents Charles III and his wife, but it does not date from that period, of course. The scene is that of the oath before the Diet, at the moment of the trial for treason. The classical costumes are purely conventional. . . ." This sudden intrusion of external reality in the form of a factual report of a historical event involving historical personages serves to underline and intensify the fantasy of the film. Its function is, I believe, to show the viewers how little real facts or the physicality of objects mean to life lived inside the dream world which characterizes the depths of the human psyche, or how little they influence its propensity for creating fiction out of pure subjectivities. As Robbe-Grillet remarks, "The story told will seem the more realistic, the truest, the one that best corresponds" to the spectator's "emotional life as soon as he agrees to abandon ready-made ideas, psychological analysis, more or less clumsy systems of interpretation which machine-made fiction or films grind out for him *ad nauseam*, and which are the worst kinds of abstractions." *Marienbad* is a composition of visual and emotional images, purposefully repetitive the way music is, completely sealed off from the external world and, therefore, pure fiction.

Till now I have discussed particular instances of the novel, drama, and film. In turning to the field of painting I shall make my approach more general. Under the impact of abstractionism twentieth-century painting has passed rapidly through a whole series of shifting styles. (The "tradition of the new," as Harold Rosenberg, the art critic, has baptized it, appears to be the only common rallying point observable on the painting scene today. His phrase may turn out to be a critical euphemism for "obsolescence.") If we examine three recent styles—Abstract Expressionism or "action painting," "Pop" Art and "Op" Art, all of which have come to the fore since about 1950—we find that each has a unique relationship to the problems I have been discussing, each tells us a great deal about the approach of these painters to their art and to the world around them. We discover that Abstract Expressionism is a completely internalized style of painting, "Pop" Art completely externalized, and "Op" Art between the two, in a neutral zone.

The color explosion which was Abstract Expressionism seems to have been born of the fusion of post-Cubism, early Expressionism, and Surrealism. The canvas, though grown immense in size, has been reduced to a two-dimensional flat surface, the object and the figure have disappeared (except in rare instances), and only color forms—some casual, some precise, some completely formless, some purely decorative and ornamental—exist to delight the eye. Abstract Expressionists are contemplative like Rothko, aggressive like deKooning, or like Pollock, spontaneous and released. Whatever their differences as artistic personalities, they have one thing in common: they are painting themselves—projecting in color and line, however controlled or chaotic the composition, their internal landscapes. Among painters today the Abstract Expressionists are the only "composers." They work with pure subjectivities, creating pure visual fictions.

Pop Art and Abstract Expressionism represent two totally different views; and there would appear to be no real point of contact between them. If Abstract Expressionism draws its images from the internal landscape of the action painter's psyche, his inner world, then Pop Art draws its images from the man-made environment. Primarily the Pop Artist is a reporter of visual facts, producing facsimiles and replicas of objects, artifacts, scenes, and symbols of a technological urban society. Even if Pop Art is considered as a form of criticism and satire, revealing the emptiness of the contemporary world of advertising, merchandising, and mass media, the work itself conveys nothing about the painter to the viewer. His comment is made from a safe distance; he is not involved or engaged. He is merely reporting the present visually crass, frighteningly dull and ugly scene. The soup can, the flag, the sex goddess, the gas station attendant are nothing more than images of things that exist but which have no vitality in art. Pop Art is a form of sheer redundancy, telling us nothing we don't already know about ourselves. The work is caught in the materiality of the environment, reporting but unable to transform the facts into visual fictions. Since the Pop Artist is merely a visual reporter, not an interpreter, his work remains outside himself—sterile but brightly colored, dull but technically slick.

Op (for optical) Art occupies that neutral zone between Abstract Expressionism and Pop Art, between the fiction of the internal landscape and the fact of the external, man-made landscape. It is concerned only with the fact that we see only with the process of visual perception itself, i.e., the physiology and neurology of vision. The Op Artist leans heavily on psychological and physical experiments, dealing with problems of visual perception and the effects of optical illusions. He is a special kind of technician or engineer, producing visual patterns and designs calculated to produce vibration and movement in the viewer's eyes. If the Pop Artist detaches himself from his own psyche in order to identify his work directly with man-made environmental facts, the Op Artist appears to have detached himself not only from his psyche but from the world around him as well, and is content to locate himself somewhere between, in the mechanics of the process of visual perception itself. Nothing could demonstrate better than Op Art the tendency of abstractionism to depersonalize and dehumanize the act and art of painting.

Now to return to music: let us probe deeper into the relationship between aural fact and fiction. There are, generally speaking, three levels which require our attention: first, the raw data of aural perception—the whole spectrum of sounds from indeterminate noise to individual, discrete pitch deriving from man-made or natural sound sources; second, the perceptual process of hearing itself—taking in sounds and organizing them into aural patterns; and third, the creation of aural relationships which we call "music." Taken separately and together, the first two levels—the raw data of aural perception and the perceptual process of hearing—comprise the aural facts of music; only the third involves the creation of aural fiction which emerges from the mysterious interaction between sound, its motion through time, the way we hear, and the creative imagination of the composer.

Let me try to illustrate: I am walking by the seashore. The ocean is rolling in, pounding the beach with heavy breakers. The sound I hear is a steady, low roaring and hissing which varies in its intensity but not in its quality. So long as my attention is completely drawn to the continuous, unrelenting sound of the ocean I literally hear nothing else. For me the sound of the sea at this point is an aural presence, a single aural fact. If I begin to broaden the range of my listening, I become aware of a series of staccato like shouts and cries of children playing on the beach. These sounds, higher pitched and without any specific rhythmic pattern, combine now with the ocean's *basso* roaring and hissing to form a new aural pattern: a continuous deep background from the sea interrupted by a random pattern of short, high, punctuating human sounds. My range of aural facts has now increased. At this point, the way I hear, the process of aural perception, organizes them into a pattern of continuity and simultaneity. (The remarkable property of the human aural mechanism lies precisely in its power to take in simultaneous sounds of varying qualities of strength or intensity and timbre differentiation and establish a configuration, a pattern in which they retain their identity.)

The number of different sounds I take in can be increased indefinitely to include the sharp, keening glissando cries of the seagulls wheeling in the sky, the mechanical sounds of an occasional plane that passes overhead, or the cars a few blocks away. The aural field becomes denser and denser but does not lose its factuality. If I do no more than continue to let these sounds happen to me—let them cross the threshold of my hearing passively—both the sounds and the way I take them in remain at the level of aural fact. The moment, however, I wish to impose upon them my desire for a particular kind of order, i.e., try to arrange the sounds as they happen outside of me in such a way that once across the threshold of my hearing they become something I want them to be in my ear, I begin the process of composing, I establish the possibilities of aural fiction.

I can do this in several ways: By an effort of concentration I can raise any of the sounds I hear to the foreground of my attention, automatically pushing everything else into the background. I can do this in a continuous pattern of changing foreground and background configurations, trying to make different relationships between whatever sounds present themselves to me. Or I can try to make shapes, i.e., phrases, of the sounds as they intersect each other, converge, and break off; I can try to establish a rhythm of events, i.e., try to find a sequence of their succession. Or I can concentrate on the color relationships of the whole field of sounds, their registral position (high, middle, or low), or their dynamic levels (from soft to loud). Or I can try to combine all of these things, hearing all together in one grand ensemble: the sounds of nature, the human sounds, the mechanical sounds; their foreground-background relationship; their shapes; their rhythm; their color. What I am trying to do is to internalize what is happening around me.

So long as I have no control over the sound sources, however, my efforts will be frustrated. Only if I can tell the ocean and the children and the planes when to sound and when not to am I in control—and only then can I completely internalize them as sound sources and compose them as I wish into music. However, if I stop short of the need to internalize and simply continue to give myself up passively to the audition of all the sounds around me, I would still be "making music" according to the view held in avant-garde circles today. The avant-garde has unwittingly claimed the realm of aural fact for itself. While its music is obviously not composed in the manner of my example, the attitudes and methods of composers and experimental music are remarkably similar to "composing at the seashore"—they generally view sound as pure sensation, external to the psyche, and meant only for the ear. They create situations in which "random" sound events comprise the variable form of the composition and leave it to the listener to make up whatever patterns he can out of them. The experimental composer usually stops short just this side of aural fiction, taking an essentially passive attitude to the body of aural facts which comprise his field of operations. I do not know whether it is impotence or modesty which prevents them from involving their psyches in their music, but it is clear that they remain apart from it, detached. It is not surprising then, that almost without exception experimental music lacks vitality and interest and tends to weary and frustrate the listener rather than reward him for his effort. Aural facts by themselves have only momentary value. New sounds *do* pique one's curiosity, but once heard they are no longer new; something else must emerge to sustain one's interest. A successive series of shapeless events made up only of aural facts is not a work of art. It lacks the shaping power and the heat of the crucible of the human imagination.

In order to compose, to create aural fiction, sounds and their movement must be internalized. They must happen inside the composer's mind and take fire from his imagination. The form into which they are ultimately cast will be the form which the listener will perceive once he has grasped it in its entirety. The vitality, energy, subtlety, force, serenity, and passion that the composer injects into his work, all these qualities belong to the aural fiction he is creating and help to generate the alchemical transformation of sounds into music. Aural fiction is inconceivable without a syntax of relationships embracing the external world of sound and the internal world of man, the field of aural phenomena and the field of human forces.

The deepest level of the creation of aural fiction is that level where the making of the art work, the shaping of the musical composition, invokes the field of human forces—emotional and mental—and involves the creation of illusions. These illusions, though magical and immaterial, are nevertheless *real*. They can be felt—intensely so—but they cannot be measured or quantified. They are the "pure subjectivities" of music. Every real composer is master of them. The creation of these illusions supersedes style and language; long after style and language have been historically supplanted, these aural illusions, these pure subjectivities, continue to exert their fascination.

Since a full-scale discussion of these aural illusions would comprise a course in composition itself, I can only mention here those which I feel are absolutely basic. At the same time, I shall try to indicate their power and influence in the process of making the artwork. There are four essential aural illusions: the illusions of continuity, of growth, of aural depth, and of musical space. While I speak of them as though they were separate and distinct from each other, I want to make clear that in the process of composition itself they are interrelated and interdependent. Whatever happens in one affects all the others. Their mutual interaction is constant.

The most difficult problem for the composer is to create a continuous, unfolding succession of musical events which is varied yet unified, constantly changing its character and quality, yet coherent. If music were physical (like architecture for example) the continuity of events would be to a certain extent guaranteed by their spatial deployment. But music is, as someone has said, "drawing in air," constantly vanishing the moment it is traced. Only the memory can retain the shape and sense of the motion of events and the way they follow each other. To create the illusion of continuity, therefore, the composer must master the shaping of the individual phrase, the linking of chains of phrases which seem to open and close, the articulation of series of these phrase chains into larger units—until ultimately the form of the work has emerged into an organic whole which we perceive as a total unit, "all of a piece." The problem of creating this illusion of continuity is intensified by the necessity to create, at the same time, the illusion of growth—the sense that the substance of the musical discourse is pulsing with inner life, extending itself here, dissolving there; starting off again in a new direction, expanding and intensifying only to be interrupted by a new element; or going on to spread itself in a climactic flood of sound. Each action and reaction requires the utmost skill and control on the part of the composer. The growth of the work, in the sense I am describing here, traces the emotional curve of the work, its psychological trajectory, which influences and is influenced by the continuously unraveling chain of local events. The use of juxtaposition and discontinuity, to which I referred earlier, is an expansion of the possibilities of continuity and growth. The juxtaposition of opposites—of discontinuous emotional gestures for example—is as much a part of the growth process and of continuity as the predictable chain of similar gestures. The illusions of continuity and growth belong to the fantasy world of the human mind, the heart, and the psyche; they partake of the dream life where juxtaposition and discontinuity are the rule. If there are, indeed, models of continuity and growth in the natural world, they long ago implanted themselves in the human brain which is (perhaps as a result of millenia of human experience) itself a model of the world as human beings know it. The creation of the illusion of continuity and growth in music is deeply rooted in our subjective relation to motion and time, to human existence itself.

The illusion of aural depth involves the interior structure of musical configurations in which layers of sound are imagined and heard in a kind of aural perspective. Every configuration has its mass or density but, depending on whether it is composed of only one unified layer of sound or two or more differently articulated moving layers of sound, the sense of aural depth will be sensed as flat or deep. We can speak of aural depth only by analogy with space; nevertheless our experience confirms its presence and validity in the process of composition and the perception of music. Some configurations of sound are opaque, thick, achieving maximum density; others are transparent. Sometimes we feel the force of gravity exerting itself on the music, producing a sense of weight and ponderousness; other times we feel the suspension of this force which results in a feeling of weightlessness.

The creation of the illusion of aural depth not only receives powerful influences from the process of growth and continuity but also influences in its turn the most remarkable (for me) of all aural illusions—the illusion of musical space. In the twentieth century, the opening up and penetration into this region of the musical imagination has created the possibility of new configurations of musical sound and has profoundly affected the process of continuity and growth. A total preoccupation with creating the illusion of musical space is constricting to the composer, chiefly because it tends toward immobilizing the flow of time and stabilizing the growth process. But if the composer recognizes that it is an expansion of the range of aural illusions, he commands a new and powerful resource. All of these aural illusions—of continuity, growth, aural depth, and musical space—belong to the field of forces which are at the direct disposal of the composer because they are rooted in his mental and emotional structure. They are his to command once he discovers their existence and can exercise their use with discipline, control, and imagination.

The fate of contemporary music depends to a great extent on its ability to rid itself of the nihilistic, neo-dada aspects of abstractionism, to transform the new facts of contemporary musical experience into new fictions. This can happen only if the contemporary composer wins his battle with abstractionism by converting its negative tendencies into positive ones, only if he is able to create new, organic contexts in which the aural illusions which go to make up aural fiction are raised to levels where the making of the artwork (itself a kind of dreamwork) becomes simultaneously the making of magic.

The Fantastic and the Logical:
Reflections on Science, Politics, and Art

The dilemma confronting us at present demands careful and close examination leading (one hopes) to accurate diagnoses of problems, their sources and causes. A tall order, to be sure, and one to which I address myself with some trepidation, hoping more to be able to suggest rather than prescribe ways out of our dilemma.

What I want to show is that while we may be (and undoubtedly are) the immediate agents of our own distress, our dilemma has been compounded by the fact that those potentially fatal flaws in our own nature are the result of an incomplete or as yet uncompleted process of evolution and development; that we must include both our flawed and uncompleted nature in our considerations, difficult though that may be; and that we can only hope for amelioration of our distress by ever-increasing acts of self-awareness and, therefore, responsibility. This is true, I believe, even if it turns out that amelioration lies in some remote future where self-transformation has finally achieved a measure of reality—or, at the very worst, that amelioration is ultimately not possible because we lack sufficient self-knowledge and capacity to effect such transformation. I believe it is, in the immediate present at least, possible to begin by tracing out basic errors in preferred thought patterns and basic misreadings of the nature of man himself, particularly as these misreadings relate to the possible limits of his relation to his physical environment, his expectations and uses of consciousness and perception, and his purposes and functions in the cosmic scheme of things.

A useful metaphor here is T. S. Kuhn's *paradigm in crisis*, i.e., the process by which science transforms itself from one state of mind to another, a process which amounts to a revolution or reconstruction of goals and methods. Since we need no less than a revolution in our approach to human existence, it will be helpful to consider Kuhn's notions to see to what extent they can help us measure the nature of our own existential crisis.

> The transition from a paradigm in crisis to a new one from which a new tradition of normal science can emerge is far from a cumulative process, one achieved by an articulation or extension of the old paradigm. Rather it is a reconstruction of the field from new fundamentals, a reconstruction that changes some of the field's most elementary theoretical general-

izations as well as many of its paradigm methods and applications. . . . When the transition is complete, the profession will have changed its view of the field, its methods, and its goals. (*The Structure of Scientific Revolutions* [Chicago: University of Chicago Press, 1970], pp. 84–85)

The reasons for paradigm change which are of primary importance, both in the story Kuhn is telling of how science transforms itself and matures and in my metaphor, are essentially rooted in the concept of *anomaly*. An anomalous situation arises when "new and unsuspected phenomena" emerge to confront the normal process of research for the scientist, or the normal process of conducting his economic, political, and cultural affairs for man in general.

Anomaly, then, emerges in the form of internal contradictions of the governing paradigm, contradictions which build up internal pressure and eventually demand change and transformation.

But anomaly is not a bloodless, cerebral matter. It demands its price. For the scientist it creates growing crisis at the heart of his view of science. As Kuhn remarks:

The emergence of new theories is generally preceded by a period of pronounced professional insecurity. As one might expect, that insecurity is generated by the persistent failure of the puzzles of normal science to come out as they should. Failure of existing rules is the prelude to a search for new ones. (Pp. 67–68)

For man it creates growing crisis *in all departments of existence*. The anomalies which threaten life itself, and which have grown before our very eyes to gigantic proportions, are well known. We need only think of the energy crisis, the ecological crisis, the economic crisis, or the inner-city crisis to realize how mired in hopeless confusion and potential and real suffering American society is at this very moment, and to recognize that these interrelated crises flow from a paradigm or paradigms which no longer fit the needs of people or contemporary conditions.

Kuhn's remark, "failure of existing rules is the prelude to a search for new ones" (p. 68), fits the case absolutely. Answering his own question "Why should a change of paradigm be called a revolution?" (p. 92) Kuhn develops a parallelism between political and scientific revolution. It is my belief that the parallelism can be extended to include an even more fundamental, far-reaching revolution in modes of thought about how man should exist, what he is and can be, and what his relation to himself and the cosmos ought to be and can become.

To continue with Kuhn,

Political revolutions are inaugurated by the growing sense . . . that existing institutions have ceased adequately to meet the problems posed by an environment that they have in part created. In much the same way, scientific revolutions are inaugurated by a growing sense . . . that an existing paradigm has ceased to function adequately in the exploration of an aspect of nature to which that paradigm itself had previously led the way. In both political and scientific development the sense of malfunction that can lead to crisis is prerequisite to revolution." (P. 92)

Drawing the "genetic parallel," as he calls it, Kuhn further states:

Political revolutions aim to change political institutions in ways that those institutions themselves prohibit. Their success therefore necessitates the partial relinquishment of one set of institutions in favor of another, and in the interim, society is not fully governed by institutions at all. Initially it is crisis alone that attenuates the role of political institutions as we have already seen it attenuate the role of paradigms. In increasing numbers individuals become increasingly estranged from political life and behave more and more eccentrically within it. Then, as the crisis deepens, many of these individuals commit themselves to some concrete proposal for the reconstruction of society in a new institutional framework. At that point the society is divided into competing camps or parties, one seeking to defend the old institutional constellation, the others seeking to institute some new one. And once that polarization has occurred, *political recourse fails*. Because they differ about the institutional matrix within which political change is to be achieved and evaluated, because they acknowledge no supra-institutional framework for the adjudication of revolutionary difference, the parties to a revolutionary conflict must finally resort to the techniques of mass persuasion, often including force. (P. 93)

Tightening the parallel significantly one more notch, Kuhn goes on to say:

Like the choice between competing political institutions, that between competing paradigms proves to be a choice between incompatible modes of community life. Because it has that character, the choice is not and cannot be determined merely by the evaluative procedures characteristic of normal science, for these depend in part upon a particular paradigm, and that paradigm is at issue. When paradigms enter, as they must, into a debate about paradigm choice, their role is necessarily circular. Each group uses its own paradigm to argue in that paradigm's defence." (P. 94)

At this point it has to be said that in the case of both political and scientific revolutions, as seen from Kuhn's point of view, it is the search for truth, or a particular localized truth, which emerges to challenge existing rules and patterns of procedure; one must affirm at the very least the efficacy and validity of this search in the affairs of men—however mistaken events may prove them to have been, or however inadequate their ideas turn out to be in the face of problems newly emerging from the very inadequacy itself. The sole exception in the realm of political life to this search for truth, i.e., efficacy in society's self-ordering and self-regulating its daily existence as related to political institutions and the laws by which society maintains itself and its individual members— and for me a very great exception, in fact, *the* great exception—is the search for power, a deadly game which still exerts its fateful attraction over mankind. We all know Lord Acton's famous dictum which equates power with corruption; it need only be added for emphasis that the process of exercising such power necessarily involves the perversion and subversion of the "general good" all the while justifying and rationalizing such acts in the name of that same "general good." Whether or not power emerges from a real crisis or a fabricated one makes little or no difference to how such power eventually imposes itself. It may reaffirm an old political paradigm, i.e., claim to be saving "The System" at the very moment it subverts it, or it may ruthlessly replace the old one with a new one in the name of saving "The People." Either way all areas of existence are eventually affected by the new rules flowing from the paradigm which governs the power structure—some obviously more than others. Since I am referring in a general way to the basic twentieth-century experience of European (and now American) political life, we will have to contend with it as potentially a basic flaw in man's nature, as we attempt to suggest directions and possibilities for more adequate paradigms to govern men's behavior toward each other and to their common existence.

In addition to our awareness of this flaw in man's nature, which emerges as the search for raw power and necessarily results in corruption, perversion, manipulation, and acts of repression and violence, there is another important distinction which has to be made in regard to Kuhn's parallelism of political and scientific revolution. Scientific paradigms may transform themselves from one view of the world to another, resulting in new possibilities of research methods and goals, problems and solutions. But they transform only the men who claim them and not the phenomena themselves. By that I mean that the subject of science, which is the cosmos itself and all it contains which is perceptible to man, his senses, and his instruments, remains beyond the reach of science per se since it is the primary given which includes human existence. More than that, man in his present form appears to be a possibly miniscule aspect of that mysteriously created given. However large he may loom in his own egocentric eyes, he remains only a small part of a still unknown and possibly unimaginable universe. This too must be taken into account when attempting to develop new paradigms for his future development and direction. The notion of man as a godlike creature, which has arisen today with the new genetics, may only be a newer and more recent version of hubris—tempt-ing the Fates—and not truly representative of the scientific community in general, which seeks understanding and insight into the cosmos rather than domination over its mysteries. If the subject of science is the given universe, of which man finds himself only a fractional or partial aspect—or, put another way, if man is himself a creation of the very same universe he seeks to under-stand—the subject of politics is society, which is man's own creation though still biologically rooted. Between the two is an incalculable difference not to be set aside or overlooked for the sake of a neat, verbally packaged parallelism. I grant that this does not alter the "genetic" nature of paradigm change (as Kuhn calls it), since in both instances the parallelism he attempts to elucidate deals with a mental process of man rather than the subject matters of science and politics. But this only allows us a further insight into the difference be-tween the two subject matters. Science, however crisis-ridden it may be with respect to a traditional paradigm, is always in relation to something beyond and outside itself—the created universe; whereas politics, whether stable or unstable, is always in relation to man himself and has no external referent except the idea of "the State" which is not a reality but an abstraction. And even if we accord the idea of "the State" a measure of reality in the sense that once established it undoubtedly affects the lives of individuals, "the State" is simply another way of looking at man; thus we are locked into a tautology. If the subject matter of science is the cosmos and the subject matter of politics is man, we have no difficulty in recognizing the objective nature of the former and the subjective nature of the latter. This distinction is of paramount impor-tance for it is my belief that it is the objective nature of science which has allowed it to succeed and the subjective nature of politics which constantly produces failure and disaster.

At this point I should now like to introduce the idea of art and, by considering its subject matter, draw the comparison I have been making even more finely. Art is the single human activity which manages to combine the objectivity of science with the subjectivity of politics. The objectivity of art springs from the ordering of individual perceptions projected toward something beyond the individual. That something must necessarily be the artwork itself, which at-tains a level of reality by becoming a given for study and perception by others not involved in its making. The ordering of perceptions by the artist is not only itself ultimately an objective act leading beyond himself, but is at the same time an ordering of selected effects which spring from perceptual awareness, link-ing the central nervous system of the artist to the universe which has endowed him with his senses. The subjective aspect of art arises from the peculiarly unique windows of perception with which the artist is endowed and his ability to transform private and personal experience of existence into an imaginative structure fixed in some degree of permanence. The act of making art becomes the transformation of the private into the public, of the subjective into the objective, of vague or sharp personal sense impressions, reactions, responses into clarified forms which touch the universal.

As with politics and science, art itself undergoes its style or paradigm crises, and among the various crises I mentioned earlier which affect our material existence we must now also count a crisis in art which affects our mental-perceptual existence. Whether art can also transform itself by discovering a new and healthier basis from which to proceed is directly tied to the larger question I am addressing: can man find a way out of his present confusion, can he find the way to transform himself by discovering a new paradigm or paradigms for existence?

This sketch of the comparison among art, politics, and science requires one more important distinction to be made, this between science and art. There have been many efforts recently to find the ways in which both art and science relate to each other. They are, when at their best, both instances of supreme acts of imagination. The "new and unsuspected phenomena" which Kuhn rightly points out occur in science and have their counterparts in art as well. That both science and art are fundamental creative acts carried out by individuals is the clearest link between them as manifestations of human mental/spiritual capacity. Where they differ, however, they differ, in my opinion, widely and fundamentally. For science must perpetually contend with the refractory nature of the universe which does not give up its secrets easily. The universe is the objective, given reality which would be there were we here or not.

Kuhn's point about paradigm change in scientific evolution underlies the fact that—whether science operates cumulatively or not—science attempts to produce an increasingly inclusive, accurate, and verifiable picture of natural phenomena; where any aspect of that picture must give way to a truer, more inclusive, or more refined way of understanding natural phenomena, to that extent science is engaged in proof and demonstration of theories and hypotheses. Art, on the other hand, simply makes individual statements which cannot be superseded by better ones; art does not progress. Whether an artwork lives into some form of posterity or dies in the shadows of oblivion, it in no way attempts to prove or demonstrate a prior, communally accepted theory or hypothesis. When art does attempt such a posture—which unfortunately is characteristic of some of today's art and therefore a sign of the confusion among its practitioners—it is no longer art but a form of manufacture, or a pseudoscience. I want also to emphasize the fact that artworks of different epochs go on living side by side, in contradistinction to science where paradigms succeed as well as supersede each other.

In the sense I am trying to develop here, art becomes a separate reality for (but not from) human perception, in its own way a transformation of human experiences and capacities into objectified (but not quantified) structures. It is man's way of recreating that part of the universe available to his senses; though related to the universe, it is still separate from it. Once born, art simply *is,* just as the cosmos is. Art is, to that degree, man's most concrete way of approaching the reality of his personal response to the cosmos—in my opinion, even more concrete than science—and, though not necessarily superior for that reason, certainly more accessible. Art links man's given senses to the given universe directly and primarily through imagination. Both givens, man's senses and the universe, are aspects of the same unimaginable mystery. *Art is to man as man is to nature:* mirror images which reflect powers and forces which are hidden from material view but manifested in material form. Music may be a way of ordering the same electromagnetic forces that the physicist can only approach indirectly through the subtlest and most refined instruments. Should a physicist be successful in uncovering their secrets, he can perhaps harness them for physical purposes, but he cannot then reorder them into new structures for human perception. This is, as I see it, the essential difference between science and art; they come together again, however, at that point where each in its own way attempts to intensify the objective reality of human existence, to open the doors of perception onto what lies outside of man as well as inside.

In my effort to sketch some aspects of a possible paradigm which could theoretically point a way toward resolution of confusion, a way out of the present cul-de-sac of cultural and societal pathology, I must raise the ghost of Blake's term "the Spectre," which for Blake is the same as an abstract idea. By examining the process by which abstract ideas come about and enslave those who hold to them, I can begin to explore the difference between what I am calling the "fantastic" and the "logical" and how the two manifest themselves in human existence.

Blake believed that most, if not all, of the social and moral ills were the result of the "mind-forg'd manacles" which men impose on themselves and each other, which are the "spectres" of the reasoning, logical, unimaginative mind. Consider the first two stanzas of the first draft of Blake's poem "London":

> I wander thro' each dirty street
> Near where the dirty Thames does flow,
> And mark in every face I meet
> Marks of weakness, marks of woe.
>
> In every cry of every man,
> In every infant's cry of fear,
> In every voice, in every ban,
> The mind-forg'd manacles I hear.

In the name of these abstractions, e.g., the state, the church, men have committed every act of violence imaginable; they have done so with perfect impunity under the rationalized protection of the very abstractions which lead them, in times of crisis, to go out and murder and torture in the name of defending "the state" or "the faith," or commit genocide to retain "racial purity." Whatever the reasons for man's aggressive behavior—genetic, instinctual, or acquired under societal pressure—the link between his seemingly endless passion for killing and his passionate loyalty to abstract ideas raises serious questions about the continued belief in the virtues of a logical approach to the problems of existence, as well as the powers of reason in general. Before leaving this part of my discussion consider these stanzas from another poem of Blake—*Urizen*, chap. 9—which capture poetically and awesomely the state of man locked into the narrowness of rationally blinded perception:

1. Then the Inhabitants of those cities
   Felt their Nerves change into Marrow,
   and hardening Bones began
   In swift diseases and torments,
   In throbbings and shootings and grindings
   Thro' all the coasts; still weaken'd
   The Senses inward rush'd, shrinking
   Beneath the dark net of infection;
2. Till the shrunken eyes, clouded over,
   Discern'd not the woven hipocrisy;
   But the streaky slime in their heavens
   Brought together by narrowing perceptions,
   Appeared transparent air; for their eyes
   Grew small like the eyes of a man,
   And in reptile forms shrinking together,
   of Seven feet stature they remain'd.
3. Six days they shrunk up from existence,
   And on the seventh day they rested,
   And blessed the seventh day, in sick hope,
   And forgot their eternal life.
4. And their 30 cities divided
   In form of a human heart.
   No more could they rise at will
   In the infinite void, but bound down
   To earth by their narrowing perceptions
   They lived a period of years;
   Then left a noisom body
   To the jaws of devouring darkness.

5. And their children wept, and built
   Tombs in the desolate places,
   And form'd laws of prudence
         and call'd them
   The eternal laws of God.

Blake has described here what I call "rational madness." Before I go on to describe this aberrational propensity which is for me synonymous with the idea of abstraction, let me offer two concrete instances of forms of rational madness, the one fictional (from Melville), the other actual. Claggart, Captain Vere's first mate and the natural enemy of Billy Budd, pursues Billy with a fanatic intensity which is certainly obsessional—but the method by which he hopes to bring Billy down is entirely rational, i.e., within his "legal" authority as Billy's superior. My second example is too well known to require discussion at all: I refer to Hitler.

There are, I am sure, those who would prefer simply to think of such creatures as psychologically irrational or perhaps even clinically insane, and spare reason the onus of being linked with their type. But this would be precisely what we must no longer allow ourselves the luxury of doing: namely, to dissociate what we consider to be the glory of man, his rational capacity, from acts of criminal intent, premeditated and carefully executed with a methodical "cool," within an orderliness of procedure that belies its cruel and ruthless ends. (Instead of thinking of man's aggressive nature as an aberrational passion brought on only in the heat of a moment's anger or fear or frustration, it seems to me more realistic, and closer to the record of history, to recognize that collective aggression is most often a matter of careful planning. When the Germans marched on France through Belgium in 1914, they put into operation plans which had been drawn up at least thirty years earlier. One can imagine the plans carefully developed and collated over the years by the military staffs of the United States, the Soviet Union, and China and linked to the greatest potential technological weaponry ever devised, now sitting in files in Washington, Moscow, and Peking.)

My remarks are not intended to derogate the rational capacity of man but to show in a general way the misuse of this capacity when abstracted away from concrete awareness. Since paradoxically, it is the imagination of man which tends toward the concrete and reason which tends toward the abstract, it becomes evident that we need very seriously to undertake an examination of the function of both in human affairs, their interrelationships and their differences, in order to discover a better balance between the two and to begin to recognize that the mass of men have, by experience and education and example, been taught to distrust their imaginative faculties almost completely. This is hardly the place to go into the question of our educational system, but it seems sufficiently clear by now that it is designed to glorify reason and the utilities of reason at the expense of the uses of imagination. This may well be part of the fallout of a society now dominated by a scientific technology and habits of thought, mental paradigms which have developed to a crashing climax over the past four hundred years. If I question the validity of this paradigm, I am doing no more than pointing once again to the evidence on all sides of the wrongheadedness and confusion it has wrought among us, literate and illiterate, educated and uneducated. Those of us who are literate and educated suffer differently from this paradigm and its consequences than those less fortunate; though there is no doubt the latter suffer the physical consequences just as fully, if not in fact more. Let me give you an example of what I mean.

The biologist Jacques Monod in his book, *Chance or Necessity* (New York: Alfred A. Knopf, 1971), attributes the distress of the present day to the conflict between what he calls an ancient animist tradition (which still hangs on stubbornly) and the logic of science. He maintains it is the incompatibility of the two world views which has induced much of the trouble; and therefore he proposes a solution which rests on what he calls "an ethic of knowledge," a body of ideas which, apparently drawn from areas of logic and science, strips man of any nonsense that the world is governed by a God or Creative Spirit or Prime Mover, leaving man alone in the universe to deal with himself and his problems only through the austerity of logic and abstraction. Clearly Monod is on the side of the logical rather than the fantastic and would remove the latter from human consideration entirely. Because he attributes the success of science to the powers of reason primarily, he assumes (erroneously as far as I'm concerned) that reason can be successfully applied to man's other problems. However, reason is not in my view a sufficient power with which to guide human endeavors; and the history of recent years suggests that when it is made the sole basis for human behavior it proves to be a dangerous power. Under improper motivation—improper because oriented toward gain in power, money, control, or domination, or toward buttressing loyalties based on abstractions—"reason" turns into arrogance, legalized "morality," suppression of human rights, criminality in the name of this or that high and noble purpose, over and over again. Even to argue, as I anticipate, that obviously I am not talking about that "reason" which leads not to truth and balanced assessments and evaluations, but to its perversion into pure rationalization is to ignore the limitations and insufficiencies of the whole of rational power—which is only one part of the mind and may turn out to be the smaller part at that. The safeguards against the abuses of reason do not lie in better reasoning, but in balancing reason with what I call the fantastic.

I believe we are ready now to consider more fully what I mean by the fantastic. There is sufficient anthropological and archaeological evidence to indicate that ancient man—I am referring to such widely separate studies as carried on by Mircea Éliade in the mythologies of the ancient Near East and Alexander Marshak in the symbolic notational systems of men twenty to forty thousand years ago—viewed the world in ways which must strike a modern as nonrational and fantastic (though not without their own peculiar logic). Primarily we are dealing with the sources of whatever animist traditions the modern world inherited in the more attenuated, even dessicated forms provided by the Judeo-Christian tradition. While on the one hand it is possible to believe with Monod that peopling the world with spirits, gods, and ghosts represents a form of primitive, mythopoeic mentality and leads away from a true grasp of the realities facing man, it is equally possible on the other hand to consider that animism is an imaginative function at root which creates symbols, images, and metaphors for forces intuited as greater than man, forces to which man is subject and must therefore propitiate somehow. Animism of this kind still lives on the highest possible imaginative plane in the work of William Blake who, in his *Prophetic Books*, invented his own mythology of cosmic creatures through whom man worked out his destiny. Animism of a newer variety lives in the science fiction and science fantasy of our own day, which projects on the cosmic screen incredible spirits and creatures often more intelligent and advanced than man—again through whom man will work out his destiny, win or lose. (The most amazing and, in a way, shattering of these tales may well be Arthur Clarke's *Childhood's End*, in which we see the final destiny of our variety of homo sapiens accomplished through a transformation which possibly even the ancients might have thought somewhat fantastic and bizarre; then again I'm not too sure that they couldn't have fit it into their systems without too much discomfort.)

By taking a closer look at an example of animism, I believe we can get still closer to my idea of the fantastic and its deep relation to man. It appears that among the Sumerians and the Mesopotamians generally, the world view held that "man's relation to the gods and the cosmos was that of obedient servant. Man was created purposefully to toil for and propitiate the gods in order to maintain harmony between earth and the universe."[1] (This view, incidentally, was also that of the ancient Vietnamese as reported by Frances FitzGerald in her book *Fire in the Lake* [Boston: Little, Brown, and Co., 1972].) "In cultivating the land,' man produced food not only for his own survival but also for the 'care and feeding' of the gods. The king was elevated above the rest of mankind in the sense that he was the useful mortal charged with the task of leading mankind in its servitude."[2] This view is corroborated by one of the authorities Rochberg-Halton quotes, Speiser, who says, "The outstanding feature of kingship in ancient Mesopotamia is the ruler's subservience to the gods throughout the long recorded history of that composite civilization."[3]

If we refract these ideas current in the ancient Near East through the terminology of our own day, what do we see? First of all, a recognition that man is not alone in the world he inhabits. Secondly, that the forces he designates as gods are more powerful than he is. On this particular point, it is worth mentioning that the Sumerians recognized forces even higher than the gods, that the gods were, in turn, responsible to these forces higher than themselves (not unlike the Overlords in Clarke's *Childhood's End* who recognize higher beings in the cosmic hierarchy). Just as man's responsibility was to the gods, the gods were responsible to cosmic law or *Kittum*. (On the stele containing Hammurabi's code of law there is an image of the god Shamash handing the *Kittum* or cosmic law to Hammurabi.) Thirdly, that man is not only the "obedient servant" who cares for and feeds the gods; he is also responsible for the earth, his home, and is, therefore, in a sense its custodian and caretaker. Fourthly, that as chief custodian of the planet earth he also has the additional responsibility of maintaining harmony between the planet earth and the universe, presumably the solar system. Even if this latter responsibility seems, at first glance, implausible to us who have been the first to land on the moon, on second thought it gains in plausibility precisely because we *have* been to the moon and now have a glimmer of the local nature of our satellite and sister planets—and if there is no intelligent life on any of these who, then, *is* responsible for the harmony between man's home and his immediate cosmic neighborhood?

Viewed from this angle suddenly one gains enormous respect for those "primitive" Sumerians who laid it down as fundamental that man, the humble, obedient toiling creation of the gods, was ecologically responsible, that man had a place and function in the cosmic scheme of things and, at that, a very important place and function. Compared with the hubristic arrogance of modern man, endowed with his incredible science and technology, the ancient Sumerians strike me as men of enormous wisdom, a wisdom we lost along the way and must now regain if we are to maintain not the gods, or even harmony between earth and the cosmos, but simply a toehold on our traditional birthplace.

Frankly, the vision of a polluted, exploited earth is only a magnified picture of the ruination of any of our large inner cities, many of which (e.g., Newark, Washington, etc.) look more as if they were ravaged by war than by slow deterioration and neglect, misuse and unconcern. If a civilization based on logic and abstraction, science and technology, and hypocritical religious mouthings results in what we see daily around us in the physical decay of our own cities—the places where we live and work—then I can only conclude that there is something dreadfully wrong with the mental paradigm (or interrelated paradigms) of a civilization which is bent on its own destruction, which even now, when the evidence of that destruction is incontrovertible, rationalizes its own position in a ridiculous posture of self-defense as though *it* were more important than the species man or the planet earth. In this we see the spectacle of an ultimate abstraction which can only end in disaster and death. Perhaps we need a revitalized animism, a new sense of the fantastic, in order to offset and correct the mad course we seem locked into, an animism which once again places us in relation to higher and more potent forces, an animism which offers us a valid place and function in the cosmic scheme and opens us up to a larger perspective of life—one which discovers the fine, but absolutely essential, balance and integration of the within and the without, the subjective and the objective, the imaginative and the rational.

The cornerstone of the new paradigm I am suggesting is the fantastic nature of man himself. All ancient cultures of the old and new worlds of the West—the Near East, the Egyptians, the Greeks, the Mayans, the Toltecs—believed that man was the creation of a God or gods, that man was a creature of the cosmos, that his origins partook of powers beyond the merely physical. Even the Old Testament, the most recent collation of ancient lore whose origins cannot be traced, speaks of God fashioning man in his own image. In the centuries which led finally to the dawn of science these beliefs grew paler and thinner until they were more mythic memories than active beliefs. Darwin's theory of evolution replaced even these pale memories (in the form of myths and religious dogma) with a different kind of story, fantastic in its own way, to be sure, but of an entirely different category, more in the nature of a biography of a physical process which necessarily leaves out the unverifiable derivation of man from divine or cosmic sources. I should like you now to consider the possibility that the apparent logic of Darwin's theory is simply the rational side of the ancient belief in cosmic origins from which man derives his fantastic nature.

It is now a paradigm of physics that the cosmos is held together by electromagnetic forces of which gravitation is one manifestation. Recently it has been discovered that each human being carries with him his own electromagnetic field. Research into areas of ESP and psychokinesis has led to photographing the electromagnetic aura which human beings give off. Even more startling is one of the discoveries of biofeedback studies: namely, that the alpha, beta, delta, and theta waves which the human brain produces under certain conditions, ranging from active thinking to various stages of quiescence finally leading to sleep, correspond directly with the electromagnetic field waves of solar system origin and probably beyond.

With the aid of modern physics, which itself is increasingly concerned with the fantastic, I am convinced we can reaffirm the ancient belief in the cosmic origins of man: Man is a walking, thinking, breathing, feeling, self-aware piece of the cosmos. He is indeed fantastic because, mysterious creature that he is, he is the child of even more mysterious forces. Each of us is a conscious piece of earth reflecting on itself and capable of reflecting on each other. Even more, the forces of gravity which hold the solar system and undoubtedly all cosmic bodies in mutual relation and union are translated into human terms, psychological, physiological, and biological, in the mysteries of love and sex.

The creation of man—the earth's supremely aware creature endowed with consciousness—is nature's way of achieving self-awareness, nature's way of opening up through evolutionary processes increasing areas of perception of her own world, which moves in concentric circles outward to embrace the solar system and beyond to the stars.

When we speak or sing, we are giving voice to nature's urge to communicate and express. When we paint or sculpt, we are giving concrete form to nature's urge to see herself in transformed structures. When we move in time and space, we are giving expression to nature's urge for greater mobility. When we think and give structure to our thoughts in written form, we become nature's scribes, recording events and memories so that the urge of our species toward ever-greater clarity and understanding can be achieved in order that nature may someday realize herself through us. The central nervous system and its incredibly subtle, interrelated perceptual capacities—all of which are windows and approaches onto the cosmos—is nature's circuitry printed on human minds which we use but do not fully comprehend as yet.

Consciousness, therefore, is a total ensemble, an interface between the world of internal perception and the world of external phenomena. Consciousness is not definable by the rational capacity alone, which is only one aspect of the total ensemble whose ultimate mystery is memory. I suspect that the rational capacity is nature's way of providing human consciousness with a clearinghouse, a traffic control center, an engineering mechanism devoted to seeing that things get done in a reasonably orderly fashion. But if the rational capacity is consciousness' manager, the specific channel through which consciousness flows outward, it does not follow that the rational is more significant or important than all the other aspects of mind—which must include intuition, ESP in its many facets, the dream life of the sleeping state as well as the daydream life of the waking state, memory, and what we call "imagination" (which I suspect is a transformed state of some or all of the aspects I've just enumerated). The work of the imagination is always specific and concrete and its possession is not restricted to the artist alone. When the imagination is at work (and everyone who has used his imagination to produce work—artistic, scientific, or otherwise—will confirm this, I'm sure), it makes maximum use of our rational powers, because these are the powers which produce structure, order, and relationships. But it is the imagination which supplies the substance to be given structure and shape. The danger to which I have already alluded, of believing only in the power of reason, is that reason has a propensity to order that leads away from the concrete to the abstract and can only be brought to heel by the imagination, which ensures the balance and presence of living concreteness.

We have reached that point in our evolution where our very survival as a species is in question. The crisis which has brought us to this state will be resolved one way or the other, and, if self-transformation is the only road to survival, we must begin to construct the elements of a new paradigm which will ensure that process of self-transformation.

The principle of the conversion of energy into matter and back again to energy is well established. Blake's "Energy is eternal Delight" is an earlier, poetic intuition of that physical law. Somewhere between the two—the physical principle and the poetic intuition—the human imagination coupled with its powers of reason must take hold and attempt the fantastic task of self-transformation. The hunger for self-transformation already exists among the young people of our time. Even though the forms that hunger takes sometimes strike me as misguided, the need is there; it is felt intensely, and it cries out for realization and resolution. I do not believe that the transformation is an overnight affair, to be accomplished in a single generation. It will take tremendous and consistent effort to carry out the process of becoming more fully human; it is one of man's blessings that once he is clear about what needs to be done, he is capable of marshaling the energy which the task requires. The fantastic nature of man needs first to be recognized as such; then (hopefully) it will be able to release itself completely from the bind of its current crisis and make its place and function in the cosmos secure and productive once again—productive of that complex materiality which it needs for physical survival but, more important, productive of that nonutilitarian complex of the products of consciousness without which man cannot be what nature intended. For, in the end, there may be no visible purpose to life at all if viewed only from the side of the cosmos; nevertheless, viewed from the side of the cosmos man is part of an incredible, unimaginable structure which I believe he was created to come to know, understand as best he can, and serve—and which, as fantastic as it may seem, may serve man in ways yet to be discovered, in ways yet to emerge to man's consciousness.

NOTES

1. Francesca Rochberg-Halton, "Deification of Kings in Mesopotamia," manuscript, 1974.
2. Ibid.
3. E. A. Speiser, "Authority and Law in Mesopotamia," in *Oriental and Biblical Studies: Collected Writings of E. A. Speiser,* ed. J. J. Finkelstein and Moshe Greenberg (Philadelphia: University of Pennsylvania Press, 1967), pp. 313–23.

The Marvelous in Art

*To make the external internal, the internal external, to make nature
thought and thought nature . . . body is but a striving to become mind.*
                                                                —Coleridge[1]

*Thus the chemical student is taught not to be startled at disquisitions on
the heat in ice.*
                                                                —Coleridge[2]

In his novel, *Fifth Business,* Robertson Davies asks:

> Why do people all over the world, and at all times, want marvels that
> defy all verifiable facts? And are the marvels brought into being by their
> desire, or is their desire an assurance rising from some deep knowledge,
> not to be directly experienced and questioned, that the marvelous is
> indeed an aspect of the real?[3]

Josef Pieper, the contemporary German philosopher, quotes Thomas
Aquinas in his essay, "The Philosophical Act": "The reason . . . why the
philosopher may be likened to the poet is this: both are concerned with the
marvellous."[4] Pieper wonders at (i.e., philosophizes) the nature of man's
capacity to wonder, to marvel. With Aquinas, he attributes this capacity to
the reason that "because man's mind is ordained to knowledge of the first
cause of the world [God], he [man] is capable of wonder."[5] He finds further
corroboration of the relation of the poet and the philosopher to the marvelous and the capacity to wonder in a poem of Goethe's seventieth year, where
Goethe says, "Zum Erstaunen bin ich da" ("I am here to marvel"), and also
in a remark recorded by Eckermann ten years later, where the poet says,
"The very summit of man's attainment is the capacity to marvel."[6] Pieper is
careful to distinguish the "enormous, sensational things" of this world from
the world of the marvelous, and remarks of the former, "that is what a
dulled sensibility requires to provoke it to a sort of *ersatz* experience of wonder."[7] For Pieper the real experience of wonder acts upon a man like a
shock, shaking and moving him to a state in which the newly awakened
awareness of living in the incomprehensible becomes the cause and focus of
his wonder. In a fully awakened state, such a man could say with Goethe, "I
am here to marvel."

But it is not only the poet and philosopher—and we may add the composer, the sculptor, the painter as well as the architect and the scientist—but also "people all over the world, and at all times" who desire the marvelous, whether it is "brought into being by their desire," or their desire is "an assurance rising from some deep knowledge, not to be directly experienced or questioned, that the marvelous is indeed an aspect of the real."

When the architect Louis Kahn used to talk about "measuring the immeasurable," he set for us all a philosophic conundrum which can only be unraveled not by posing another similar conundrum like "comprehending the incomprehensible," but by translating the word *measuring* into an act of desire whose profound intent has the sole purpose of reaching over, through the imagination, to some as yet unknown portion or aspect of the marvelous—that which is immeasurable and imponderable because creatively limitless in form—and representing it in a newly fashioned, finite image. To penetrate through consciously willed perception—the act of imagination—into the realm of "the real" (of which the marvelous is an aspect) is a qualitative act of "measuring" which is the only way open to the artist. The energy which fuels and drives the artist's quest to raid the infinite, to wrest from it one of its secrets, to know a little more of the unknowable, is his desire to bring into living actuality in finite form something of the world of the marvelous, the world of the real. Even the scientist who quantitatively "measures" the phenomena of the created world cannot be denied the qualitative side, the imaginative side, of his equally powerful urge to measure the immeasurable, to discover the root structure of material and mental reality through means other than those the artist employs.

In trying to guess what people—the art public if you will—want, or expect from art, I don't think it is too farfetched to suggest rather strongly that what they want is the same thing the artist or the scientist wants: to experience the world of the marvelous, grasp if they can, if only for the briefest moment, something of the real. That, I believe, is what draws and pulls them to the experience of art, because in art they sense that behind and beyond the immediacy and finiteness of any given work or series of works lies a still larger realm; through the direct experience of the artwork, they intuit that they may be put in touch with that larger realm, the desire for which haunts them all their lives as an indefinable yet palpable hunger. Art mediates between their desire, their hunger, and the experience desired, the experience hungered for. Their desire and hunger exist as an inner emptiness which cannot be and is not satisfied by the daily round of existence. They long, in varying degrees of intensity, for authenticity of being, for that sense of ontological fullness of life. In their experience of art, they seek not only self-transcendence but corroboration, through the artist's vision, of the possibility of leaving behind the crushing literalness of the world of modern society, which presses in on them from all sides daily, and of opening themselves to the reality which art mysteriously channels into their lives.

In rejecting the literalness of their lives (all too occasionally perhaps), people are acting out that to which the artist devotes himself almost exclusively: the search for larger meaning through training of the powers of perception and sensibility, the effort to gain entry into that world of the marvelous, the reality which lies beyond the scrim of routine existence (yet which, at the same time, infuses that routine existence with its essence)—if only we are not deadened to it by accepting the counterfeit coin of the literal as "real."

The world of the literal is a world from which perception has fled. It is the circumscribed world of the factual—the world of routine, of business, of taxes, of governmental bureaus, of corporate law, of political polls, of media polls, of statistics, of body counts. It is the shriveled, starved product of centuries of the Cartesian duality which separates mind from matter and reduces the power of reason to its lowest form of usage and operation. It is Blake's world of the "Spectre" and the "mind-forg'd manacles." The idolatry of the world of the literal is the Cartesian wedge which modern man has allowed to separate imagination from thought, thought from feeling, and feeling from being. The literal arises when we see an "object" as separate from and unconnected with other objects. It derives from the process which converts human beings other than ourselves into manipulable objects and therefore—by the same token— ourselves into objects manipulable by others. The literal denies that, though a tree, a star, a stone, a plant, a man, a woman are outwardly separate from each other, they are inwardly made of the same stuff, infinitesimally small parts of a vast, intricate web of interrelationships which binds them to the whole and to each other.

The marvelous points away from the literal to the imagination which, as Coleridge saw it, is the primal energy that created and sustains the universe. The imagination which informs the world of nature and man is the source and realm of the marvelous, its vital energies streaming through all its "multeity" (Coleridge's term) of forms, yet binding them into oneness and unity.

Music has an ontological intent: to represent the perfection of being. It is this ontological intent which, in saturating the way music projects itself in sound—

in its patterns and designs—we unknowingly (mostly, but sometimes with a clear knowingness) use as the qualitative measure for determining and judging what is called "greatness" in music and in art generally. It is the saturation of his music with ontological intent that makes Bach "great" and the lack of this saturation with ontological intent that makes Stravinsky's music merely "clever." It is the saturation of their music with ontological intent that allows us to hear in Mozart the radiance of pure being and in Beethoven the power of utterance in being.

> *Music is the one corporeal entrance into an incorporeal realm which*
> *comprehends us but which we cannot comprehend.*
> —attributed to Beethoven

"Corporeal" and "incorporeal" stand to each other as flesh to spirit; or matter to mind; or the finite to the infinite. Stated this way, these become fixed, static dichotomies. The key word *entrance* provides the active, dynamic element which converts the frozen state of these dichotomous pairs into a fluid, polar movement of energized passage in two opposite directions. Music, corporeal substance, enters into the incorporeal realm, a realm where the corporeal is dissolved into "spirit" or energy. Something finite has entered the infinite, which is the unimaginable totality (by our knowledge) of all possible finitudes already created by nature and man and those yet to be realized either in nature or man. To say that the incorporeal realm "comprehends us" is to say that the finite is both a part of the infinite and, at the same time, includes the infinite within it. (Otherwise, how could the finiteness of music "enter" the infinitude of the incorporeal?) But to say that "we cannot comprehend" the incorporeal realm is to point to the limitation of our human understanding and senses. How then can we, who are lacking in the means to "comprehend" (i.e., to know directly) the incorporeal realm, make something, like music, which can enter that realm? We do so through the power of imagination, an imagination which, as Owen Barfield describes it, is

> a varying interplay between active and passive elements in the *relation* between self and world, of such a nature that the two elements them- selves may change, the one into the other. Or, we may say, between man and nature. Only, in using those terms, we must remember that the boundary here presumed between man and nature is by no means the currently fancied one. It is not the boundary of a fixed outness. Within *that* schema the only possible mental interaction between active man and passive nature occurs at or within the skin. Whereas the interplay, which is imagination, though it is involved with body and space, is not their creature; and it would be as true to say it occurs in nature as to say that it occurs in man. . . . The life of nature is at all levels a power of "separa-

tive projection" and separative projection ("the eternal act of creation")
is what the act of self-consciousness—what the act of imagination—is.
The underlying reality (sub-stance) of things is thus not matter, nor any
equivalent inanimate base, but immaterial relationship.[8]

Imagination, in the sense Barfield means it, is the "growing point" of mind,
the nonsensory faculty of man, which by projecting itself in sensory, corporeal
form (music) enters the nonsensory world of the spirit which sustains both
mind and matter.

Though they were contemporaries, Coleridge and Beethoven did not know
each other; yet they were both sensible of the relation between the corporeal
and the incorporeal, between human consciousness and world consciousness.
And while I doubt Beethoven knew of Coleridge, it is clear that Coleridge
knew of Beethoven and could find grounds for comparing, in an analogous
way, their mutual experience in making art.

> Music seems to have an *immediate* communion with my Life. . . . It con-
> verses with the *life* of my mind, as if it were itself the Mind of my Life.
> Yet I sometimes think that a great Composer, a Mozart, a Beethoven
> must have been in a state of Spirit much more akin, more analogous to,
> mine own when I am at once waiting for, watching, and organically
> constructing and inwardly constructed by, the *Ideas,* the living Truths,
> that may be reexcited but cannot be expressed by Words, the Transcen-
> dents that give the Objectivity to all Objects, the Form to all Images, yet
> are themselves untranslatable into any Image, unrepresentable by any
> particular object.[9]

In Coleridge's view, imagination was divisible into primary and secondary
levels. Coleridge held

> primary Imagination . . . to be the living Power and prime Agent of all
> human Perception, and as a repetition in the finite mind of the eternal act
> of creation in the infinite I AM. The secondary Imagination [he consid-
> ered to be] an echo of the former, co-existing with the conscious will, yet
> still as identical with the former in the *kind* of its agency, and differing
> only in *degree,* and in the *mode* of its operation.[10]

Coleridge's "primary imagination" is that vital power of the universe
which creates nature *and* man. The reflection of this living power of primary
imagination in man and "co-existing with the conscious will" operates in
man's self-consciousness, in what Coleridge calls "secondary imagination."

The two levels are identical in kind, "differing only in *degree* and in the *mode*" of their operations. Man and nature are thus the products of the same world—imagination—and, as parts of that world, contain in them the living power of their mutual source. Though not identical, they are connected as parts of a whole, therefore one with each other, and one with the whole from which they emanate as distinguishable, separate projections. As I see it, what Beethoven meant, reinterpreted in the light of Coleridge, is that through music, a product of secondary imagination, man enters into the world of primary imagination, the former being the "echo" or "reflection" of the latter. While Beethoven's statement—that there is a higher consciousness which "comprehends us but which we cannot comprehend"—points up sharply the limits of human consciousness, nevertheless it does not deny but may even reinforce the sense of his statement: that we belong to, are a part of, a higher world consciousness which we are unable to experience directly in our present state of development. Beethoven's *aperçu* stands within the range of Coleridge's ideas and Barfield's exigesis of them, just as the entire ensemble of these ideas has startling links to the recently emerging paradigm of the new physics.

Barfield's "immaterial relationship" lies at the heart of the new physics, which has set aside the centuries-old Cartesian duality and division of mind and matter. Fritjof Capra writes in his book, *The Turning Point,* that the conception of the universe held by some of the bolder new physicists comprises two major themes: the one, that the universe is "an interconnected web of relations" and the other, "that the cosmic web is intrinsically dynamic."[11] Quantum mechanics and relativity theory have confirmed each other in presenting a new picture of world phenomena. Subatomic particles

> can no longer be pictured as small billiard balls or small grains of sand. These images are inappropriate not only because they represent particles as separate objects, but also because they are three-dimensional images. Subatomic particles have to be understood dynamically, as forms in space and time . . . as dynamic patterns . . . of activity which have a space aspect and a time aspect. Their space aspect makes them appear as objects with a certain mass, their time aspect as processes involving the equivalent energy. Thus the being of matter and its activity cannot be separated; they are but different aspects of the same space-time reality.[12]

In the 1960s Geoffrey Chew proposed the S-matrix theory, which rests on the idea (as expressed by Capra) that

> nature cannot be reduced to fundamental entities, like fundamental building blocks of matter, but has to be understood entirely through self-

consistency. All of physics has to follow uniquely from the requirement that its components be consistent with one another and with themselves. This idea constitutes a radical departure from the traditional spirit of basic research in physics which had always been bent on finding the fundamental constituents of matter. At the same time it is the culmination of the conception of the material world as an interconnected web of relations that emerged from quantum theory.[13]

Moreover this theory, which rejects the idea that there are "fundamental building blocks of matter," also rejects the idea that there are any "fundamental entities whatsoever."[14] In it, "the universe is seen as a dynamic web of interrelated events. None of the properties of any part of this web is fundamental; they all follow from the properties of the other parts, and the overall consistency of their interrelation determines the structure of the entire web."[15]

The most striking, indeed startling, idea to have come from quantum mechanics is the idea "that the observed patterns of matter are reflections of patterns of mind."[16] As Capra states it, "the fact that all the properties of particles are determined by principles closely related to the methods of observation would mean that the basic structures of the material world are determined, ultimately, by the way we look at this world."[17]

Among the new physicists there are those who believe that "consciousness may be an essential aspect of the universe."[18] This idea is embodied in a recent theory developed by David Bohm "whose starting point is the notion of 'unbroken wholeness.'"[19] Bohm's "aim is to explore the order he believes to be inherent in the cosmic web of relations at a deeper, 'nonmanifest' level." This order, according to Bohm, is "implicate" or "enfolded" in what he calls *holomovement* "out of which all forms of the material universe flow. The aim of his approach is to study the order enfolded in this holomovement, not by dealing with the structure of objects, but rather with the structure of movement, thus taking into account both the unity and dynamic nature of the universe."[20] Bohm has moved a giant step beyond the earlier quantum-mechanics realization, that material phenomena, *as observed,* are affected by the mind of the observer, to the conviction that consciousness is "an essential feature of the holomovement,"[21] and therefore must be taken into account *explicitly* in his theory. According to Capra, Bohm "sees mind and matter as being interdependent and correlated, but not causally connected. *They are mutually enfolding projections of a higher reality which is neither matter nor consciousness* [emphasis added]."[22]

We have come full circle and now find ourselves enclosed ("enfolded," in David Bohm's term) in a web of ideas which all point in the same direction and back again: from the finite to the infinite; from the separate projection of all phenomena to their unity in an interrelationship of oneness; from materiality to immateriality; and from the marvelous, which comes from our sense of wonder, to the real. That Aquinas, Pieper, Kahn, Beethoven, Coleridge, Barfield, Capra, Chew, and Bohm are all talking about the same thing (but in various and different terminologies, from differing points of view, and from perhaps differing purposes) is in itself no small cause for wonder. The past and the present meet in them, as do art, philosophy, and science, in their mutual obsession with the reality which surrounds and sustains us, and in their mutual conviction that this reality is both of itself (while simultaneously interpenetrating the world of nature) and of man (with its power and vital energy). It is at this level that the great art of the past projects itself and needs to be perceived. It is at this same level that the art of the present must also be projected and perceived. Modernism has done little to satisfy the hunger for experience of the marvelous, which is timeless and ahistorical. We stand on the threshold of an epoch which has put Modernism behind it. Whatever the art of this new epoch may be capable of, we can ask nothing better of it than to reveal once again, in new ways and through new images, the realm of the marvelous.

NOTES

1. Owen Barfield, *What Coleridge Thought* (Middletown, Conn.: Wesleyan University Press, 1971), p. 80.
2. Ibid., p. 83.
3. Robertson Davies, *Fifth Business* (New York: Penguin, 1977), p. 199.
4. Josef Pieper, *Leisure: The Basis of Culture* (New York: Random House, 1963), p. 69.
5. Ibid., p. 101.
6. Ibid., p. 100.
7. Ibid.
8. *What Coleridge Thought*, p. 76.
9. Coleridge's Notebook 52, quoted in *What Coleridge Thought*, p. 118.
10. *What Coleridge Thought*, p. 74.
11. Fritjof Capra, *The Turning Point: Science, Society and the Rising Culture* (New York: Simon and Schuster, 1982), p. 87.
12. Ibid., pp. 90–91.
13. Ibid., p. 92.
14. Ibid.
15. Ibid.
16. Ibid., p. 93.
17. Ibid.
18. Ibid., p. 95.
19. Ibid.
20. Ibid., p. 96.
21. Ibid.
22. Ibid.

On the Renewal of Music

- *The Avant-Garde and the Aesthetics of Survival (1969)*

- *Reflections on the Renewal of Music (1972)*

- *On the Third String Quartet (1974)*

The Avant-Garde and the Aesthetics of Survival

It takes some sense of history, however vague or dim, just to utter the term *avant-garde* in relation to the aesthetic and stylistic problems of art. Implicit in the term for me is the handy, if fanciful, image of Zeno's "irreversible arrow of time," and it is generally assumed that the avant-garde either sits on the point of that arrow, penetrating to the next unfolding moment of time, or perhaps even occupies the whole of the arrowhead itself, its sharp cutting edges ending in the point which will tear into the fabric of the future. Before we begin though we are already faced with two irreconcilable paradoxes: first, the shaft of the arrow, though propelling the arrowhead and its point into the future, is itself still in the past and will always remain in some past relative to the position of the arrowhead and its point; and second, the point of the arrow can never, if Zeno is right, reach the future toward which it is presumably traveling, and must therefore remain in a seemingly motionless present, always in transit, never able to reach the future it longs for. Thus every "wave of the future" movement is, at least theoretically, an illusion because the future is always beyond our grasp; nor can it ever be reached except as a new "present." Every "new" movement in the arts (or culture generally) is attached to its history and the past, no matter how much its initiators and supporters would like to disclaim it; in the instance of that part of today's avant-garde, which actively wishes it could cut itself free from any and all ties with past history, memory, or cultural associations, we see the peculiarly pathetic twentieth-century phenomenon of the disaffected human spirit trying desperately to dissociate itself from itself and its own works. Whatever part of time's arrow we travel on—shaft, arrowhead, or point—we are in some relation to the other parts, and the awareness of one position affects our awareness of the others. We can see this readily enough in any number of instances chosen at random from Western culture: for example, the cool, underplayed gestures of Claude Debussy cannot be understood except as a reaction to the overblown, super-sensuous gestures of Wagner; Monteverdi's assertion of a *seconda prattica* requires an understanding of the Neo-Platonism of the Florentine Camerata and the *prima prattica*, reaching back for approximately 150 years, for which Artusi, Monteverdi's reactionary contemporary, was the spokesman; the theory and practice of cubism makes no sense except as viewed in the possible light of Einstein's relativity theory and especially against the long-standing theory and practice of perspective; color field painting, theoretically extending itself in all directions, is a very recent reaction against the much older tradition of the "picture" as an enclosed, graphic projection or representation separated from everything else around it by the limit of the surface on which it is painted; aleatory or indeterminate structure can only be understood as a principle or aesthetic of artistic behavior against the historical background of determinate structure, whether we are thinking of painting or music; and so on. We take the past with us wherever we go, and only cultural provincialism (which is frequently the lens through which enlargement of the present is exaggerated to mammoth proportions, automatically excluding any glimpse of the past) makes it possible—now as in the past—to claim that only that present is pre-eminent and valid, only that present has reality for those living in it, and that all other past "presents" have ceased to exist or have meaning. There is no greater provincialism than that special form of sophistication and arrogance which denies the past, and no greater danger to the human spirit than to proclaim value only for its narrow slice of contemporaneity. One last point on the subject is worth mentioning: if the theory of curved space is correct, the irreversible arrow of time, like Halley's comet, must at some point in its trajectory retrace positions in space it has already passed through many times before. The idea of cosmic return, eternal recurrence, so deeply embedded in Oriental thought, may, in the end, find a form of potential proof in this most recent hypothesis of Western astrophysics. And then King Solomon's doleful remark, "There is nothing new under the sun," will take on implications surely disheartening to those who believe that only by changing constantly, only by progressing to the "new," can human culture save itself from atrophy and stagnation.

I think the notion of "progress" and the "new" expressed culturally in our time is nothing more than the old hunter instinct of man who, in order to survive physically, was forced to follow game wherever it went. That restless, primitive instinct of the hunter still lives on in science's pursuit of "the truth" and the avant-garde's pursuit of "the new." The avant-garde is already the hapless victim of an increasingly rapid spiral of change endemic to our society generally, breathless in its haste to keep up the peculiarly Western illusion that only the new can release fresh human energy and vitality, only the new can vivify existence. By its own definition the avant-garde must constantly give way before the pressure of the next wavelet it generates. Nothing can grow; nothing can stand. Everything "new" must make way for everything "newer." Thus our culture moves so fast that no style can enjoy the traditional luxury of slow or even painful emergence from embryonic style to full maturation; no style is nurtured now for even a full generation. The last musical style of significance to enjoy some duration, some temporary stability, was serialism—and that lasted less than two full generations, from 1923 to about 1965. In our time we have witnessed the dizzying rate of changes in stylistic fashion every ten years, every five years, every year, every six months. If this continues it is possible that even a single work will be sufficient grounds for declaring a style finished, exhausted. The avant-garde is geared to a kind of Don Juanism, a form of sensationalism, which permits no loyalty, no attachment, no affiliation beyond the moment—there is only the passion to possess briefly. Change for its own sake has become a virtue entirely unto itself; stylistically speaking, one must plant one's flag and move on, otherwise be left behind in the mad race to nowhere. But the image of Don Juan is always shadowed by the specter of Il Commendatore. No matter how many sweet moments of conquest there may be, no matter how many Donna Annas and Donna Elviras, the stone guest eventually arrives for supper. Though the avant-garde mentality may prefer to push them aside, to make believe they are not really there, there are always consequences to human action. Even in game playing one wins or loses. The fate of Don Juan is legend.

I want to delay for a little later a discussion of what the pressures are, as I see them, which have induced this mad pace of change in our society and culture. Clearly the avant-garde is not the agent or cause of these pressures, but rather its victim and effect. Still, a basic question comes to mind and I should like to examine it now: can art (and presumably the avant-garde) itself be an agent of change? Can it influence or affect its human environment?

In the last of the essays collected under the title *Against Interpretation* (New York: Dell Publishing Co., 1967), Susan Sontag makes the point that "art today is a new kind of instrument, an instrument for modifying consciousness and organizing new modes of sensibility." According to Sontag, what she calls "the Matthew Arnold notion of culture," which "defines art as the criticism of life—this being understood as the propounding of moral, social, and political ideas," has been overtaken and replaced—although not everyone is aware of it—by "the new sensibility" which "understands art as the extension of life—this being understood as the representation of [new] modes of vivacity." These new modes of vivacity (or extensions of man's senses) comprise what she calls "an erotics of art." For, as she remarks, "we are what we are able to see (hear, taste, smell, feel) even more powerfully and profoundly than we are what furniture of ideas we have stocked in our heads." Sontag's ideas about "an erotics of art" draw a fine line between an aesthetic of pure sensationalism and seeming anti-intellectualism. But a new and different relationship between the mind and senses exists for her, one in which

> sensations, feelings, the abstract forms and styles of sensibility count. It is to these that contemporary art addresses itself. The basic unit of contemporary art is not the idea, but the analysis of and extension of sensations. (Or if it is an idea, it is about the form of sensibility.) Rilke described the artist as someone who works "toward an extension of the regions of the individual senses"; McLuhan calls artists "experts in sensory awareness." And the most interesting works of contemporary art

(one can begin at least as far back as French symbolist poetry) are adventures in sensation, new "sensory mixes." Such art is, in principle, experimental.

Taking Ortega y Gasset's famous phrase "the dehumanization of art" as a positive rather than negative indicator of, and point of departure for, what she calls "the exploration of the impersonal (and transpersonal)," Sontag asks:

> What other response than anguish, followed by anesthesia and then by wit and elevating the intelligence over sentiment, is possible as a response to the social disorder and mass atrocities of our time, and—equally important for our sensibilities, but less often remarked on—to the unprecedented change in what rules our environment from the intelligible and visible to that which is only with difficulty intelligible, and is invisible? Art, which I have characterized as an instrument for modifying and educating sensibility and consciousness, *now operates in an environment which cannot be grasped by the senses.* (Emphasis added)

> Here is where art (among other things) enters, and why the interesting art of our time has such a feeling of anguish and crisis about it, however playful and abstract and ostensibly neutral morally it may appear. Western man may be said to have been undergoing a massive sensory anesthesia (a concomitant of the process that Max Weber calls "bureaucratic rationalization") at least since the Industrial Revolution, with modern art functioning as a kind of shock therapy for both confounding and unclosing our senses.

Presumably the mission of the avant-garde is, as Sontag sees it, both instrumental, in the sense of modifying, organizing, and educating the sensibilities, and therapeutic, in the sense of opening up the reservoirs of potential feeling, awareness, and perception. Her position would come very close to William Blake's were it not for the fact she is still at heart—for all her talk about the extension of the senses—a rationalist; but most of all because she fails to understand art as a transcendent intrusion on a world already replete with instruments and institutions for modifying and organizing and educating humankind, most of them power-based, and all of them benignly convinced of their own efficacy for the improvement of man. To reduce art to a program for change is, in my opinion, to indulge in a form of critical wishful thinking. Sontag's dream of the awakened twentieth-century sensibility and intelligence remains her own private dream; it cannot make contact with reality. Ideally, who of us would not like to see art reach into and affect, in the most efficacious way possible, the concrete and diverse existences of untold numbers of human beings? Which of us does not dream privately of the ultimate humanizing power of art in a world hopelessly off center, somehow helping to right things, to bring them back to more human proportions?

There is a letter which Rilke, deeply shaken by the outbreak of World War I, wrote a friend in June, 1915, where he reveals the depths of his despair and shock at the realization that his art, and the art of his time, had had no effect at all on the tragic course of events.

> . . . that such confusion, not-knowing-which-way-to-turn, the whole sad man-made complication of this provoked fate, that exactly this in-curably bad condition of things was necessary to force out evidences of whole-hearted courage, devotion and bigness? While we, the arts, the theater, called nothing forth in these very same people, brought nothing to rise and flower, were unable to change anyone. What is our metier but purely and largely and freely to set forth opportunities for change,—did we do this so badly, so half-way, so little convinced and convincing? That has been the question, that has been the suffering for almost a year, and the problem is to do it more forcefully, more unrelentingly. How?!

That single, mournful phrase: "we . . . were unable to change anyone." And poor Rilke can only think that, by doing it more "forcefully, more unre-lentingly"—if one could but find the way to, the "how" of it—perhaps then art could and would reach into the hearts of men and help to alter things so as to divert future catastrophe. But all the arts which flourished between World Wars I and II did not change anyone or anything, did not prevent a second world-engulfing holocaust. And now we stand bewildered before our own destiny, still unable to avert disaster, still lacking in the means to humanize ourselves, certainly not able to believe that art is potentially such an instrument for change as would miraculously call off the Eumenides, which now pursue us because we have provoked them by our peculiarly unbalanced and passion-ate belief in reason, by our insistence on the pursuit of scientific truth, by our greedy acceptance of the deadly technology which science has bestowed on us out of misguided notions of its own efficacy.

The essential inescapable fact of our day is the dominance of science and its penetration of and applications to human culture in every sphere of exis-tence. It would appear that with but rare exceptions the basic model for con-temporary art is the rational methodology of science, a model taken at virtually face value, unquestioned as to its premises or consequences. I agree with Sontag that "the parallel between the abstruseness of contemporary art and that of modern science is too obvious to be missed" and the "spirit of exact-ness," the "sense of 'research' and 'problems'" which characterizes contem-porary art "is closer to the spirit of science than of art in the old-fashioned sense." Taking it a step further, today's avant-garde art is not only closer to the spirit of science than to the spirit of old-fashioned art but derives from, feeds on, depends on the spirit of science.

The linking of art with science in this manner has subordinated man's faculty for fantasy to his reason, and where once what Blake called "the poetic imagination" held autonomous sway, now rational intelligence (as opposed to an imaginative intelligence) has become the overlord. Just as the physical survival of man has been placed in grave jeopardy by science and its technological extensions, so the survival of art as an authentic value in human life is jeopardized by the uncritical acceptance of a scientific mentality as the paradigm for artistic behavior. This flies in the face of what is already known about the nature of human intelligence; as we shall see, precision and exactness are not the primary characteristics of the human brain.

The avant-garde's assumptions that it has broken through the old limits which presumably bind the mind and spirit of man—limits which tie art and culture to history, memory, correspondences, associations, identity, structure, order, value judgments (including moral ones); its claim to have opened up to exploration uncharted, infinitely expanding areas of new sensations and qualities, to have discovered, invented, or both, viable new relationships and forms—these assumptions are rarely challenged any more; if and when they are, the challenge usually issues from humanists who do little more than assert their own personal objections, leading the discussion nowhere. It becomes necessary, therefore, to find another, perhaps oblique, way to get at the ramifications of the special problems posed by the avant-garde. By one of those unique ironies that sometimes do work in our favor I believe I have discovered just such a way, and from a totally unexpected source: the theories of a renowned mathematician, John Von Neumann, whose little but powerful book of lectures on *The Computer and the Brain* (New Haven: Yale University Press, 1958) provides what I believe to be the right key to unlock an understanding of the avant-garde mentality and simultaneously and paradoxically lend courage, possibly even comfort, to the humanist. Whether other implications for avant-garde art other than music may suggest themselves, I am primarily concerned here with drawing the widest possible parallels between Von Neumann's ideas and the principles and practices of contemporary music.

Von Neumann, considered the father of the computer, describes computers as automata which employ *parallel* and *serial* schemes of operation. A parallel scheme is operative where "a number in the machine is represented by a sequence of ten-valued markers (or marker groups) which may be arranged simultaneously in different organs of the machine—in parallel." A serial scheme is operative where a number in the machine, represented as described above, may be arranged to appear "in temporal succession, in a single organ of the machine—in series." Von Neumann then compares the computer and the human nervous system, i.e., the brain, with respect to these two modes of operation.

> Natural componentry favors automata with *more*, but *slower*, organs, while the artificial one favors the reverse arrangement of *fewer*, but *faster*, organs. Hence it is to be expected that an efficiently organized large natural automaton (like the human nervous system) will tend to pick up as many logical (or informational) items as possible *simultaneously*, and process them simultaneously, while an efficiently organized large artificial automaton (like a large modern computing machine) will be more likely to do things successively—one thing at a time, or at any rate not so many things at a time. That is, large and efficient natural automata are likely to be highly *parallel*, while large and efficient artificial automata will tend to be less so, and rather be *serial*.

Von Neumann's remarks suggest a number of observations with respect to music. Quite obviously, music has the structured capability of being both highly parallel and completely serial. All harmonic and polyphonic structures embody parallel, i.e., simultaneous, streams of pitch relations. The continuous flow of their temporal movement—even where breaks in the form of silence or rests occur—embodies serial succession. Only in the instance of monophony, i.e., unaccompanied, single-voiced melodic structures, is the parallel mode suppressed and temporally successive pitch relations, i.e., serial, define the mode of projection. Given the essentially parallel structure of the human nervous system—its ability to deal with many things at once or many things together in what I shall call an "ensemble" relationship—it is apparent that the natural structure of the central nervous system, the human brain, is adapted to receiving parallel musical structures, i.e., ensembles of simultaneously organized levels of pitch and rhythmic relationships, directly and without the aid of intermediary functions. The central nervous system is also capable of receiving any order of successive serial events organized on the melodic plane. In fact, because it is serial and not parallel, it may be easier for the human nervous system to respond to, to register, to follow, and comprehend a monophonic/melodic structure. This last observation may offer a clue to why most ethnic music and popular musics tend more toward the melodic (often developing highly ornate and subtle forms of improvisatory systems of tropes or ragas or variations) than toward the harmonic or polyphonic (although there are clear evidences of primitive steps taken toward the parallel, i.e., the ensemble, relationship in such musics). It would appear, then, that greater conscious effort is required to develop and integrate the two modes fully—the parallel and the serial; and here is undoubtedly the clue to the evolution of Western art music. It is conceivable, even possible, that the logic of melodic structure (organized in series) is absolutely *necessary* on at least one clearly perceivable level, in order for our nervous system to be able to organize a continuous stream of ensembles (organized in parallel). Since it is the serial mode which establishes successive connections between the individually synchronous aspects of parallel structures occurring simultaneously, it would appear to be a reasonable assumption that, lacking a perceivable logic in their serial order, ensemble relationships occurring in rapid (or even slow) succession would tend to overburden and tire the nervous system, however attentive it might be to the business at hand, and therefore produce varying degrees of fatigue, frustration, dissatisfaction, anger, and even rage—or simply total indifference. (The continued pleasure in the music of the past may have its true source not in cultural reasons per se but in the very structure of our central nervous system. Which is to say that the continued performance and popularity of Mozart, Beethoven, Chopin, Tchaikovsky, and Brahms among others rests on the fact that their music is organized at high levels of clearly designed parallel, or ensemble, relations which in turn are dominated, controlled, and guided by clear serial patterns of melodic thought. So it is that even twentieth-century composers like Stravinsky, Bartók, and Prokofiev have established themselves solidly in the repertoire, not because we have grown accustomed to having their music around, but because there is a deep connection between how their music is made and how we are made. The answer to the question of why Schoenberg is not yet fully accepted into the repertoire, even though his music has been around as long certainly as Stravinsky's, may lie precisely in an understanding of these matters under discussion.)

Before going on I would like to draw some tentative conclusions. It seems to me that where what is received activates and animates the human nervous system, *corresponds* to its natural order of functions (parallel/serial), there we should expect to find the highest degree and most synchronized release of energy—and therefore flow of communication, uninhibited and undisturbed, between the source of the stimulus (in this case music) and the receiving, responding system (in this case the human nervous system). Conversely, therefore, where what is received disturbs and inhibits this flow of communication, i.e., the taking in and organizing of sense impressions of external phenomena and the registering of them in forms of logical response and synchronization of energy release—and does not correspond sufficiently or at all with the natural order of the central nervous system's functioning—the chances are very good, indeed excellent, that the central nervous system is likely to suffer temporary "breakdown," an inability to relate to the musical messages streaming into it from outside. In short, as the saying goes, "we don't get it." Now, suddenly, if what I am outlining here has any plausibility, we are faced with a number of possibly unanswerable, certainly very difficult to answer, questions: was the optimum of musical communicability reached by the composers of the nineteenth century (granting some spillover into the twentieth); and are we forced to remain within the general frame of their solutions not so much for cultural as for biological-genetic reasons? In other words, does the correspondence between the natural parallel/serial functions of the human nervous system and basic parallel/serial functions of musical structure impose types of limitations which must eventually constrain today's composer to respect that correspondence or suffer the consequences? What are the risks facing a composer who runs counter to the natural functions of the central nervous system and literally goes so far as to destroy their correspondence with musical structure? What are the real limits of music? How far can one go before music disappears and only unintelligible sound is left?

The second major aspect of Von Neumann's essay on the computer and the brain deals with the problem of memory in the central nervous system, a problem I consider absolutely fundamental to any serious discussion of music and especially of the music of the avant-garde.

> The presence of a memory—or, not improbably, of several memories— within the nervous system is a matter of surmise and postulation, but one that all our experience with artificial computing automata suggests and confirms. It is just as well to admit right at the start that all physical assertions about the nature, embodiment and location of this subassembly, or subassemblies, are equally hypothetical. We do now know where in the physically viewed nervous system a memory resides; we do not know whether it is a separate organ or a collection of specific parts of other already known organs, etc. It may well be residing in a system of specific nerves, which would then have to be a rather large system. It may well have something to do with the genetic mechanism of the body. We are as ignorant of its nature and position as were the Greeks, who suspected the location of the mind in the diaphragm. The only thing we know is that it must be a rather large-capacity memory, and that it is hard to see how a complicated automaton like the human nervous system could do without one. (Pp. 60–61)

Von Neumann goes on to describe possible embodiments of memory functions: nerve cell connections which relate to variability of stimulation criteria and involve past history of individual cells or connections (axons) with other cells; genetic memory in which "chromosomes and their constituent genes are clearly memory elements which, by their state, affect, and to a certain extent determine, the functioning of the entire system"; self-perpetuating traits of chemical composition of certain areas of the body which may be possible memory elements; nerve cell systems "which stimulate each other in various possible cyclical ways" which also constitute memories made up of active elements (nerve cells)—a type of memory system, in fact, in "frequent and significant use," according to Von Neumann, and the first one to be introduced into computing machine technology.

Obviously musical structures *in themselves* cannot physically constitute memory functions as such in any of the ways Von Neumann talks about. Nevertheless it is not implausible to suggest that there are certain levels of musical structure, pattern, and design which function within the structure in much the same way as memory systems seem to function in the nervous system. This speculation leads us in an entirely different direction from thinking about what happens when the design of a structure activates memory responses in a listener—although in the end the two tracks of thought must be brought together if my speculation is to produce a reasonably plausible result. In almost every piece of music from the beginnings of Gregorian chant to at least about 1950, we find structural devices and patterns whose fundamental purpose is *self-perpetuation*. These forms of musical self-perpetuation, like Von Neumann's genetic memory-bearing chromosomes or self-identifying, chemically stable memory elements in certain areas of the body, are absolutely essential to establishing the identity of a work, whether on the implicit or explicit level. Lacking such identity, a work could hardly be said to exist as an organic entity. And this is presumably what a work of art is: an identifiable, organic unit possibly bearing relations to or having associations with other similarly structured units but unquestionably and distinguishably different from them. Where the definition of the profile of identity is very high, there we will undoubtedly find self-perpetuation operating on every important level; where it is low, undoubtedly the urge toward self-perpetuation is minimally present and poorly organized. This is very likely the difference ultimately between what we used to call a "good" piece of music and a "poor" or "mediocre" piece. What are the devices for structural self-perpetuation at the disposal of the composer? They fall essentially into two groups: one which operates at the level of the pitch and/or rhythmic motive which is where, musically speaking, primal cellular identity must be located; the other is on the level of large-scale form where complex, cumulative shapes and gestures must also achieve perceivable identity. The process of self-perpetuation takes place on both levels simultaneously through forms of repetition, variation, and recall which literally saturate the parallel/serial structure. The whole craft of traditional composition rests on these principles; and while I'm certain Bach would have been no less surprised than Beethoven or Brahms or Mozart or Wagner to be told he was producing works based on the principle of structural self-perpetuation, he would have understood immediately what was meant once the principle was made clear to him. For the fugue is the example par excellence of an internally self-perpetuating organic unit of identifiable elements, and the sonata form is an enlargement of the application of the principle carried out on a scale of considerably increased structural dimensions. Even twelve-tone music attempted to carry out this principle; where it failed was in dissociating its specifically intended identifiable form, the row or series, from physical perception. Its actual units of perception, i.e., motives, rhythms, intervals, chords, even melodies where they occur as obviously traditionally structured contours and shapes are, with but few exceptions, usually too low in definition to act as recognizably perceptible self-perpetuating elements. It is in the post–twelve-tone period we are in now that we have been hearing more and more about the irrelevance of memory to the new music.

When we move from the principle of self-perpetuation physically built into the structure of a work to a consideration of how the varying degrees of presence of this principle affects memory functions in a listener (not to mention performer), the whole area of discussion bursts wide open. I take it as a reasonable assumption that, given (1) a human nervous system which contains memory functions, i.e., whose nerve cells are so constituted as to retain relations among discrete bits of information, and (2) that kind of music whose structure is founded on perceptible, self-perpetuating forms of repetition, variation, and recall, the two would appear to be in direct correspondence with each other and a high level of identity perception would result from contact between them. To put it simply, an attentive and serious listener could theoretically remember what he hears; in fact, as musicians have been demonstrating for generations, the same listener could actually remember every detail of a composition with sufficient study and effort. A high level of redundancy and a low one of information are essential if a work is to be committed to memory. The opposite automatically increases the difficulty, and where the simple act of hearing is concerned it should be clear that, the higher the level of information and the lower the level of redundancy, the less intelligible the potential act of perception and the greater the difficulty of remembering what has been heard. It is possible to conclude tentatively that where parallel and/or serial functions in music are structured along the lines of self-perpetuating forms of identity they will correspond at some level or levels to the memory functions of the central nervous system; and that where this correspondence increases or decreases along lines of profiles of identity, clarity of perception will vary with the change in relationship. Conversely, where parallel and/or serial functions in music are not structured on the principle of self-perpetuating forms of identity, it can be said they will probably deviate completely from the memory functions of the central nervous system and will, conceivably, produce a physical block of the nervous system, a form of perceptual blackout, a nonfunction with respect to memory. Otherwise said, if the memory system of the human brain is made for a high degree of determinate function, i.e., specific perception and handling of intelligible, identifiable pieces of information, it is plausible to assume that anything not clear, anything vague or amorphous or nonspecific, anything indeterminate as to pattern, shape, or identity will frustrate the memory capacity of the nervous system itself and will simply fall victim to its own inability to make contact with the memory function. It should seem obvious that the nervous system seems not to be able to respond to what is not intelligible or graspable—which is simply another way of saying it doesn't care about what does not reach or get through to it; nor can it learn what it can't remember or remember what it can't learn. It would thus seem that music must structure itself along the lines of self-perpetuating forms of repetition, variation, and recall if it is to become intelligible and retainable by the memory functions in the nervous system.

If my speculations have any plausibility at all, the implications for the present state of music and the direction of composition for the future are enormous. Clearly much of today's music has foredoomed itself to extinction. For example, all forms of strictly aleatoric music which invoke chance operations and improvisatory pieces which are not based on already stated or culturally known external referents but rather on internal rules of a game devised for those specific works alone do not, on principle, address themselves to the human nervous system and its memory functions. Because they reject structural forms of self-perpetuation there is no way in which they can achieve identity, and therefore no way in which they can be remembered because there is nothing to remember. They can only be heard as dissociated aural sensations in passing; they cannot be *listened to*—if listening means actively focusing attention for the purpose of perceiving an order or structure with the tacit faith that there is something there to grasp, to take in and hold on to. Composed music whose performance depends on shuffling the deck, so to speak, operating on the principle of altering the successive appearance of fixed events by some principle of choice, and can only achieve a very low definition of profile of identity. Inevitably, such music turns off the central nervous system because it frustrates the physical system on the levels of both its serial mode and memory elements. Any given single performance of such music might stand a chance of intelligibility, providing its fixed, composed elements correspond at important levels to the central nervous system. But once a second or third performance takes place (for the same listener) and the succession of events is altered, any meaningful relationship of correspondence between the shifting order of the fixed elements and the functions of the central nervous system becomes attenuated and begins to break down. Any system of composition which bases itself on precompositional matrices—total serialism, stochastics, information theory—which depend solely on arbitrary rationalizations of rules of the game, cannot achieve a direct and meaningful correspondence to the functions of the central nervous system, for the very reason that whatever music it produces depends for its understanding not on the perceptual functions built into the nervous system but on a post-intellectual comprehension of its externally predetermined rationalizations. In such cases the "ear" has been bypassed and ignored. Intuitively the central nervous system recognizes that what it is being asked to relate to is a by-product of processes which exist at levels which are secondary to its alpha language and belong to a category other than music. Self-extinction, then, is built into much of the avant-garde music of our day; and no amount of training or conditioning in its perception, no amount of repeated hearings can eventually overcome its essential lack of correspondence with the primary functions of the human nervous system.

The last section of Von Neumann's book, "The Language of the Brain not the Language of Mathematics," contains some of the most remarkable statements I have ever come across, statements which have powerful implications for culture in general and the arts and music in particular.

> Pursuing this subject further gets us necessarily into questions of language. As pointed out, the nervous system is based on two types of communications: those which do not involve arithmetical formalisms, and those which do, i.e., communications of orders (logical ones) and communications of numbers (arithmetical ones). The former may be described as language proper, the latter as mathematics.
>
> It is only proper to realize that language is largely an historical accident. The basic human languages are traditionally transmitted to us in various forms, but their very multiplicity proves that there is nothing absolute and necessary about them. Just as languages like Greek or Sanskrit are historical facts and not absolute logical necessities, it is only reasonable to assume that logics and mathematics are similarly historical, accidental forms of expression. They may have essential variants, i.e., they may exist in other forms than the ones to which we are accustomed. Indeed, the nature of the central nervous system and of the message systems that it transmits indicates positively that this is so. We have not accumulated sufficient evidence to see that whatever language the central nervous system is using, it is characterized by less logical and arithmetical depth than what we are normally used to. . . . The statistical character of the message system used in the arithmetics of the central nervous system and its low precision also indicate that the degeneration of precision, described earlier, cannot proceed very far in the message systems involved. Consequently, there exist here different logical structures from the ones we are ordinarily used to in logics and mathematics. They are, as pointed out before, characterized by less logical and arithmetical depth than we are used to under otherwise similar circumstances. Thus logics and mathematics in the central nervous system, when viewed as languages, must structurally be essentially different from those languages to which our common experience refers. . . . When we talk mathematics, we may be discussing a secondary language, built on the primary language truly used by the central nervous system.

Thus the outward forms of our mathematics are not absolutely relevant from the point of view of evaluating what the mathematical or logical language truly used by the central nervous system is. However, the above remarks about reliability and logical and arithmetical depth prove that *whatever the system is, it cannot fail to differ considerably from what we consciously and explicitly consider as mathematics.* (Pp. 80–82, emphasis added)

I think it is a reasonable assumption to make that music is a secondary "language" system whose logic is closely related to the primary, alpha logic of the central nervous system itself, i.e., of the human body. If I am right, then it follows that the perception of music is simply the process reversed; i.e., we listen with our bodies, with our nervous systems and their primary interacting parallel/serial and memory functions. The potential perceptual meaning for each of us individually of musical stimuli, i.e., message systems, increases with the increase of conscious attentive awareness. If this is true—the question is how to corroborate it—the implications are very great and far-reaching. At the very least, the pulse-trains which transmit messages in the nervous system suggest a direct correspondence with the logic of musical events characterized by structural continuity based on self-perpetuating forms of repetition and recall. The fact that these pulse-trains function periodically suggests that music itself may be a direct expression or reflection of the fundamental language of the human nervous system. Periodicity of metric and rhythmic movement, and the larger periodicities and rhythms of the musical phrase and of formally articulated structure, were fundamental identifying characteristics of Western art music until only very recently. Perhaps we have here a direct clue to one of the basic reasons for the essential failure of much new music to communicate itself directly to even the most sympathetic listeners. Its insistence on suppression of the pulse, its conscious avoidance of periodicity on all levels of structure and movement, and its consequent inability to perpetuate itself as a growing, identifiable, organic structural entity apparently go against the grain of the natural functions of the central nervous system. Everything Von Neumann tells us about the way the human nervous system functions suggests it is a goal-directed system, i.e., anti-entropic; its natural capacities for logical processes and its high degree of logical reliability appear to confirm this. It is then plausible to conjecture that any music which consciously frustrates the goal-directedness of the nervous system, which denies clarity of structure, which suppresses perceptible periodicities, which is lacking in self-perpetuating characteristics, which turns it back on identity as an essential feature of its design, must ultimately pay the price in terms of perceptual failure and cultural self-extinction. To play with entropy in art is to play with a self-consuming fire.

In the sense that Von Neumann characterizes spoken languages (as well as logics and mathematics) as historical accidents, secondary language offshoots of the alpha language of the central nervous system, it becomes reasonable to consider all musical systems and styles in the same light, especially in view of their historical multiplicity. Apparently, *any* coherent system of music which possesses a high degree of identifiable internal consistency, which produces clarity and coherence in its structural forms, can be transmitted as message systems to the human nervous system with the expectation that it will be received, i.e., perceived, by the nervous system directly and be understood—if only at the most primitive levels at first. It is not necessary to know how Mozart composed, or what the theory of functional tonality is, to have a direct experience of the clarity and coherence which characterize his music. Nor does one have to be from Madras or Bombay to respond eventually on basic levels to the virtues of Indian music. (Obviously study and intensified experience of any such musical system potentially increases and enhances the joy of response and understanding.) The essential requirements, then, of a musical system, regardless of its cultural, historical, or ethnic origins, no matter how much it may differ from all previous historical or other contemporaneous systems, is that it correspond and relate to the central nervous system in fundamental, direct ways—clarity and coherence being the necessary ingredients of that correspondence and relationship. It follows then that the advanced music of our time that is characterized acoustically by generalized bands or conglomerations of sounds bordering on the noise spectrum will lack the specificity of pitch relationship which the human nervous system evidently requires for direct comprehension. A total reliance on such aggregates or constellations, as they are sometimes called, must in the end short-circuit or anesthetize the central nervous system. Sounds which abandon clarity through this process of generalization move toward nonidentity; relations between such sounds degenerate rapidly into mere succession, an accident of time so to speak. When the human nervous system is confronted by music characterized chiefly by perceptual disorder, lack of identity, and avoidance of periodicity, it loses interest, becomes indifferent, and ends up rejecting what it cannot relate to—and understandably so.

If we were to hypothesize a "new" art music, one which does not yet exist or may never exist, but which would nevertheless *be* music and therefore related to historical musics (like a hypothetical language to historical languages), we would, I believe, have to proceed along the following lines in projecting a theory of its structure: (1) it would require parallel/serial functions, i.e., ensemble relations moving along a line of coherent melodic continuity; (2) it would require memory functions in terms of self-perpetuating repetition, variation, and recall which would literally saturate the parallel/serial structure to produce coherent relations of organic consistency, thereby creating directly perceivable, comprehensible levels of identity; and (3) it would require logical relations which would be goal-directed and direction-producing in accord with the inherent teleology of the central nervous system. It appears I have described a "tonal" system. In fact, ironically enough, while my investigation of possible correspondences between music and the central nervous system has brought me a long way around, it has brought me to a possible theory of a musical system which appears to have profound connections with historical tonality. If that is the case, then I can only conclude that historical tonality, however it is defined and regardless of the number of different "styles" it evolved, is a musical system whose basic language characteristics are traceable to the alpha language of the central nervous system. Whatever the ultimate truth of my speculations may be, I think it entirely reasonable to suggest that the sources of coherent musical structure lie deep in the human body, in the central nervous system, and that, just as performers perform with their bodies and listeners listen with their bodies, composers compose with their bodies. The lack of recognition of these basic observations on the part of the present musical avant-garde explains why they have preferred to deal with sound *as* sound rather than with sound as the physical medium of music. It also underscores my conviction that the trivialization of music into mere unintelligible sound structures constitutes the essence of the musical avant-garde mentality and foretells its ultimate demise.

The only "new" thing that is worth talking about, and that art makes possible, is the infusion of private vision into the stream of public consciousness. The private cosmologies of a Beethoven and an Ives are, in my view, worth more than all the new technology, all the new devices, all the new materials spawned in our time, put together. They are the lifeblood of the world and of the society of men. Without such periodic infusions the world of art—and the world itself—grows anemic and listless, apathetic. Each new infusion is a reminder of the ever-present possibility of the transcendent nature of experience, of the profound connection to the alpha language of the human psyche and the central nervous system which is its ground. Rational knowledge coupled with sensory experience of the transcendent is the only proper food for the education of the human spirit. A profound sense of man's capacity for fantasy and for acting out such fantasy through art is one of the best training grounds for those who hunger to reach as close to the sources of life as the human central nervous system will permit. While we are living here we need to know, in our very flesh, what it is that we are. All other forms of rational knowledge which deviate from or deny the transcendent nature of private vision, which anesthetize fantasy and art, myth and symbol, while no doubt necessary for certain transactions on the routine and material side of things, need to be readjusted to the nature and requirements of human existence.

A new balance needs to be discovered. It is not the world which needs remaking but ourselves. In remaking ourselves it would be well to remember that for countless milennia before the dawn of the age of science man survived without science as we know it. Instead of science he had a profound relation to the cosmos, however fantastic or superstitious that relation may appear from our vantage point. He survived not through rational knowledge or science and technology but through cosmology which peopled his imagination with myth and symbol, poetry and metaphor, image and story and song. He ritualized his existence, propitiated the gods, surrounded himself with magic. He developed the arts of language, music, dance, painting, sculpture. He learned the rhythms of his world and fitted himself into them. He survived. . . . And we? What are our chances? Can we survive our rational madness, our science and technology, our obsession for progress and change, our avant-garde, our aberrant passions for new sensations, our refusal to accept the limits of our own being? The same attitudes of mind and spirit which have brought us to this pass will not lead us out of it. We must reconnect ourselves with the alpha language of the central nervous system which is itself, I believe, a secondary derivative of the alpha language of the cosmos, and bring the two into correspondence again, into direct connection and relationship with each other. The lesson of the avant-garde should be, if we read it correctly, to show us in concrete ways how far removed we now are from any real contact with ourselves or the cosmos, how far we have wandered from home—and that it is time to try to get back, not to some historical past, but to an awareness of the mysterious creatures we are—a secondary, living, organic "language" of the alpha language of the cosmos.

Reflections on the Renewal of Music

*Now that I've worked my way through Brahms, I've fallen back on
Bruckner again. An odd pair of 2nd-raters. The one was "in the casting
ladle" too long, the other, not long enough. Now I stick to Beethoven.
There are only he and Richard (Wagner) and after them, nobody.*
—Gustav Mahler, in a letter to his wife Alma, 1904

When Mahler called Bruckner half-baked and Brahms overdone, he was exercising his very strong sense of skepticism regarding the value of their achievements. Obviously, judgments produced by the skeptical temper are not
necessarily true for all people. Yet, for an artist, they are basic to decisions he
must make for himself. They affect his views, not only of the work of others,
but of his own as well, and determine to a great extent what he will willfully
take, i.e., borrow or "steal" from another artist, how he will allow himself to be
influenced, and what he will accept into his personal canon.

The capacity for self-indulgence is the measure of the lack of self-critical
faculties, rationalizations notwithstanding, whether offered in the guise of
aesthetics or not. Skepticism, therefore, is one of the primary requisites of
mental awareness, the sharpness of a natural or developed acumen which tests
everything in order to discover what is good or authentic. The development of
critical powers leads to the capacity to make discriminating judgments without
which there is no taste—and without taste there is no art. For what we call art
is ultimately, however else it may be defined, the habitual exercise of projecting fine judgments of subtle and specific perceptions. That is why the grossly
generalized and nonspecific perceptions of today's avant-gardists fall outside
the range of art (and have been dubbed "anti-art"). The self-declared avant-
gardist lacks, among other things, precisely that skeptical temper of mind
which develops the critical powers leading finally to taste, subtlety, grace,
proportion—in a word, art.

Jorge Luís Borges's[1] notion that history may be the record of the infinitely varying individual inflections of a universal mind contains more than one
refutation of commonly held beliefs. Among them is the belief in the necessity
or desirability of originality,[2] the motive force which seems to supply the
energy for change itself and offers the justification for asserting the aggressive
tendencies of the ego, whether in art, politics, business, etc. From Borges's
notion one can proceed directly and easily to the consideration of how influence—which produces resemblance, replication, reminiscence through emula-
tion of manner or substance, or both—operates from one man to another, from

one epoch to another, even to the inclusion of outright borrowing, i.e., exact repetition. But, then, in the case of direct borrowing, from whom is one taking if not from one's larger self? (Providing, of course, one accepts Borges's idea that each of us is, indeed, a single individual filament of a vast, interconnected cosmic nervous system, one cell of a complex, far-flung organism.) Narcissistic individualism, which thrives chiefly on the belief in originality and rationalizes the excesses of self-indulgence, is thus a kind of metaphysical cop-out.

By an act of pure fantasy the Florentine Camerata reached across centuries to the drama of ancient Greece and came up with monody and opera. If ancient Greek drama had persisted without change into the time of the late Renaissance, Baroque and subsequent opera might never have occurred. How different is modern opera from Greek drama as it was actually performed? We shall never know. But in the mental space carved out by the historical loss of the actual practice of Greek drama there grew a myth of how it had been; out of that myth and the urge to resuscitate Greek tragedy, music renewed itself. We are still living off the energies of that act of renewal.

Another of the many refutations of commonly held beliefs, implicit in Borges's idea of history, is the long-cherished notion of the linear causal progression of human events buttressed in our time by the dizzying speed of the changes by which science and technology have "advanced" our civilization. To be a victim of the idea of change for its own sake, as endemic to the course of man's motion through time, is nothing short of a curse on the artist. For it deprives him on every side of the reality and value of the past experience of human beings whose earlier contributions must be considered as valid as his own (but for different reasons) if his own are to be considered valid by others who will come later. If one wipes the slate clean of others, in order to satisfy some misguided notion of being "contemporary," one's own fate is, by the same token, equally guaranteed null and void. There is no virtue in starting all over again. The past refuses to be erased. Unlike Boulez, I will not praise amnesia.

The history of music leapfrogs its way across the centuries. The "perfect art" of the polyphonic Netherlanders, overridden by operatic monody, lives in renewed form in Schoenberg and Webern; the fugal art of Bach, overridden by the sonata, comes to life again (albeit imbued with a new psychology and purpose) in Beethoven, the master of the sonata; the ground bass variation technique, overridden by the harmonic variation, is reborn in Brahms's Fourth Symphony; Stravinsky resurrects pseudo-Pergolesi in *Pulcinella;* Webern, in his *Klangfarben* version of Bach's ricercar from *The Musical Offering,* virtually writes a new work; Ives's *Concord* Sonata treats the motto of Beethoven's Fifth Symphony as an underlying presence; and so on. All such acts of renewal through uses of the past renew both that past drawn upon and that present in which the act occurs. Far from being acts of weakness or signs of the depletion of creative energy, they reveal a profound wisdom about the paradox of time, which does not consume itself and its products as if it were fire, but gathers up into itself everything which has occurred in it, preserving everything as the individual mind preserves its individual memories. The myth is more important than the fact.

It is not at all true that this is the "Age of McLuhan" any more than it is the "Age of Schoenberg," "of Stravinsky," or of anyone else. This is the cliché language of the media and of simple-minded critics and historians who need to pin tags on phenomena. Nor is it at all true that there is a single tradition which operates along the track of a main line with station stops at Bach, Beethoven, and Brahms. If one can accept in whole or in part the idea of a universal mind, endlessly producing a repertoire of recurring images and forms, one immediately appreciates the rule of human conduct and culture: an emergent procession of varieties of parallel, simultaneous patterns of living and believing, frequent juxtapositions of opposites in these patterns, frequent and violent overt conflicts between such patterns, subtle conflicts and tension between related but different patterns, and so forth.

Like every other time, ours is a vast mix which refuses to be reduced to neatly packaged verbal categories. If Brahms does not belie the "Age of Wagner" concept, then Debussy does; if not Debussy, then Verdi. Verbal consistencies are no more fruitful than aesthetic ones. To insist on either verbal or aesthetic consistency is to limit the world, at any given moment of individual perception, only to what that individual eye can see, ear hear, mind perceive; it is especially to refuse the contradictory evidence of other observers and other consciousnesses which are equally limited. Like the nineteenth century, the twentieth presents us with nothing but contradictions, and only the partisan thinks he sees clearly.

Schoenberg probably suffered more from a sense of ongoing linear change and the pressure of historical consciousness than any other major composer of the twentieth century. He was overly concerned with his ultimate position in history and as a result became too self-conscious about how he worked and how his work affected others. When history becomes the criterion for the evaluation of oneself and others, it tends to corrode and destroy. Taken as an abstraction, history is a constant danger to human thought and life.

In his story "The Aleph," Borges describes a poet and his work, in a way the very model of a certain variety of contemporary composer, in these words: "He read me many another stanza, each of which obtained his approbation and profuse commentary, too. There was nothing memorable in any of them. . . . I realized that the poet's labor lay not with the poetry, but with the invention of reasons to make the poetry admirable; naturally, this ulterior and subsequent labor modified the work for him, but not for others." Like a stain on the tissue of time, the self-indulgent verbiage of proclamation and justification will remain as sometime documents of our collective confusions; but the work which it attempted to make "admirable" will have long since faded from the field of memory.

The desperate search in the second half of the twentieth century for a way out of cultural replication, i.e., being influenced by others, borrowing, leapfrogging, has let loose a veritable Pandora's box of aberrations which have little or nothing to do with art, but everything to do with being "successful" historically or commercially. Even the critics, no longer willing to be left out or behind, have joined in the hue and cry for "the new"; they celebrate and rationalize it. Self-indulgence is now the rule. By a series of typical paradoxes only powerful creative spirits like Brahms, Mahler, Bartók, and Stravinsky have remained skeptical of everything but authentic values and, therefore, continue the process of cultural replication by refracting all previous music through their individual, particular natures; the avant-gardists, wanting to start all over again, make anarchic hash of music, justifying themselves partially by invoking the philosophies of the East and (among others) the doctrines of noncausality and indeterminacy.

What was advertised as the "exhaustion of tonality" at the end of the nineteenth century and described by historians, beginning typically with *Tristan* and tracing the demise through the new Viennese school, may simply have been an incapacity on the part of composers to continue to produce a viable tonal music which could stand comparison with the best work of the eighteenth and nineteenth centuries. Even if we grant the emergence of new perceptions and sensibilities, it does not follow that authentic values must be cast aside every time a new device or procedure is discovered. Culture, like time, its guardian, proceeds by slow accretion and eventually absorbs everything of value. By the same token nothing of value is ever lost. This is the only faith that a serious artist can live by, provided that he has made something worth preserving, even though he will never really know the fate of his work.

We live within two distinct yet interrelated realities: the world of nature which includes man as a biogenetic reflection of nature's urge toward consciousness, and the world of man which includes art as a spiritual reflection of that self-awareness nature has given him. Art is neither a mirror nor a substitute for the world. It is an addition to that universal reality which contains natural man and shows the infinite varieties of ways that man can be. William Faulkner put it much more simply when he said that art was a way of declaring that "Kilroy was here." However we phrase it, art preserves the reality of man's presence on earth. It is part of his urge toward the physical survival of the race and the spiritual immortality of the individual. Its fantastic nature does not change this striving one iota. On the contrary, it intensifies, confirms, and purifies it; for man, though he may be a failure in the realms of social and political order, is primarily and essentially a craftsman and maker of symbols and metaphors. This is his true gift, his real nature.

What cannot be remembered cannot be preserved. The true intent of art is to preserve human consciousness. The Homeric epics and the Old Testament—to cite just two examples—existed, we are told, in centuries-old oral traditions before being written down more than two thousand years ago. If the dislocation of tradition which afflicts us had befallen the ancient Greeks and Hebrews, we would not know the poetic glories of the *Odyssey* and the *Iliad* nor the vast sweep of human experience recorded in the Pentateuch. We would be bereft of two of the richest sources and deposits of human metaphor and symbol. Why, then, do composers today think that music which they admit cannot be remembered earns them, merely because they wrote it, the right to preservation and transmission? They produce for obsolescence while secretly hoping for immortality.

It is curious that *Le Sacre* is the subject of rhythmic analysis, *Wozzeck* of structural analysis, and more recently *Lulu* of harmonic and intervallic analysis, not to speak of rhythmic and metric analysis. They are treated as though the balletic and theatrical impulses which brought them to life are as nothing compared with the formal designs and patterns which articulate their audible surfaces. The primal energy and sensuality of *Le Sacre*, the heartbreak of human noncomprehension and cruelty of the human condition which are basic to *Wozzeck*, the heartlessness of lust and poison of soullessness depicted in *Lulu*—all this is disregarded as though it were of no account. The passions of man, which are the very heart of theater and theater music, seem to escape or to embarrass those who write about music today. The gestures which embody dramatic functions and form the real and audible stuff of music remain, analysis notwithstanding, the only reasons why these works have entered their respective repertoires and will undoubtedly remain there. As obvious as all this is, or ought to be, it is completely overlooked by legions of composer-theorists who are lost in the labyrinth of academic abstractions.

There can be no justification for music, ultimately, if it does not convey eloquently and elegantly the passions of the human heart. Who would care to remember the quartets of Beethoven or Bartók if they were merely demonstrations of empty formalisms? What claim would Chopin have on us if he had merely given us the abstractions of shape, gesture, and motion through time? Debussy was being celebrated only a few years ago as one of the patron saints of pure instrumental timbre as a compositional virtue. (How he would have writhed to be reduced to the size of his idolators!) More recently, interest has been shown in Varèse's penchant for symmetry; all well and good—but one could hardly claim that this describes or explains in any meaningful way the passion, bite, and force of his rhetoric, the real reasons we value him. The insistence by all on ignoring the dramatic, gestural character of music, while harping on the mystique of the minutiae of abstract design for its own sake, says worlds about the failure of much new music. Like mushrooms in the night, there has sprung up a profusion of false, half-baked theories of perception, of intellection, of composition itself. The mind grows sterile, and the heart small and pathetic.

The enlargement of mental perspective teaches us that consciousness, whose core is the central nervous system, is radial, not linear. Earth-time embraces man through his entire slow, tortuous advance up the ladder of evolution. No matter how far up that ladder he may climb, no matter how far away from his beginnings he may find himself as the decades, centuries, and eons elapse, he will bear within him all that he ever was. What profit is there, then, for man to shorten his perspective to man-time, that tiny scale of measurement by which men count their days and actions? Man-time is a distorting mirror in which, by ever so slight a shift of position, men can create false images, reduce the significant to smallness, inflate the insignificant to largeness. Music without a cosmology will not move the soul; nor will it illumine the heart.

The cosmogony of the ancients and primitives, expressed in magic, rites, and rituals, which invested the world around them with signs and symbols of the unknown, paradoxically ensured the survival of these peoples; for through their seemingly unsophisticated notions they preserved the sense of awe and mystery in the face of a cosmos into which man had seemingly stumbled. And we? Because we have lost that precious sense of the magic and mystery of existence, we have no cosmogony—physics and astronomy are poor substitutes. Because we have no cosmogony, we are faced with the problem of whether man can survive his own thoughtlessness and arrogance, his collective hubris. Mahler was the last composer to intuit that music belongs to cosmogony and is supported by it.

The renewal of music depends on the renewal of the art of composition itself. If we value Wagner and Brahms for the power of their harmony, why, then, have we given up harmony? If we value Mozart and Chopin for the elegance of their melodies, why, then, have we given up the melodic line? If in the combination of many voices a radiant polyphony emerges, why have we given up counterpoint? Ballet cannot exist without rhythmic pulsation and periodicities, any more than opera can exist without the accompanied aria. Both are rooted in myth, fairy tale, real or imagined history, the embodiments and extensions of man's passionate nature. Nontheatrical music is not necessarily less dramatic. It must still move and touch us. The enlargement of the timbral palette is made at the sacrifice of the melodic phrase, the rhythmic period. If there is value in this enlargement it will come only with its direct and concrete association with discernible, memorable melodies and rhythms, polyphonic combinations, and textural composites which articulate that longing for a reality which is man's best and perhaps only true claim to existence. History will not help us; but the past, which is ever-present, can.

The renewal of music is linked to the survival of man. In his prophetic introduction to *Magister Ludi* (published in 1946) Hermann Hesse refers to the treatise of an ancient Chinese philosopher who describes "the music of decline" as a reflection of the chaos and disorderly state of men's affairs. It is painful to consider that ours may be such a "music of decline." Man the human being must learn to reconcile himself to a universe in which he is or is not a welcome guest (how can one tell?) simply in order to survive physically—which means acknowledging the limits of his biogenetic nature, as well as the delicate balance of nature itself and his relation to that balance. In the same way, man the musician must learn to reconcile himself to the limits of music, which inhere in his central nervous system, and to stop torturing sound into shapes and gestures whose meanings (if they have any) suggest that man has lost the power of musical speech and has reduced himself to inarticulateness. To sing is to project the subtle inflections of the human psyche; to dance is to project the subtle inflections of the human body and its musculature. The renewal of music lies in the direction of reasserting both, simply and directly.

The gestures of twentieth-century music do not invalidate those of the eighteenth or nineteenth centuries, any more than Western music invalidates Indian music or vice versa. When authentic, they are extensions of the psychology of musical expression. In no way can it be claimed that they supersede the vast continuities, the grander and more serene gestures of tonal music. They are primarily investigations of previously unexposed and unexplored areas of the human psyche and have value insofar as they articulate those areas of sensation, feeling, and emotion with clarity of means and eloquence of utterance. These narrow, attenuated gestures of our time often tend to be peripheral to the major, earlier gestures of music and describe, as it were, a series of vague and tenuous probes and lines of movement, extending from the ghostly shadowlands of the surreal to the gravity-free, time-frozen sensations of cosmic space-longing, from the randomness of causality-free projections to the overdetermined, tightly woven structures of total organization. There is no contradiction in suggesting that the renewal of music depends on the fullest possible use of the human imagination, the only recognizable limit being the central nervous system, which potentially includes, therefore, all the gestures, old and new, of which music is capable. Translated into practice, this would mean the use of every device and every technique appropriate to its specific gestural repertory in combination with every other device and technique, until theoretically all that we are and all that we know is bodied forth in the richest, most diverse music ever known to man: *ars combinatoria*.

NOTES

1. Argentine poet and philosophical essayist (b. 1899). In "Pascal's Sphere," which appears in *Other Inquisitions, 1939–1952* (Austin: University of Texas Press, 1965), pp. 5–8, Borges remarks, "Perhaps universal history is the history of the diverse intonation of a few metaphors" (p. 8).
2. A unique discussion of the belief in the necessity of artistic originality can be found in Leonard B. Meyer's *Music, the Arts and Ideas* (Chicago: University of Chicago Press, 1967), especially pp. 54–67, 188.

On the Third String Quartet

When I wrote my Third String Quartet I had no idea it would call forth the quantity and kinds of critical comment that followed its first performances and recording. Some critics rejected the work out of hand on the grounds that its combination of tonal and nontonal musics simply did not add up to being "contemporary." Some seemed fascinated but still puzzled by the phenomenon of structural fusion of past and present. The majority of writers, however, welcomed it even though they were uncertain whether the direction that the quartet pointed to could or would be followed up.

The acceptability of such a work hinges no doubt on whether one is able to reconcile a juxtaposition of musically opposite styles. In order to effect such a reconciliation, one has to be persuaded, first, that the idea of history as "progress" is no longer viable and, second, that the radical avant-garde of recent years has proved to be bankrupt. Both conditions lay behind the impulse that generated my quartet. Both were determining factors in my choice of ideas, levels of musical action, and the structure of the work itself. Far from seeing tonality and atonality as opposite "styles," I viewed them as significant aspects of an enlarged language of musical expression with branching subdivisions of what I like to call "dialects"—a particular way of stressing or inflecting parts of the whole spectrum of Western musical language. These dialects can be presented singly or in combination depending on what one wants to say and the particular size, shape, and character of the work one wants to say it in. In the quartet the dialects range widely from diatonic, key-centered tonality to forms of chromaticism which veer toward nineteenth-century or early-twentieth-century practices (but still structurally tonal) to a more atonally oriented chromaticism; from predictable to unpredictable periodicities of phrase structure; from simple to complex metric pulsation; and from continuous to noncontinuous gestural relationships between phrases, sections, and movements.

By embracing the earlier traditions of tonality and combining them with the more recently developed atonality, I found it possible to release my music from the overintense, expressionistic manner inherent in a purely serially organized, constant chromaticism, and from the inhibition of physical pulse and rhythm which has enervated so much recent music. With the enlargement of this spectrum of possible means came an enlargement of perspective which potentially placed the entire past at my disposal. I was freed of the conventional perceptions which ascribe some goal-directed, teleological function to that past, insisting that each definable historical development supersedes the one that has just taken place either by incorporating or nullifying it.

In this view, the invention of classical twelve-tone methodology—and later total serialism—not only superseded everything that came before it but literally declared it null and void. Obviously, I rejected this view—though not without great discomfort and difficulty, because I had acquired it, along with a number of similar notions, as a seemingly inevitable condition of the twentieth-century culture in which I had grown up. The demanding effort to evolve and maintain a personal kind of transcendentalism still occupies me; but that effort has resulted in being able to compose whatever kind of music I feel deeply and intensely.

I am not aware that anyone has yet attempted a full-scale answer to the questions my quartet seems to have raised. Perhaps wisely—because I believe the issues involved are complex beyond imagining, and therefore certainly not susceptible to the kind of either/or, binary thinking so characteristic of the contemporary mind. To live with paradox and contradiction is not and has not been our cultural or intellectual way. I suspect that what my quartet suggests to others, and what I began to accept for myself at least fifteen years ago, is that we can no longer live with monolithic ideas about art and how it is produced. Nor can we take as artistic gospel the categorical imperatives laid down by cultural messiahs or their self-appointed apologists and followers of whatever persuasion.

On the contrary, the twentieth century has pointed—however reluctant we may be to accept it in all areas of life, social as well as political, cultural as well as intellectual—toward a difficult-to-define pluralism, a world of new mixtures and combinations of everything we have inherited from the past and whatever we individually or collectively value in the inventions of our own present, replete with juxtapositions of opposites (or seeming opposites) and contraries. In other words, not the narrow, pat, plus/minus, monoview of the rational-minded, but the web of living ideas which combine in strange and unexpected ways much as the stuff of biological matter does; not the self-conscious aesthetic or morality which excludes so much for the sake of "purity," but the sensed (if not quite yet articulate) notion that stretches to embrace everything possible to one's taste and experience, regardless of its time or place of origin. This not only makes it mandatory to see the "past" as continuously viable and alive in our "present" but also to be able to perceive large chunks of time as unities which create a vast physical-mental-spiritual web enfolding our individual lives, actions, and feelings.

I believe we are the filaments of a universal mind which transcends our individual egos and histories. The degree to which we partake of that universal mind is the degree to which we identify with the collective imagery, fate, wisdom, and tragedy of our still struggling species. By ourselves we are virtually nothing—but by opening ourselves to the transcendent collectivity of mankind and its experiences, we share in a totality which, however mysterious its sources, dimensions, and ultimate fate, sustains us.

Pluralism, as I understand it, does not mean a simplistic array of different things somehow stuck together in arbitrary fashion but a way of seeing new possibilities of relationships; of discovering and uncovering hidden connections and working with them structurally; of joining antipodes without boiling out their tensions; of resolving the natural tensions of contradictory terms on new symbiotic hierarchic levels—more than all of the above, a way of preserving the uncertainty of the artistic enterprise which itself demands that, out of the tensions and anxieties attendant upon it, we struggle for clarity and order, to gain not a permanent certainty (which is not possible anyhow) but a momentary insight into how it is possible to resolve the chaos of existence into a shape or form which takes on beauty, perhaps meaning, certainly strength. Art is a way of fighting the encroachment of the forces which diminish us. Through art we are all Don Quixotes battling Time and Death.

Granting pluralism, how is a composer to deal with it? From the inside out, i.e., from the internal psychic imagery which becomes the musical gesture to its artistic manifestation. Gesture, singly or in combination, successive or simultaneous, is the determining factor—not style, language, system, or method.

Given the very strong possibility that music is rooted in our biological structure—as are spoken language and mathematics—the gestures of music can only proceed authentically from one direction: from inside. That is where they get their energy, their power, their immediacy. The conscious effort to give voice to the vast range of these gestures becomes the act of composing, and inevitably demands not only freedom of choice but freedom of combination. If Beethoven, for example, had not felt this way, we would not have the late quartets—those glories of our civilization. There is surely no logic to a movement such as the "Heiligedankgesang" of Op. 132, with its combination of alternating Baroque chorale variations and eighteenth/nineteenth-century idealized dance which hides vestiges of the old courtly minuet; or to the insertion of a German folk dance in the more metaphysical surroundings of Op. 130 which Beethoven capped with the grandest fugue of them all. There's no rational way to understand Ives's placing a diatonic fugue in C major cheek by jowl with the layered musics of the other movements of his Fourth Symphony; or his juxtaposition and overlay of chromatic on diatonic, diatonic on chromatic, in his two gems, "The Unanswered Question" and "Central Park in the Dark." (Consider the juxtaposition of the intensely chromatic fugue and essentially pandiatonic last movement in Bartók's *Music for Strings, Percussion and Celesta*.)

The determination to write the Third Quartet the way I did (and other works similar in nature but cast differently, because of different gestural needs, balances, and projections) stems from my personal way of understanding composers like Beethoven, Bartók, and Ives, but is not limited to them. If, in the need to expand our sources—pluralism of gesture, language, and style—we lay ourselves open to the charge of eclecticism, we need not concern ourselves. Other and earlier forms of eclecticism may also be charged to medieval music or to early classical music or to Bach or to Mozart (who seemed thoroughly eclectic to his contemporaries), or to Stravinsky.

Some of the critics who have commented on my quartet have wondered out loud whether the work would "last." How can anyone tell? It is not important. Culture is not the additive product of a series of discrete, specific events or works. It is, like the biology that it rests on, a self-renewing, self-sustaining organism that proliferates, spreads, unites, subdivides, reunites, dies individually but lives collectively. The cultural mechanism for continuity (posterity; immortality) resides in human memory and the preservation of what is authentic and has, therefore, captured a piece of human wit or wisdom (as possible in music as in painting, as in literature). The cultural mechanism for renewal resides in the courage to use human passion and energy in the direction of what is authentic again and again. The ring of authenticity is more important than the clang of originality. Whatever is authentic about the twentieth century will be preserved, and we need not worry about it. Given that certainty, we can safely leave it alone and get back to the business of writing music without falsely institutionalizing the means we use to produce it. But we must be sure that it *is* music; i.e., that we write what we believe in, write it consummately well and that we intend it at least for the delectation and edification of the human ear and heart—beyond that, if possible, for the purification of the mind.

To quote from my notes to the recording of the Third Quartet: "I am turning away from what I consider the cultural pathology of my own time toward what can only be called a *possibility:* that music can be renewed by regaining contact with the tradition and means of the past, to re-emerge as a spiritual force with reactivated powers of melodic thought, rhythmic pulse, and large-scale structure."

Selected Bibliography

Adorno, T. W. "Modern Music is Dead." *The Score* 18 (December, 1956).

Anhalt, Istvan. "Record Review." *Canadian Music Journal,* Winter, 1961, pp. 34–39.

Barfield, Owen. *What Coleridge Thought.* Middletown, Conn.: Wesleyan University Press, 1971.

Beckett, Samuel. *Waiting for Godot.* New York: Grove Press, 1954.

Blake, William. *The Poetry and Prose of William Blake.* Edited by Geoffrey Keynes. London: The Nonesuch Library, 1967.

Borges, Jorge Luís. *The Aleph.* New York: Dutton, 1970.

Boulez, Pierre. "Schoenberg is Dead." *The Score* 6 (May, 1952).

———. "At the Ends of Fruitful Land." In *Die Reihe.* Vol. 1, *Electronic Music,* pp. 19–29. Bryn Mawr, Penn.: Theodore Presser Co., 1955.

Broch, Herman. *The Sleepwalkers.* New York: Pantheon Books, 1948.

Cage, John. *Silence.* Middletown, Conn.: Wesleyan University Press, 1961.

Capra, Fritjof. *Science, Society and the Rising Culture.* New York: Simon and Schuster, 1982.

Davies, Robertson. *Fifth Business.* New York: Penguin, 1977.

Delacroix, Eugene. *The Journal of Eugene Delacroix.* New York: Viking Press, 1972.

Dreiser, Theodore. *An American Tragedy.* New York: Modern Library Giant, 1956.

Dürrenmatt, Friedrich. *The Physicists.* New York: Grove Press, 1965.

Eimert, Herbert. "A Change of Focus." In *Die Reihe.* Vol. 2, *Anton Webern,* pp. 29–36. Bryn Mawr, Penn.: Theodore Presser Co., 1958.

Éliade, Mircea. *Cosmos and History.* New York: Harper Torchbooks, 1959.

FitzGerald, Frances. *Fire in the Lake.* Boston: Little, Brown, and Co., 1972.

Freud, Sigmund. *Moses and Monotheism.* Translated by Katherine Jones. London: Hogarth, 1951.

Gredinger, Paul. "Serial Technique." In *Die Reihe.* Vol. 1, *Electronic Music,* pp. 38–44. Bryn Mawr, Penn.: Theodore Presser Co., 1955.

Greenberg, Clement. *Art and Culture.* Boston: Beacon Press, 1961.

Grout, Donald Jay. *A History of Western Music.* New York: W. W. Norton, 1960.

Heller, Erich. *The Disinherited Mind.* New York: Farrar, Strauss, and Cudahy, 1957.

Hesse, Hermann. *Steppenwolf.* New York: Henry Holt and Co., 1929.

———. *Magister Ludi.* New York: Henry Holt and Co., 1949.

Hodeir, André. *Since Debussy.* New York: Grove Press, 1961.

Kuhn, T. S. *The Structure of Scientific Revolutions*. Chicago: University of Chicago Press, 1970.

Langer, Susanne K. *Feeling and Form*. New York: Charles Scribner's Sons, 1953.

Lévi-Strauss, Claude. *The Raw and the Cooked*. New York: Harper Torchbooks, 1970.

Lewis, Wyndham. *Time and Western Man*. Boston: Beacon Press, 1957.

Meyer, Leonard. *Music, The Arts and Ideas*. Chicago: University of Chicago Press, 1967.

Mann, Thomas. *Dr. Faustus*. New York: Alfred A. Knopf, 1948.

Monod, Jaques. *Chance or Necessity*. New York: Alfred A. Knopf, 1971.

Olson, Charles. "Projective Verse." In *The New American Poetry 1945–60*. Edited by Donald G. Allen. New York: Grove Press, 1960.

Pascal, Blaise. *Pensées* and *The Provincial Letters*. New York: Modern Library, 1941.

Pieper, Josef. *Leisure: The Basis of Culture*. New York: Random House, 1963.

Rilke, Rainer Maria. *Duino Elegies*. New York: W. W. Norton, 1939.

———. *Wartime Letters of Rainer Maria Rilke (1914–1921)*. New York: W. W. Norton, 1964.

Robbe-Grillet, Alain. *Last Year at Marienbad*. New York: Grove Press, 1962.

Rochberg, George. "The Music of Arnold Schoenberg, Vol. VII." Liner notes, Columbia Records. M2L 367. Stereo M2S 767.

Rosen, Charles. *The Classical Style*. New York: Viking, 1971.

Rosenberg, Harold. *The De-definition of Art*. New York: Horizon Press, 1972.

Rufer, Joseph. *Composition with 12 Notes*. New York: Macmillan Co., 1954.

Schoenberg, Arnold. *Style and Idea*. Edited by Leonard Stein. New York: St. Martin's Press, 1975.

Sessions, Roger. *The Musical Experience*. Princeton, N.J.: Princeton University Press, 1950.

Sontag, Susan. *Against Interpretation*. New York: Dell Publishing Co., 1967.

Stockhausen, Karlheinz. "Structures and Experiential Time." In *Die Reihe*. Vol. 2, *Anton Webern*, pp. 64–74. Bryn Mawr, Penn.: Theodore Presser Co., 1958.

Strunk, Oliver. *Source Readings in Music History*. New York: W. W. Norton, 1950.

Tovey, Donald Francis. *Beethoven*. London: Oxford University Press, 1944.

Von Neumann, John. *The Computer and the Brain*. New Haven: Yale University Press, 1958.

Weiner, Norbert. *The Human Uses of Human Beings*. 2d rev. ed. New York: Doubleday Anchor Books, 1954.

Whitrow, G. J. *The Natural Philosophy of Time*. London: Thomas Nelson and Sons, 1961.

Zuckerkandl, Victor. *Sound and Symbol*. New York: Pantheon Books, 1956.